*f*P

ALSO BY PHILLIP LOPATE

To Show and To Tell

At the End of the Day

Notes on Sontag

Two Marriages

American Movie Critics: An Anthology From the Silents Until Now

Waterfront: A Journey around Manhattan

Rudy Burckhardt

Getting Personal: Selected Writings

Writing New York: A Literary Anthology

Totally, Tenderly, Tragically

Portrait of My Body

*The Art of the Personal Essay:
An Anthology from the Classical Era to the Present*

Against Joie de Vivre

The Rug Merchant

Bachelorhood: Tales of the Metropolis

Confessions of Summer

The Daily Round

The Eyes Don't Always Want to Stay Open

*Being with Children: A High-Spirited Personal Account
of Teaching Writing, Theater, and Videotape*

PORTRAIT INSIDE MY HEAD

~ *Essays* ~

PHILLIP LOPATE

Free Press
New York   London   Toronto   Sydney   New Delhi

Note: Certain names and identifying characteristics have been changed.

Free Press
A Division of Simon & Schuster, Inc.
1230 Avenue of the Americas
New York, NY 10020

First Free Press hardcover edition February 2013

FREE PRESS and colophon are trademarks of Simon & Schuster, Inc.

From *The Poems of Charles Reznikoff: 1918–1975* by Charles Reznikoff. Edited by Seamus Cooney. Reprinted by permission of Black Sparrow Books, an imprint of David R. Godine, Publisher, Inc. Copyright © 2005 by Charles Reznikoff.

For information about special discounts for bulk purchases, please contact Simon & Schuster Special Sales at 1-866-506-1949 or business@simonandschuster.com.

The Simon & Schuster Speakers Bureau can bring authors to your live event. For more information or to book an event contact the Simon & Schuster Speakers Bureau at 1-866-248-3049 or visit our website at www.simonspeakers.com.

Designed by Jill Putorti

Manufactured in the United States of America

10   9   8   7   6   5   4   3   2   1

Library of Congress Cataloging-in-Publication Data

Lopate, Phillip.
  [Essays. Selections]
  Portrait Inside My Head : Essays / By Phillip Lopate. — First Free Press hardcover edition.
     p. cm.
  I. Title.
  PS3562.O66P66 2013
  814'.54—dc23

                                                          2012041141

ISBN: 978-1-4516-9586-1
ISBN: 978-1-4516-9631-8 (ebook)

Contents

PORTRAIT INSIDE
MY HEAD

Introduction

In Defense of the Miscellaneous Essay Collection

Reader, you have in your hands a motley collection of essays, personal and critical.

The advantage of the heterogeneous essay collection by a single author is that it shows you how a particular mind moves through the world. If you are attracted to an essayist's mentality and way of speaking, ideally you can surrender happily to his or her take on various subject matters, the more diverse the better. Let us see how our author will tackle this particular memory, neurotic tic, political or social problem, book, movie, play, comic strip, rock band, without requiring an overarching theme.

If there is a consistent theme in this particular collection, it is the discovery of limitations, and learning to live with them. The recognition of one's limits, painful as it may be, can have salutary side effects. In my case, it absolves me of the need to be both a hero and a coward, an explorer and a stay-at-home, a saint and a villain, a loyal husband and a Don Juan, a political activist and a skeptic, a spiritual mystic and a rationalist atheist, a performing athlete and a sports fan, a great if excruciatingly self-demanding literary stylist and a prolific if merely good-enough writer. Granted, we are all composed of numerous shards, and incorporate many contradictory selves in our makeup. But over the course of time, we choose, or the choice is made for us by fate, circumstance, whatever name you care to give it. The acknowledgment that one is tied to a fairly predictable set of behaviors and responses, and is not an amorphous blob of open receptivity, can certainly be a source of strength, even as it implies some rigidity. I concede that we probably use only a small portion of our human potential. Americans are accustomed to think that a person has almost unlimited capacity for growth. *Anything is possible; if you want it enough, go for your dream.* While it may be un-American to say so, just speaking for myself, I have learned over the course of a lifetime that I am quite limited, and I find that knowledge reassuring. Though I continue to learn new things and accept new challenges, I am no longer in the process of becoming: I may be an unfinished man but I am more or less *a closed book.* What better way to show that finality than in a collection largely of personal essays? For the personal essay is uniquely suited to expose this continuous bumping up against limits, against the borders of the self—which is one good reason I cling to it.

At the same time, I consider the essay to be a wonderfully fluid form, possessing the freedom to wander in search of sudden discovery. It has a long, glorious history as a literary testing ground of intellectual thought and psychological self-portraiture; and a heterogeneous assemblage of essays offers an ideal field in which to demonstrate the form's range. The risk is to be told that "collections of multi-purpose, previously published prose are often bitty and unsatisfying," as one *TLS* reviewer phrased it. Yet I persist in putting forth a collection that will include my musings on movies, literature, friendship, sex, urban history, city form, and the nail parings of daily life, so that the reader can enjoy the fluent play of a single consciousness, a sensibility flowing through disparate subject matters. I persist because I know the truth, which is that, deep down, you love essays. You may be ashamed to admit it. But you love essays, you love essays, you are getting very sleepy, you *lo-o-ove* essays . . .

An essay collection is a distinctly different adventure from a memoir. A fiercely accomplished essayist I know was advised to dismantle her collection of personal essays and restructure it as a memoir. She spent a year trying to do so, only to decide in the end that it wouldn't work, that the original form had an integrity that it made no sense to camouflage. Emily Fox Gordon, in "Book of Days," put her finger on one difference between the two genres when she argued that the memoir seems to have a built-in redemptive bent by the very nature of the author's having survived to tell the tale, the how-I-got-over aspect. In her words,

> The memoir and the personal essay are crucially different forms. The memoir tempts the memoirist to grandiose self-representation. The essay, with its essential modesty, discourages the impulse. . . . The erratic zigzag of essayistic thinking—what has been called thinking against oneself—makes the essay proof against the triumphalism of memoir by slowing the gathering of narrative momentum. The essayist *transects* the past, slicing through it first from one angle, then from another, until—though it can never be captured—some fugitive truth has been definitively cornered.

When I was editing my anthology *The Art of the Personal Essay,* I was uncomfortably aware that I might be drawing an overly pronounced distinction between personal and formal essays, by including just those examples from my authors that were most personal. William Hazlitt was a well-known drama and art critic as well as one of the most relentlessly self-scrutinizing essayists; George Orwell wrote about Henry Miller, Mohandas Gandhi, and Charles Dickens, not just about his school days; James Baldwin's first collections included pieces about "Everyone's Protest Novel" and the movie *Carmen Jones* along with his signature autobiographical essay, "Notes of a Native Son"; and Virginia Woolf wrote hundreds of pages of exemplary literary criticism and reflections on current affairs. It was not that these writers compartmentalized their personal and analytical essay sides: everything that interested them carried a personal watermark, just as every attempt to understand their experiences was inflected with the detached, analytical intelligence they employed as critics. The books we read, the movies we see, the public spaces we inhabit, the historic cataclysms and bizarre tabloid scandals that preoccupy us are as much a part of our autobiographies as the familial struggles, substance-abuse problems, or other illnesses that test our psyches.

As recently as the 1950s and 1960s, it was understood that an essay collection like *On the Contrary* by Mary McCarthy would and should include her musings on the Broadway play season, Gandhi, the Kinsey Report on American sexual behavior, and Simone de Beauvoir, along with some amazing memoir pieces such as "My Confession" and "Settling the Colonel's Hash," while Leslie Fiedler's miscellany *An End to Innocence: Essays on Culture and Politics* would range in lively fashion from Alger Hiss, Senator McCarthy, and the Rosenbergs to *Roman Holiday, Huckleberry Finn*, F. Scott Fitzgerald, and a travel journal through Italy. The motley character of these assortments was part of their allure. I don't see why those pleasures should be only a thing of the past, any more than poetry or short story collections would be considered passé.

Is my polemic beginning to sound transparently self-serving? I am only advocating the pleasures of the genre in which I toil and the unsung delights of the miscellaneous single-author essay collection, not arguing for my place in the essay pantheon. I am no Hazlitt by any stretch of the imagination. Still, I take heart from what my hero once wrote, after watching some Indian jugglers tossing up four brass balls:

I ask what there is that I can do as well as this? Nothing. What have I been doing all my life? Have I been idle, or have I nothing to show for all my labor and pains? Or have I passed my time in pouring words like water into empty sieves, rolling a stone up a hill and then down again, trying to prove an argument in the teeth of facts, and looking for causes in the dark and not finding them? Is there no one thing in which I can challenge competition, that I can bring as an instance of exact perfection, in which others cannot find a flaw? The utmost I can pretend for is to write a description of what this fellow can do. I can write a book: so can many others who have not even learned to spell. What abortions are these Essays! What errors, what ill-pieced transitions, what crooked reasons, what lame conclusions! How little is made out and that little how ill! Yet they are the best I can do. I endeavor to recollect all I have ever observed or thought upon a subject, and to express it as nearly as I can. Instead of writing on four subjects at a time, it is as much as I can manage to keep the thread of one discourse clear and unentangled. I have also time on my hands to correct my opinions, and polish my periods; but the one I cannot, and the other I will not do.

That *Hazlitt* could have thought so poorly of his efforts! But what really sticks in my mind is his last statement: he will not polish and perfect his essays. Is it because he is obstinate and lazy, or because the nature of the essay form is such that—unlike the poem and the short story—it does not readily permit of crystalline perfection? It is too open to the incidental, too impure, too forgiving. Maybe that's why I love it so much. I am not a perfectionist, neither by temperament nor by prose style. I am drawn to the shagginess of the essay, its discontinuous forms of consciousness, and for much the same reason, to the unavoidable yet unapologetic unevenness of the miscellaneous essay collection.

It was Charles Lamb, that other great English essayist, who warned of the dangers and the requirements involved in such an enterprise, in a review of his friend Hazlitt's *Table Talk*: "A series of Miscellaneous Essays, however well-executed in the parts, if it have not some pervading character to give a unity to it, is ordinarily as tormenting to get through as a set of aphorisms, or a jest-book." Lamb cited Plutarch, Montaigne, Samuel Johnson, and Hazlitt as those who were able to get away with it: that is, impart a pervading character or unity to an essay collection's heterogeneous parts. The bar had been raised very high indeed. Let us lower it a little, for pity's sake and my own.

I

THE FAMILY ROMANCE

Tea at the Plaza

What is important to an adult and what matters to a child are so often at variance that it is a wonder the two ever find themselves on the same page. Parents may feel an occasional urge to spend money extravagantly on their offspring, only to discover that it means very little to the children themselves. You buy an expensive antique Raggedy Ann doll for your kid that she tosses in a corner, thinking it ugly and musty, meanwhile being enthralled by the shiny plastic action figure they give out free at McDonald's. And yet, if you're like me, you keep falling into the trap of costly, unappreciated presents, perhaps because they're not really for your child but for the child-self in you who never got them when you were growing up.

I remember, when my daughter, Lily, was four, my wife, Cheryl, and I sprang for a family carriage ride through Central Park in the snow. We had such an idyllic Currier & Ives image in our heads, and it seemed such an ideal treat for the holidays—all the more special because we were dyed-in-the-wool New Yorkers and usually stayed clear of what the tourists went in for. "Let's just do it!" we cried impulsively, determined to play at being tourists in our own city. Yet I could not help noticing the reluctant, even alarmed expression on Lily's face as she climbed, or was lifted, into the barouche, behind the bewhiskered coachman with the tall shamrock hat, stationed across from the Plaza Hotel. We started off at a slow trot; the carriage entered the park, my wife and I entranced by the vista, and Lily beginning to whimper and complain that she was cold, until she spotted a merry-go-round, the prospect of which excited her far more than an actual horse giving her a ride. As we neared the merry-go-round, Lily became so insistent that we had to ask the coachman to stop the carriage. I forked over what felt at the time like major dough for a fifteen-minute trot, grumbling as she ran to the carousel.

I vowed under my breath that I would never be such a patsy again. But we had not yet gotten out of the business, my wife and I, of manufacturing exorbitant "perfect memories" for our daughter to cherish all her days. So we took her to Broadway shows, and to the *Nutcracker* ballet (where she fell asleep), and we began—at first vaguely, then with more urgency—plotting an afternoon's high tea at the Plaza's Palm Court. Somehow that corner at Fifty-Ninth Street and Fifth Avenue was the Bermuda Triangle that kept sucking us into fantasies of civilized luxury. You must understand that this was not a case of passing on some proud family tradition: my father took me not to Brooks Brothers for a fitting of my first suit but to the back room of a Gypsy shop that probably trafficked in stolen goods. I grew up in working-class Brooklyn, and never entered the Plaza when I was a child, nor did Cheryl, who hailed from hardscrabble upstate New York and might, if she were lucky, get to order a hot chocolate with whipped cream at the local luncheonette. But our child was a middle-class New York child, thanks to our fatiguing efforts to claw our way up the social ladder, and, by God, we were bound and determined to give her all the social graces and sophisticated experiences that befit her, if not our, station in life.

So, with somewhat grim if hearty countenances, we got Lily and ourselves all dressed up, and took her into Manhattan for the thrill of a lifetime. We did not ride the subway from Brooklyn, mind you, as that would have spoiled the general effect, but drove in and, unable to find a parking spot on the street, left our car in a garage a few blocks east of the Plaza, in what must be the most expensive parking area in the planet. But hey! Who cares about the expense? We're treating ourselves! We entered the regal steps of the Plaza, which had on powerful electric warmers, and stood in line at the perimeter of the majestic Palm Court.

I had already called ahead and knew they did not take reservations over the phone; but fortunately the 4:00 p.m., midafternoon line was not that long, and we were assured of seating. In fact, business seemed relatively slow, for a treasured landmark. We oohed and aahed at the fabulous high ceiling, the palm trees, the piano, the marble floor, and the fashionably or laughably costumed Ladies Who Lunched. Lily nodded, smiling and looking dutifully about, but seemed a bit cool toward it all, as if she were indulging her parents' naïve enthusiasm. Once seated, we took up our menus stiffly. The waitress wrote down our orders—three specials with all the trimmings, o spare not the clotted cream, the crème frâiche, the clabber, or what have you, the peach cobblers, the jams, the crustless cucumber sandwiches, the savorics, the petits fours, the works! All that centuries of human ingenuity had found to include in this cozy English tradition of High Tea, we wanted.

"Think of it, Lily, Eloise herself ran through this very same room!" I said.

"But she's not real, is she?" said my knowing six-year-old.

"No, but still—"

"Of course she is!" insisted my wife, ever eager to prolong childhood credulity, be it about Santa Claus, the Tooth Fairy, or Eloise. She darted me a scolding look, warning me away from shortening our daughter's childhood with my "realism."

So we kept it Nice; we were all on our best behavior, and commented favorably, when the food came, on the beautiful tea service, the exquisite arrangement of edibles, the deliciousness of everything—it short, it was a dull conversation, but appropriately so, duly dull. We were proud of ourselves for adhering to the parts assigned us in this civilized ritual, for coloring within the lines. No one would ever guess we lived in Brooklyn.

We had stuffed ourselves, and now Lily began getting restless, as children will in that postprandial moment. Enough with the talk, she wanted action. I commiserated with her squirminess—more to the point, I felt childishly restless myself, and so I volunteered to take her for a walk about the floor. "Should I come, too?" asked Cheryl.

"No, stay and enjoy the last of your tea." (I was already deep in the throes of performing a Good Deed.)

It was fun to walk around with Lily and stick our noses into every corner of the nearby bar, the cloakroom, and the lobby. We pretended to be spies; she picked a person to trail after, then darted away madly in the opposite direction and hid, giggling. In our last go-round we came upon a family—a mother and her three young daughters in dresses, the youngest of whom was holding a clutch of balloons. Probably she was celebrating her birthday. Lily was instantly enchanted—not by the birthday girl, by the balloons. They were plump, filled with helium, and had marbleized patterns outside and little silver jingling bells inside. How she wanted one of those balloons! I could tell it meant everything to her at that moment; so I went over to the mother and asked her if my daughter might have one. The word *borrow* would have been dishonest, as we had no intentions of ever returning it. No, have it for free, just like that, is what I meant; it was a brazen request to make of a perfect stranger, and fortunately the kind woman understood what was at stake and acquiesced. "Which one would you like?" she asked Lily. Stalled between the pink, the blue, and the red, Lily finally chose the red. The woman then turned to her daughter and asked ceremoniously, "Would you mind giving this little girl one of your balloons?" The girl, obviously a well-brought-up child, gravely assented, and Lily walked away holding its string, happy—in ecstasies—as happy as I'd ever seen her.

We were both pretty high, delighted with our luck, when we sat back at the table. There is something marvelous in a place like the Plaza about getting something for free, even if it's just a twenty-five-cent balloon. My wife wanted to know the whole story, and Lily began telling it, with her usual dramatic flair and embellishments. As she was gesticulating to make a point, she lost hold of the end of the string and the balloon floated up to the ceiling. How many seconds it took to make its ascent, I could not begin to tell you, but the subjective experience was one of quite extensible duration: just as in a car crash your whole life, they say, flashes through your mind, or just as a glass rolling off the table takes forever when you can do nothing to arrest its fall, so my accumulated past of error, catastrophe, and missed opportunity fluttered before my eyes while I watched the balloon drift up, up, languidly taking its time.

Was I passing on my destiny of disenchantment and lost illusions to my daughter? It was too horrible to contemplate. What is even more unconscionable is that a part of me wanted to laugh.

This despicable urge to laugh arose in me, in spite of (or maybe because of . . .) the fact that Lily had started wailing. Piercing sobs issued from her as she watched her balloon (which had only been *hers* for five minutes) escaping further and further. The diners at nearby tables stopped midfork, perhaps readying themselves to intervene in the event they saw evidence of child abuse; when they satisfied themselves that there was none, they returned to their food, most likely blaming us for not being able to control our brat better. Meanwhile the captain of the waiters hurried over to see if there was anything he could do. Our waitress began making commiserating faces and noises such as one directs at a little baby. All to no avail. My wife took Lily in her lap and started calming her down.

I attended to the check, handing over my credit card and totaling up the tip, the full amount coming to two hundred dollars. I could not rid myself of feeling chagrined that that outlay, plus the garage bill, had been nullified by the loss of a little nothing balloon. "We'll get you another balloon as soon as we leave the hotel," Cheryl promised Lily, who was beginning to decelerate from wrenching sobs to puppy whimpers.

After I had gotten my credit card back and we'd put our coats on and were about to leave, I turned to the simpatico wait-captain and asked him how long it would take for that balloon to come down, thinking it might be possible to retrieve it and give the story of our outing a happy ending.

"Oh, about a week, I'd imagine," he said with a slight accent (Egyptian? Maltese?).

"And is there no way to get it down before then?"

"No way."

For some reason, this report that it would take a week to come down set Lily off on a fresh burst of wailing. Now she was inconsolable. She was like Hecuba, experiencing precociously the fullness of grief. We hastened her out of there, but she kept up loud sobbing in the street.

"Knock it off!" said Cheryl, suddenly out of patience. "You're making a spectacle of yourself, you're acting like a two-year-old!" While I completely agreed with my wife, I also, in that instantaneous switch of good cop–bad cop roles for which parents are so adept, became entirely sympathetic to Lily's woe: I knew that emotions do not have to be reasonable to shatter us, and that sobs feed uncontrollably on sobs, regardless of our efforts to stop them,

"Let her cry," I said. "I'm not embarrassed. Who cares what these people think?"

The truth was, I was strangely happy. The whole incident had struck me as funny, a cosmic comeuppance for our pretensions to being the sorts of swells who had tea at the Plaza, though it may also have been a defensive reflex arising from my powerlessness in the face of Lily's anguish. Meanwhile, Lily, as if picking up on my undertone, began to giggle, in between her sobs—a part of her perhaps recognizing that she *was* being ridiculous, a drama queen, making entirely too much of this. I think, though, that my errant satisfaction issued from a darker source: I felt myself bonding with my daughter in our now-shared discovery that life was composed, at bottom, of loss, futility, and ineluctable sorrow. There was nothing you could do about it but laugh.

Years later, that is precisely what we do do: whenever we recall the lost balloon, it is always good for a chuckle, and Lily, now a teenager, is the first to laugh at herself. But we know better than to return to the Palm Court for tea. In fact, speaking of loss, that elegant ballroom, which conjures up Edith Wharton's and F. Scott Fitzgerald's New York, and which we all thought would last forever, regardless of how slow business might be, is hanging by a thread. The new owners of the Plaza have turned a good part of the hotel into condominiums, and have wanted to gut the Oak Room and the Palm Court as well, but the landmarks preservation community has prevented them, for the time being. If someday these cherished interiors are demolished, as seems likely, I will be sad but I will not *only* be sad. The Palm Court will have gone the way of Rumpelmayer's, the legendary pink-ensconced ice cream parlor that once stood a block away from the Plaza—both institutions no longer around to torment parents with the chimera of a perfect children's outing.

The Camera Shop

Whenever I see the flags, bunting, and triangular pennants announcing a store's Grand Opening, my heart does a flip-flop at this poignant fusion of patriotism and retail, as though we were all being asked as good citizens to prop up the gross national product. I cross the street to examine the window, and stare at the proprietors with their nervous, eager air. Rarely do I go into a store on its Opening Day, however: partly because I consider myself unlucky and would not want to visit my bad financial karma on a maiden establishment, but more likely because I cannot shake the *triste* memory of my parents' camera shop.

My mother, who was given to daydreams of fortune, and impatient with her dead-end clerical job in Midtown Manhattan's garment center, had hit on the idea of starting a store in Brooklyn that would sell Brownie cameras and Kodak film, take in negatives to be processed elsewhere, and act as a booking agent for Kewpie Studios, the unfortunately named enterprise of a photographer-friend of hers, Alan K., who specialized in baby and child portraits.

Now it must be said that my mother knew nothing about the technical side of photography, but she could read a Kodak box and regarded herself as a "people person," ever ready to deal with the public. She had some retail experience, first having worked in a beauty parlor as a teenager, then having run a candy store in her twenties with my father when they were starting out as a couple. They had both remembered this candy store as one of the few happy times in their marriage: my extroverted mother had enjoyed playing confidante to the neighborhood youths, and my reserved father, while by no stretch of the imagination a people person, had gamely mixed malteds. It was agreed now that he would keep his regular job, helping my mother on weekends in the camera store.

At the time we lived in semisqualor, barely squeaking by; my parents had virtually no capital to invest in a business, and certainly no cushion to tide them over the rough early stages of enterprise. But my energetic mother found a vacant store with low rent not too far from where we lived.

In those days, when you walked up Lee Avenue a mile or so away from the center of Williamsburg, you would cross the Hasidic Jewish part to a largely African-American and Hispanic area around Myrtle Avenue, then a desperate slum. Myrtle Avenue, a gloomy street darkened by elevated trains adjacent to housing projects, had seemed to my childish imagination the furthest demarcation line, beyond which sea serpents lurked. Now we were suddenly about to operate a store on the "wrong" side of Myrtle Avenue.

I remember Opening Day, with its flags and streamers, a pleasant Saturday in June. I was eleven. My mother sent me outside as a shill to mingle with window-shoppers and drum up business. A dozen curious spectators were craning their necks and looking in, but none seemed eager to enter the shop. Some of the remarks I overheard had a skeptical tone: "Don't look like they got much in there." "They're never gonna make it." I suddenly saw our camera shop not through my mother's hopeful eyes but through a more detached, disloyal perspective: the pathetic, meager stock of Brownie cameras and other cheap models, the nondescript fluorescent lighting, the display counters lined with brown contact paper of the sort used on kitchen pantry shelves, the spare, undecorated space, the lack of furniture save for two kitchen chairs with cheap plastic backing—all gave out the impression of someone's shabby home rather than a retail establishment. The store lacked *store*ness.

(Decades later, I would encounter this same becalmed, not-quite-retail atmosphere in East Berlin shops before the Wall came down: shops that had been so long removed from a capitalist mercantile culture that they had grown disdainful of or no longer able to project a vending aura.)

Fortunately, the camera shop managed to draw some regulars, mostly doting Puerto Rican fathers, in its opening week. I remember one particular exuberant father with an upswept pompadour, a tattoo on his arm, a cigarette pack tucked into his rolled-up T-shirt sleeve, who could not resist taking roll upon roll of his daughters in their pink Sunday dresses. It was the first time I became conscious of that passionate paternal pride that Latino men sometimes take in their offspring, and it made me envious.

"Poor people like to take pictures of their children," my mother explained. While the maxim held true, its downside was equally true: poor people cannot always afford to pick up the printed rolls they have left for developing.

My older brother, Leonard, and I, who had been hanging around the store too much during summer vacation, were sent by our mother into the neighboring streets to collect payment. More than once I found myself in the nearby massive public housing project, all of whose brick buildings looked confusingly alike. I would ring the doorbell of the address on the yellow film envelope and, when no one answered, call out the customer's name. Sometimes I heard scurrying sounds inside, and the voices of black or Hispanic children probably no older than myself whispering, "It's the landlord!" or "It's the Man—don't open it!" So great was their fear of authority—welfare caseworkers, bill collectors—that even a trembling eleven-year-old like myself was accorded the power to frighten.

I had thought *we* were poor, but now I was seeing a level of poverty that shocked me. Meanwhile, every time my mother turned her back to keep an eye on her four children, since she could not afford babysitters, some neighborhood kid would run in and steal a camera. Thefts, deadbeat customers, and insufficient volume all doomed the business. Within six months of opening, the camera shop was closed.

My mother continued to operate Kewpie Studios from our apartment, making cold calls to strangers in the phone book. Ashamed, we would wince at her saccharine (to our ears) "pitching" voice and mimic it behind her back. Of course she was putting on this phony voice to keep *us*, the family, solvent, but at the time we were purely ungrateful.

Her photographer-partner, Alan K., a touchy, blade-thin guy with a wife and two bratty kids, whom I sometimes babysat for, would go out on shoots set up by my mother. Alan K. intrigued me because he had written an autobiographical novel called *The Keys to the Cage* about his sad childhood, whose traumatic secrets had been unlocked with the aid of hypnosis and Freudian analysis. Unable to find a publisher, he had paid a vanity press to print it. I am one of the few to have read this precursor of Victim Literature. He was not much of a writer (the recorded dreams were especially boring), but he took decent pictures of children, and could reasonably document a wedding, confirmation, or bar mitzvah. Eventually he and my mother quarreled, and she gave up her last connection with photography, going back to work as a clerk in the garment industry—at the time New York's largest, most dependable and forgiving employer. So ended one of those Ralph Kramdenesque schemes and pipe dreams to which my parents periodically fell susceptible, like other members of the striving working class who sought to pull themselves up by their bootstraps into the lower-middle-class Eden of proprietorship.

Recently I walked around the area where the camera shop had failed. I was surprised to find Myrtle Avenue not nearly as bleak as I remembered. Gone was the gloomy El train (torn down in 1969). The projects were still charmless and monolithic as ever. But the entire block on which the camera shop had stood was now an empty lot, tall weeds surrounded by a chain-link fence. I saw what the problem had been: location, location, location.

The Countess's Tutor

Recently I brought a friend to see the old block in Fort Greene, Brooklyn, where I lived from age eleven through high school, in the mid-1950s. Parts of the neighborhood were as funky as I remembered: its bars and fortune-tellers, processed-hair parlors, fried chicken joints, and street-corner winos unchanged. Imagine my chagrin, however, when, prepared to show off the "mean streets" of my youth, I found the crummy six-story apartment building of my early adolescence converted into condominiums, with a concierge, no less, at a lobby desk. The last time I'd bothered to check, twenty-five years before, that double-winged apartment house on Washington Avenue had looked abandoned: windows boarded up with plywood, yellow brick façades blackened like singed eyebrows by a suspicious fire. I had half-expected to see it torn down, but no, this time it was clean and gleaming, its stone-carved gargoyles displayed to perfection. I asked the concierge for permission to take the elevator to the top floor, where my family, all six of us, had lived miserably crammed together. He said yes, provided we did not disturb the present occupants. I assured him my friend and I had absolutely no desire to peer inside: just seeing the door would suffice. We rode the elevator in silence, I noting with satisfaction its dingy brown paint job. But I was in shock when I faced the old door: 6A had been changed to PH1. Had I known then that I was living in a future penthouse, how different my sense of destiny and entitlement might have been.

Something is wrong when the slum dwellings of our youth have become the prewar desiderata of the next generation. Then again, maybe the apartment building had been initially intended as discreet, middle-class luxe, and had only gone into decline mid-twentieth century, the period during which my family lived in it, and was now restored to its original economic niche.

But that was not what I was thinking about. I was remembering the last time we had been inside that door, when my mother sprayed the kitchen for cockroaches in one final skirmish before moving out. We had fought the roaches so many years, unavailingly, but at the penultimate moment of our tenancy we got hold of a powerful DDT spray gun and cleared the food out of the kitchen. At first there were only a few. Then like a locust storm the roaches began pouring out of the stove, from behind the refrigerator, across and down the ceiling. They were drop-ping at our feet, doped and spinning, and we smashed them under our shoes like raisins, two at a time. It was a regular killing field: wherever we stepped, we slaughtered.

Then I gazed at the staircase, and remembered the time I descended, with heavy heart of brother-responsibility, to defend my younger sister Joan, who said she had been robbed by two black boys. I walked her around for blocks, asking her every time we approached a knot of boys, "Are those the ones?"—as if I ever could have wrested anything from them but a beating. (Years later she confessed that no one had robbed her; she had spent the money on ice cream.)

We had moved there in the mid-1950s ostensibly because our family of six needed more room. But you don't move four growing white kids into a black slum just for the extra space. The flight from our previous Jewish neighborhood, Williamsburg (itself a run-down ghetto then), had all the stigma of exile. My parents had gotten in trouble with our last landlady and had been kicked out, simple as that. One afternoon, the landlady (who lived beneath us: always a mistake) burst into our apart-ment while both our parents were away at their jobs. She had two police-men with her. We kids had been running around half-naked—playing strip poker, as my brother and I liked to do with our younger sisters—but as soon as we saw the landlady and the cops enter we hid under our beds. "You see what I mean?" she kept saying, sweeping her arms in all directions. "It's a madhouse, a pigsty! There's no supervision, the kids run wild, it looks like it hasn't been cleaned in months. I just want you to be witnesses." I poked my head out, but they ignored me, taking flash photographs of the disarray. I began to see my family's peculiarities from an outsider's perspective. Still, what had we done? We had let the apartment get messy—by no means criminal neglect, or even destruction of property. In a less house-proud setting, no one would have thought to complain.

When the invaders left, we came out of our hiding places and roared with laughter. Partly, it was shock, but beyond that, we were genuinely convulsed, mimicking the outrage on the landlady's face, her uptight prissiness, and the cops' picture-taking gestures. My parents, though, did not find the incident funny at all. They had to take a day off from work to answer Mrs. Jacobs's charges in court. The upshot was that we were given three months to move.

So I could never get out of my mind the notion that we were living in a black section of Brooklyn as punishment—evicted from the "Eden" of Williamsburg for being slobs. My mother remained an indifferent housekeeper, after coming home tired from her clerical job, and we kids continued to run free and not bother to clean up either. But in Fort Greene, nobody seemed to care: we could mess up the place as much as we wanted. The result was that the kitchen table acquired an intriguing fecundity of detail.

The focus of our family life was the kitchen table. Hardly a revelation: I have often read accounts of ghetto upbringings, Hispanic, African-American, Jewish, Italian, which boasted of the kitchen as the warm domestic center, dispensing nourishment, conversation, and a sense of community. However, in our case the kitchen table had something sinister and pathological about it, due to the inconceivable density of objects on its surface. Originally it had been used as a pantry annex, to catch the surplus from cupboards, but what had started in one corner of the table spread to another, so that pretty soon nothing was put away except perishables. Everything else was left on the table, where we could "get at it easily": jelly jars, Ritz crackers, dirty dishes, matzo boxes, playing cards, coffeepot, crayons, schoolbooks, radio, tax records and insurance papers (which got spots of jam on them), mucilage, twine, sewing machine, vitamin bottles, seltzer canisters, U-Bet chocolate syrup, classical record albums from the Masterpiece of the Month club, and whatever else had wandered into our lives at the moment.

There is no question that the table's chaotic clutter expressed something about our family's character, but what, you might be asking, other than our being slobs? It was our Noah's ark, our survival raft, our environmental artwork; an overcompensation for our being poor, a visual refutation of material deprivation. The table also called attention to my mother's struggle against overweight: because she was unhappy with her marriage and her job and herself, she went on eating binges, absentmindedly downing whatever was left around, a whole box of chocolate-covered marshmallows at a time. But it was not only my mother who "rounded out" a meal, or assuaged preprandial hungers, with snacks that took no preparation: the whole family was addicted to noshing in a dreamy, unconscious way. My father would pop one Fig Newton after another in his mouth, staring off into space, while remaining thin as Kafka's hunger artist—which naturally enraged his corpulent wife. Father's pensive passivity, his geological resistance to housework, played its part in this assemblage. But if you asked our parents how the table came to be so messy, they would have a simple answer: the children. It was the children who never cleaned up after themselves, who expected their mother to do everything like a slave, who brought whatever homework or game they were working on to the table, for the purpose of finding company there.

In truth, we did use the table as our school desk. And even I, who had the family reputation for being a neatnik, because I tried to keep a section of the bedroom I shared with my older brother, Lenny, free from clutter, would no more have thought of cleaning off the table by myself than of pruning all the trees in Brooklyn. Still, we were ashamed of the mess, and whenever anyone came over to the house, which was rare, we apologized about the table immediately. Less and less did we invite any classmates over, fearing they would not understand. My par-

ents, on their side, seemed too fatigued by work to bother with friendships. They withdrew into themselves and gave free rein to their mania
for disappointment.

———————

Well I know I got religion—certainly
I know I got religion—certainly, Lord
Well I know I got religion—certainly
 Certainly, certainly, Lo-oord!

Sunday mornings we would awake to the ebullient, hand-clapping
sounds of gospel music from the clapboard tabernacle down the block.
We would open the window and hear a free concert of "Mary, Don't You
Weep," "Great Day in the Morning," or "I Got a Mother over Yonder"
(which we would sing sarcastically to our mother just to irritate her).
That modest-looking church used to attract renowned groups on tour.
My brother, Lenny, who was fast becoming a gospel and jazz aficionado,
would say, "Ohmigod, they're having the Blind All Stars and Claude
Jeter next month, and after that, Sister Rosetta Tharpe!"

The other church, Baptist, across the street from us, was more staid
and established: from the window of the bedroom I shared with Lenny,
I would stare down every Sunday at the dignified black parishioners, the
men in dark suits, the women in cheerful white dresses and splendiferous
hats, lingering sociably on the iron balustrade, in a manner I would now
characterize as Southern. They represented normalcy to me (an attribute
in short supply in our household). I see that the indispensable *AIA Guide
to New York City* has deemed that very church across the street architecturally noteworthy: "1860. Ebenezer L. Roberts. A pinch of Lombar-
dian Romanesque decorates a highly articulated square-turreted English
Gothic body. The brownstone water tables (white-painted) against red
brick are perhaps too harsh." Picky, picky. I've since become fairly interested in architecture, but as a child I never thought to notice and had no
clue back then that the Fort Greene neighborhood around me, which
I took to be a dilapidated slum, was actually quite handsome and dis-

tinguished, awash in "Romanesque beauties," as the *AIA Guide* put it. Perhaps all those fieldstone mansions and bay-windowed brownstones, those granite pediments, cylindrical turrets and mansards registered subconsciously, planting the seeds for my later architectural interest; but my reality growing up was much more class-bound. We were barely scraping by, and we stuck out as downwardly mobile whites in a black section that seemed mostly impoverished (although, even then, the area drew a nucleus of home-owning, middle-class black professionals).

Back then, we thought of ourselves as living on the border of Bedford-Stuyvesant, a notoriously rough neighborhood over whose turf two mighty street gangs, the Bishops and the Chaplains, rumbled. I had to be careful where I walked because I would be shaken down by roving bands of kids when I strayed beyond the streets where I was recognized. They would suddenly form a line in front of me. The curious thing was that sometimes they would let me pass, if I said the right thing, pressed the right button, sounded neither too fearful nor too flippant, but sufficiently respectful; they would laugh and say, "We was just playing with you," and let me by. Other times they took every penny I had. It didn't have to be a violent encounter if you played it right: more like a loan to a neighbor you knew would never be paid back.

Getting robbed was a straightforward transaction, almost preferable to the teasing, ominous game of "What you lookin' at?" You had to answer "Nothing" (or "You" if you were feeling suicidally cocky: I never was). But even "Nothing" would not necessarily let you off the hook. You might be told you were lying, you had been seen looking at them, and they might now smash your face in. It was always on the tip of my tongue to ask, not out of provocation but curiosity, "What if I had been looking at you? What would it mean?" It was mysterious how I could be harming anyone by my gaze. Was it like the aborigine's dread of being photographed? Or like a king whose subjects were forbidden to look upon his splendor? If you did not finesse the response correctly, you might be drawn into a fistfight. The whole point of the exercise was to challenge one's honor. Though I considered my honor not worth a thrashing, and regularly refused to take offense at the dozens of players' slights to my mother's virtue, my situation was complicated by the fact that I did love to look at people. I always felt guilty because I probably *had* been staring at the boy who called me out.

I learned the art of cowardice partly by watching Lenny, and deciding to do the opposite. One memory remains particularly vivid. Lenny and I had entered the vestibule of our apartment building, where they buzz you in. Standing in front of the doorbells was Pete, the toughest kid on the block. Everyone, adult and child, feared Pete. Even in idleness, his body conveyed a coiled power, with the muscular shoulders of a professional prizefighter. His skin was coal black, his bullet head was completely smooth: if he butted you with his skull alone it might knock you out.

"What you lookin at?" he said to my brother, baring his teeth in an almost friendly, ingratiating grin.

"Nothing, okay?"

My brother tried to get past him and put the key in the lock. Pete blocked his way. "I saw you starin at me. Why you lookin at me? You some kind of fairy? Don't lie. Be a man. Admit you was lookin at me."

I want to say, Come on, Lenny, tell him you're a fairy, apologize, whatever he wants, just get us to the other side of the door.

Instead Lenny answers, in a heated voice (I know his temper so well): "Okay, I was looking at you. What of it?"

"You want to fight?" Pete asks tantalizingly, beckoning Lenny forward with his curled hand. It's an invitation, almost like "You want to dance?" He thrusts his index finger against my brother's chest. My brother raises his fists in the time-honored manner. *Meshugana.*

"Lenny, don't fight him! Come on!"

Neither pays attention to me. Pete grabs him, fast as a cat, before Lenny can change his mind, and they tangle. Lenny's glasses fall to the tiled floor. I grab them and put them in my pocket. My brother is taller than Pete, and tries to tie him up with his long arms, but the tussle lasts only a matter of seconds before Pete breaks away and throws a combination of expert jabs at Lenny's face. My brother goes down. Pete is on him instantly, straddling him, punching him in the face, moving his fist straight down like a pile driver on Lenny's nose. I am thinking, I must save my brother, I must save my brother. I start beating Pete on the back. My arms have an eerie lassitude, my punches lack force. Pete shoves me against the wall with one arm, while the other continues to pummel Lenny. My brother's nose is gushing blood. I start to scream: "*Help!* Stop them!" Maybe someone bigger can break up the fight. Pete starts banging my brother's head against the hard tile floor. This is the worst part. I can only watch, with a sick feeling. Lenny's face is all pink, his eyes are weirdly glassy. Each time his head hits the stone floor with a thud, I register the pain. We're very close, Lenny and I: what happens to one, the other feels. At the same time, some little part of me is glad to see my brother, the tyrant of my youth, getting it. See, idiot, you shouldn't have accepted his challenge. I admire Pete, or at least his ability to fight, even as I am horrified by his lack of emotion. He seems to show no personal malice toward my brother, doesn't even know him, this is just his way of enjoying himself—beating up a white boy. Or bloodying a black boy, on a slow afternoon.

"You'll kill him! *Quit it!*" I'm yelling. An adult, Mack, the super, runs in. Pete rises with a smile, and hold his hands out, as if to say, I'm clean. He darts out the door smooth as a leopard, disappears.

I help my brother up. "I'm so sorry, Lenny. I couldn't stop him. Are you all right?"

"I'm all right. Motherfucking sonofabitch!"

"Here are your glasses."

"Next time I'll kill him," says my brother.

———

Of the three white tenants, besides ourselves, in the building, two were a highly cultivated foreign couple, the man a professor of Spanish, I seem to recall, who spent part of each year in Peru and took an interest in Inca handicrafts. You would have thought that such a refined pair, who read good books and appreciated classical music, would have been a godsend to my parents, who did the same. But not only did we never make friends with them, we ridiculed them behind their backs. The woman, Tina, was rumored to have been caught sun worshiping on the roof, naked to the waist and raising her arms to the sky. She was probably just practicing yoga. As often as I sneaked up to the tarred roof to catch her in this rite, I never saw her doing anything but innocently drawing in her notebook. Since the singer Yma Sumac had made a big splash with her exotic, scale-ascending vocals, my sister Betty Ann, who was our unofficial bestower of nicknames, dubbed Tina "Yma."

I thought Yma harmless, but I was terrified of the other white woman in the building. She lived with our black superintendent, Mack, so we called her Mrs. Mack for starters, but later, thanks to Betty Ann, the Dragon Lady, because she smoked constantly and curled the smoke up her nose, and because she had a surly, evil expression, with tiny, mistrustful eyes embedded in a porcine face rolling in fat, and huge, dimpled arms that she used to lean on, while looking out the window for Mack. She would chase us kids away when we tried to throw a pink Spaldeen ball against the cornice beneath her window. She always wore the same faded housedresses, and gave off a strong, oniony body odor. Since Mack himself was a patient, decent-looking, squat, muscular man who tolerated children and in consequence was well-liked by them, we wondered how he could have gotten stuck with such a repulsive sow. It was said that some black men had a "thing" for white women, but surely her skin color alone could not have balanced out her other defects. Yet there seemed an undeniable physical passion between them, a powerful glue; you sensed it when you saw them together.

I could certainly understand the attraction white women might feel toward black men. I looked up to blacks also, as a rule: it was the beginning of my White Negro period, and I had no difficulty romanticizing them as a superior race. Their best seemed stoically graceful and effortlessly creative, like our neighbor across the hall, Melville, who was a track star at Boys' High School and an honor student, outrageously handsome, with the friendly, obliging manner of a natural-born aristocrat. My boyhood heroes had been the Dodgers' Jackie Robinson and Don Newcombe. By the time I was twelve, my brother had introduced me to rhythm and blues; we would thrill to Mickey & Sylvia and Sam "The Man" Taylor on the radio, and from there it was but a short step to worshiping Charlie Parker, John Coltrane, Bessie Smith, and the blind gospel singers.

One day Lenny came home all excited. He had just learned that the drunk we sometimes stumbled over near the corner of our block, where Washington Avenue and Fulton Street met, the wino who slept in the alley beside the gospel church, was none other than Gil Coggins, a former bop piano player who had once recorded with Bird! My brother, who usually responded with ironic grimaces when misfortunes fell on our own family, was so touched at and angered by the fate of this black musician, at how American society undervalued its jazz artists and permitted them to end up in the gutter. He vowed to do something about it. What? I was curious to know. At the very least he would talk to the man, tell how much his music had meant to him. (For my part, after that I never came upon the sleeping ex-sideman without reverently tiptoeing around him.)

There was a difference, of course, between the demigods and the everyday blacks you came across, who might stare you down with a scowl, but here, too, I made my adjustments. After I'd lived on the block a while, it seemed to me my neighbors knew who I was, and either accepted me or just left me alone. The row of brownstones next to the Baptist church made a perfect backdrop for punchball—there was just enough room from end to end to hit a decent-size fly ball for a homer—and the black kids who lived there would let me into their games if they were short of players. "Easy out," they would taunt me. I would bunch my fist together, pretending it had the hard, bony strength of theirs. To hit a punchball far does not require massive biceps: you toss the ball up and whack it with your fist. There is a knack in the wrist, or the knuckles, which I never quite mastered, though sometimes I got lucky.

But then, just as I thought I was becoming invisible, or that race didn't matter, I would be brought up short. As I loved to sing, I had joined a Hebrew choir when my family lived in Williamsburg, continuing to perform in it after my family moved to Fort Greene. One night I was coming home from a gig at a Bronx synagogue. This was just before my own bar mitzvah; I was twelve. Though it was late, I decided to walk the mile from Fulton Street and Franklin Avenue, rather than make the several train transfers which would have put me a block from home. Franklin Avenue was an elevated train station: at the bottom of the steps awaited the one corner I was afraid of, a seedy intersection that felt menacing even on ordinary nights.

This particular night, there was a crowd at the foot of the El steps, listening to an angry black orator. He stood on a makeshift raised platform decorated with signs for the U.S. Labor Party, a Communist front. Usually I liked crowds; I trusted them, I was curious about speechmakers. But this crowd had a nasty growl to it. The orator was whipping them up about Emmett Till, the boy who had just been lynched down South. I knew about the case, because my liberal parents talked about it often; we were outraged at the bigots who had lynched Emmett Till. But suddenly that didn't matter: I had to traverse a semicircle around the crowd, making myself inconspicuous, before I could continue down Fulton Street.

"Now they took that twelve-year-old Negro boy and strung him up and choked the sweet life out of him, just because they *saaaid* . . . said he looked at a white woman. Said he *looked* at a white woman. And our government sits by, don't do a thing. Not a thing. So I ask you. What are *you* going to do about it? What you gonna do about it?"

Everyone started yelling for revenge. I tried to make myself small, harmless, childlike. The thought struck me that I was about the same age as Emmett Till. An eye for an eye. I began inching my way behind the crowd, as silently as I could, when suddenly some voices started yelling, "Hey, here's one!"

"Look at that white devil!"

"He got some nerve comin round here."

"Leave him alone," growled the speaker. "He just a kid."

"Emmett Till just a kid!" responded someone.

"Our conflict is with the ones in power. Let us not confuse the issue," the speaker said wearily. The crowd turned back to listen. I scurried up the street. He had saved my skin—whether out of compassion or ideological purity I would never know.

I had lived on Washington Avenue for three years, and was approaching fourteen, when a new white family moved into the building. By that time we had made casual friendships with many neighbors, and almost resented the presence of this new white contingent, who, we felt obscurely, had no business being here. You would think we wanted to shut the door after us and keep the neighborhood from tipping. But it was rather that, like typical American Jews, we had assimilated—albeit to a black ghetto—and the fact that these newcomers were Jews who spoke with a heavy Polish accent, looking like they'd just come fresh off the boat, made us uncomfortable. They would draw attention to our being Jewish, to the whole idea of Jewishness.

Sure enough, the Janusches were delighted when, after probing my mother in the hallway, they found out we were Jewish. Too delighted, for my taste. Confirming my worst fears, they remarked about the *"schwarzes"* around us not knowing how to "keep clean." Occasionally I saw the newcomers in the darkened, orange-walled lobby, entering while I was leaving. Mr. Janusch, a bone-slender man with a mustache, who wore a suit, tie, fedora, and topcoat, even in balmy weather; his stout wife, who seemed always to be bossing her husband, and Georgie, their pudgy ten-year-old. The boy spoke reluctantly to his mother in Polish, but whenever he saw some other kid coming, he would break out a very American whine, "Oh, Ma!"

After a few months, I got the peculiar impression that Mrs. Janusch was studying me. Why, I had no idea, but whenever our paths crossed she would eye me with a quick, shrewd look. She had a penchant for black fur collars and feathery ruffs, which set off her chubby but not unpretty face in the manner of middle-period Elizabeth Taylor. Her jet-black eyes flashed imperiously, as though she were used to giving orders in the Old Country. My sister Betty Ann had immediately dubbed her "the Polish Countess."

One day, as I was getting the mail, Mrs. Janusch pounced on me from nowhere.

"Excuse me, you go to *chader*?" she asked, using the Yiddish word for Hebrew school.

"Not anymore. I had my bar mitzvah a year ago," I said, blushing. "I go once a week to a Bible discussion group for kids who have been bar mitzvahed."

"And do you lay *tefillin*?" she asked, referring to the morning devotional prayers with leather phylacteries which are the duty of young Jewish men.

"Sometimes. Not so much lately."

"But you read Hebrew well. Your mother tells me you were in a Hebrew choir?"

"Yes, until a little while ago," I said, flattered that she should know that.

"What did you do in the choir?"

"I—sang during the High Holidays, and at weddings, bar mitzvahs, concerts."

"And why did you quit?" she asked keenly.

"I got tired of it," I lied. The truth was, my voice had changed with puberty, and besides, I resented the fact that I never got more solos. I had sounded too "American" for the choir leader to feature me; I didn't have that plaintive *shtetl* melisma.

"Everyone around here says you're very smart."

"Around here. . . ."

"Don't deny it. You know my son, George? Do you think you could teach him to read Hebrew? He knows the letters already, but . . . either he is too slow or he just doesn't bother. His father is ashamed that he can't take him to *shul* with him."

"I don't understand Hebrew either. Just a few dozen words."

"But you read it fast, yes? That's all his father wants. Besides, Georgie likes you."

"How can you tell? We've never even had a conversation."

"I can tell the way he looks at you. Mothers know. How do you say in English? 'He looks up to you.' If *you* teach him to read Hebrew, George will be interested."

"I'm not sure how to do it. I've never taught before."

"Think about it. I will speak to your mother. I will pay, of course."

She worked out a deal with my mother. I would get $2.50 a week to tutor Georgie, and, since summer vacation was about to start, Betty Ann would also get paid two dollars to make his lunch on weekdays. Two-fifty was good money for me in those days—two and a half times my weekly allowance. The choir had only paid me twenty-five dollars a year; I could make that now in ten weeks. Besides, the idea of teaching appealed to me. At school I loved to stand in front of the class and deliver a report or recite a poem. Aside from my tiresome need to show off, I had, even at that early point, a genuine pedagogic urge, which would someday lead me to a teaching career. But I was still uncertain how to go about it. Should I prepare lessons in Hebrew, use learning games? I didn't know any. I would have to bluff—a thought that planted butterflies in my stomach.

My first lesson was scheduled for a Sunday afternoon. The Janusches had asked me to come at four, but they were still finishing off their midday roast when I arrived, so they asked me to wait in the boarder's room for ten minutes. This was a small room at the end of the hall, which they had rented out to an elderly tailor. Every Sunday he went to visit his sister in a nursing home in Queens. The room had an odor of stacked dust and incontinence. On the floor were black socks rolled into balls, brown cardboard suitcases, prayer books, fabric remnant books, used tea glasses, and recent Yiddish newspapers. I occupied myself trying to puzzle out the headlines and captions on the front page. "La-zar Ka-gan-o-vitch," I translated into English the Yiddish letters below the photograph of Kremlin chiefs stiffly reviewing a military parade. Whether the Yiddish daily's slant was pro- or anti-Soviet I couldn't tell; only that it was printed in New York City and fascinated with Russia.

The room's disheveled condition stood in marked contrast to the rest of the apartment, which was immaculate, the oak or mahogany furniture highly polished, the inlaid parquet floors spotless. Yet the Janusches had suggested that the first lesson take place in the boarder's room: I wondered why. Perhaps they wanted to spare Georgie the embarrassment of their looking on. Too, the room did have the appropriately musty air of a synagogue back room.

I was sunk deep in a scratchy velveteen chair of a faded rose color, with dusky splotches where the fabric had been rubbed against the grain, when Georgie entered. I immediately stood up, closed the door behind him, and handed him a prayer book from the floor. "Read this." I pointed to a passage. He looked at me with imploring eyes, as though about to be dragged to the slaughterhouse. I was calm but stern: if anything, his fear reassured me and quickened my sense of power, making me feel less like a fraud. He began stumbling through the first syllables. Right then, I decided to spend the first few sessions simply listening to him read and gauging his level—the old diagnostic-stall maneuver, which all teachers in the dark employ. His forehead beaded with sweat as he read. I put my hand on his shoulder. "Start again. This time read just the first paragraph. Slowly, don't rush it."

He began again, and I corrected each of his mistakes in a neutral voice, while looking over his shoulder. He would bite his lip when he stumbled, or punch his arm, muttering "Dummy." He was making mistakes more from nerves than from ignorance. I knew I would have to reduce his level of fear somehow. My strategy was to get him to read one paragraph perfectly, build up his confidence this way, then move on to the next. The inspiration that struck me during the first lesson was very simple: all he needs is practice.

By the end of the hour, he could read the first three paragraphs of the daily prayer. I returned him to his parents. I don't know whether or not they had been listening at the door, but they greeted us with pleased expressions. Georgie's piglet eyes gleamed shiny yet sleepy. "Now can I play outside?" he demanded. His mother kissed him on his blond, cropped head. Then she squeezed his cheeks together and yanked his face up to her lips, giving him a real mother-son smooch. The quiet Mr. Janusch smiled his gold-toothed smile and looked away apologetically.

———————

The Janusches lived two flights below us, so that it was possible for Betty Ann to stick her head out the window of their apartment and call up the courtyard shaft, "Phee-lips! Gee-orge is ready for you," in a thick Polish accent, mimicking the Countess's mispronunciations. I would put down my library book (that summer I was making my way through *100 American Plays*, encountering for the first time the suave humor of George S. Kaufman and Philip Barry, planets remote from Fort Greene, Brooklyn) and run downstairs, where Georgie would have just finished his lunch, typically a grilled cheese sandwich and tomato soup. Betty Ann, good sister that she was, often left an extra lunch for me.

I was fired with ambition now to make George into a smooth, rapid reader of Hebrew. I had visions of his being called up to the Torah and impressing everyone. "Who is that little kid?" they would say. "Where did he learn to read so well?" But his progress was less than astonishing. Without his parents in the next room, Georgie proved harder to control—I practically had to sit on him to keep him in one place. The kid was sly and used every delaying device he could.

We would begin by chatting for a few minutes. It was then that Georgie would do his damnedest to undercut the lesson, through a combination of coyness and mischief. "Oh please?" he would beg, pressing his fingers together in a steeple.

"That's the Christian sign of prayer—that won't do you any good here. Come on, get in the other room," I'd say. Next he would try to make me chase him: daring me, he would dart toward my reach and spin away. Admittedly, Georgie was not very fast, but sometimes he could squirm out of my grasp like the greased little piglet he was. He seemed to crave rough-and-tumble physical contact with an older male; perhaps he never got enough of that from his father. His clownishness made me laugh against my will, and he used it to his advantage to stall (just as, I suppose, I used his liking for me to make him study). Other times, my amusement at him vanished without a trace, usually when he was being a little too cute or coy. Such maneuvers might charm an adult but they would fail to work on another child.

If Georgie sometimes miscalculated by forgetting I was still a child, he remembered it enough to exploit my secret weakness: that I also wanted to play. I had made the mistake one day of taking him outside for a game of punchball after he had done particularly well with his lessons. After that it was always: "Aw, why can't we just skip Hebrew this time and play punchball? I won't tell, I promise." Instantly, the nerves in my punchball arm quivered, as I imagined belting a pink ball down the block. "No, we have to study."

We eventually struck an arrangement. I would use the punchball game as a carrot to keep him, the donkey, praying. If he read x number of pages without a single mistake, we could cut ten minutes off the end of the lesson. A few times, however, I gave in to temptation and we went outside to play before our goals had been met. We would try to scare up a game with which-ever kids happened to be in the vicinity. If there weren't enough players for two punchball squads, we would resort to three-box baseball or hit the dime.

One reason Georgie was so keen on our playing outside together was that I protected him. He had already acquired a reputation on the block for being both obnoxious and defenseless. A chunky kid who tried to whine his way into every game, he seemed a walking invitation for a stiff punch. Betty Ann joked that we were really getting paid to see that the kid didn't get beat up. There was some truth in that: since Georgie was lonely and friendless, his mother had in effect hired him a couple of companions.

The synagogue for which I was preparing Georgie, the Fort Greene Jew-ish Center, was housed in a dignified, red-stone Romanesque structure with a pointed roof and stained-glass windows. The congregation, a drop-let of Orthodox Jewry in an indifferent ocean, had been forced to rent an old, abandoned church until such time as it could muster the resources to build a new synagogue. (It seems that the building has returned to use as a church, since the sign outside it today says "Eglise Haitienne.")

I usually entered the synagogue through the back door, which was a block closer to my house and opened onto a gymnasium, the unofficial domain of us teenagers. Here the Saturday-night socials for teens were held: a phonograph with a felt turntable would sit on a folding chair, and I would station myself by it, pretending that monitoring the choice of 45 rpm records engrossed me too much to dance, while the other boys tried to feel up the more precocious twelve-year-old girls. Here also the Boy Scouts met. I had gone to only one meeting of the troop's chapter, and, turned off by the unsupervised rowdiness, all these doltish Jewish boys wrestling each other sadistically on the floor, I sneaked out when no one was looking. The gym was also where the kiddush of wine and honey cake and sometimes herring was set out, on folding tables with white tablecloths, after bar mitzvahs.

You had to cross the lengthy gymnasium, with its basketball hoops, sports equipment cartons, and folded bingo tables, to enter the synagogue proper. But once there, you came upon the Old World. It was a happy accident that the church interior had duplicated the classical architecture of Eastern European synagogues: the carved wooden railings, the steps leading to the raised ark in the middle, the balconies reserved for women and girls, all of which had a curiously nautical flavor, like the deck of a clipper ship. The old men in the front benches would chant in hoarse singsong the first words of a prayer, such as *"Ashro yishraw v'seycha,"* then rock back and forth in their ancient bobbing motion, *davening*, mumbling the rest under their breaths. It was these old men who were the spiritual (though not the socioeconomic) heart of the community. They kept an eye on tradition, and would grumble at the little mistakes Rabbi Dorfman, just turned forty, made in the service, or criticize his upbeat, patriotic sermons. I shared their contempt for this nasal-voiced, smiling rabbi, with his seminary vocabulary: "Let us now partake of the repast." But the old men were no kinder to me. At my bar mitzvah, when I had not only chanted the traditional *haftorah* portion but led the whole morning service, having learned the routine in my Hebrew choir, and there was even some talk around the congregation of their using me in future as a boy cantor (to save money they would otherwise have to spend hiring an outside cantor), and I was accepting compliments all around, two of the elders crooked their fingers at me and said I should not have repeated a certain phrase more than twice, it was a sin! They knew.

These old men were small and wrinkled as dwarfs, and they seemed to have nothing to do with America. I liked them for that, and for the furious looks they gave us boys who breathlessly entered from the gym during morning service, causing the leather doors to creak. (You were supposed to stand waiting and look through the diamond-shaped window cut into the door, and only enter during a break in the service.) Except for a few grandfathers who grinned toothlessly at anything young, most of these old worshipers showed no sentimentality toward children. Perhaps because they were equally small, they felt endangered by these wild beasts that showed no reverence for the Law.

From my favorite pew, last row right, where I could watch everyone who was seated in the balcony, especially a girl I liked, Merrily Waxman, without being seen myself, I would find myself drawn to the old men and wonder what consoling thoughts collected in their minds while they read the same prayers that left me cold. I wanted to believe in God and the rest, the way they did. But all that incomprehensible Hebrew did nothing for me, and the English translation facing it was no better: incessant praise for an Almighty Deity who seemed to need to be flattered and told all the time how great He was. I knew this was not the only way to think about my religion, but it was too late, I was on the slippery slope of disbelief.

And yet I kept coming back to the synagogue. No one forced me to—certainly not my parents, who told me even on the High Holidays, "You can go, it's not for us, honey." Or my older brother, who was already proudly calling himself an atheist. But the year after a young man undergoes a bar mitzvah is a crucial time, in which he is specifically instructed to strengthen his faith. Precisely because I was no longer strapped to the conveyor belt of bar mitzvah lessons, and my participation was voluntary, it seemed to me I was duty-bound to try. I rose a few times at dawn and lashed the leather thongs of the phylacteries around my wrists and read the morning prayers. The upshot was that I felt embarrassed, as though I were attempting to acquire the mindset of a nomadic shepherd in opposition to the modern world.

Only in the synagogue did I not feel embarrassed about practicing Judaism. There I felt bored, but that seemed appropriate: everyone else was. And sometimes a mysterious shiver went through me when I put on the *tallis*, the ceremonial striped shawl; I felt a warmth which issued from more than the thin weight of the cloth. I instantly became more stoop-shouldered under that silken pressure, as though bypassing manhood and progressing straight to a pious, bent old age. When the Torah was paraded around the synagogue, I scrambled like everyone else to touch it, kissing the shawl's fringes to my lips and pressing them against the holy scroll as it marched past my aisle. I was kissing God.

———

At other times, the Jewish ritual meant nothing to me. Why was I drilling Georgie in sight-reading Hebrew? It seemed so mechanical, this skill of reading Hebrew rapidly without mistakes. What did he need it for? As far as I could tell, his parents were not particularly religious; they didn't even light Sabbath candles.

Receiving my wages one week, I noticed that Mrs. Janusch, in her black orchid summer dress, had numbers on her arms. It didn't particularly surprise me: ever since I was a small boy, Brooklyn had accumulated those who had been in the concentration camps. You would go into a hardware store and the man behind the counter would be gruff and ill-tempered, and you'd notice the numbers on his arm. The Polish Countess was not that sour type, but she was somewhat adamant. In any case, after this discovery it began to make sense to me that she would want her son to know how to carry himself as a Jew, having paid such a steep price for it herself.

Each time Mrs. Janusch counted my wages, she tried to lure me into a heart-to-heart talk about George's progress.

"Do you think he's slow?" she'd ask.

"He's all right. He's getting it."

"But he's lazy. He doesn't practice when you're not here. I wonder if he has the brains to amount to anything. No, it's not brains, that isn't the problem—"

"Certainly not, he's a smart kid."

"You mustn't think because intelligence comes easy to you," she said, "that it is the same for everyone."

I blushed. I wasn't being modest; I certainly thought I was smarter than her son. But she should not have been the one to tell me that. Why all these interrogations about Georgie? Leave the kid alone, I thought. What I didn't understand was that her constant parental concern masked her adoration of him. It was one more opportunity to talk about her beloved child. I misread it as a sort of flirtation passing between her and me. I resented her way of cornering me, especially as I found her, in spite of my initial impressions, attractive. My youthful tendency to caricature all adults as grotesque told me that she was a fat, silly foreigner; but my fourteen-year-old eyes kept being drawn to her bosom. And she would give me these shrewd, penetrating looks. It all comes back to me, the terror of that deep, probing look her woman's eyes imposed on me as a boy.

The one time Mrs. Janusch crossed the line was when she told me I was my mother's favorite. It shamed me to hear this woman, this outsider, calmly put into words what I had long suspected but dared not believe, in loyalty to my siblings; in fact, I rejected the claim with all my might. Far from feeling honored, I held it deeply against Mrs. Janusch for her invasive picking at that Oedipal thread.

———

One day, Georgie and I were taking a breather from reading Hebrew by going over some Bible stories. I had just read aloud the one about Joshua praying to have the sun stop in the sky, when Georgie said: "That's impossible. That's a cock-and-bull story."

"Why do you say that?"

"Because, if the sun stopped, everything would fall off the earth and we'd all be dead. Joshua would be dead, too." My pupil seemed so proud of his cleverness I had to smile.

"Maybe it is scientifically impossible. But don't you think that if God wanted to, He could do something that was scientifically impossible?"

"No, because that's what *impossible* means. It can't be done."

"Except in the case of miracles," I said impishly.

Georgie looked stymied. "I don't get it. You're gonna tell me—?"

"Look, we read in the Bible that the earth was created in six days. Scientists like Darwin say that's impossible. So there are two explanations. One is that if you believe God is all-powerful, He could do anything He wants. He could have made the earth in six days, and He could have strewn fossils around that looked like they came from millions of years apart. I'm not saying He did, but He could have. The other explanation is that each of those six days stood for so many thousands or millions of years. So the Bible tells the truth, but in a roundabout way."

"I get a beating when I do that."

"It's not a fib. It's a code. The Bible substitutes one thing for another. Six days means six million years. Maybe making the sun stop is code for an eclipse. Everyone got confused in the midst of battle, thinking Joshua had made the sun disappear."

"So which is right, the miracle or the eclipse?"

"That's for you to choose."

"You're the teacher, you're supposed to tell me. I'm just the smart-aleck kid."

"I don't know what the answer is. I wasn't around at the time."

"The way I see it, a code is just another way of saying it's a cock-and-bull story."

"You love that expression, don't you?"

Georgie's challenging of the Joshua story pleased me. Essentially I agreed with him, though my own doubts about the Bible arose less from scientific contradiction than from moral concerns: the stories where God came off acting like a bully. For instance, Sodom and Gomorrah: why wouldn't God go along with Abraham's plea for mercy? I had thrashed this out in one session of the study group for post–bar mitzvah kids at the Fort Greene Jewish Center. These discussions were conducted by Max Drucker, a somber, intelligent man with silver hair and a pencil mustache, whose leg wound in World War II forced him to limp with pain. It was Drucker who had suggested to my parents that I become a cantor. First, because I had a good singing voice, and, second, because cantors did not have to fight in wars but could serve on the sidelines, like chaplains. This perk did not seem to me a sufficient career motivation. But I was touched that he had thought enough of me to make the suggestion. Maybe because he did like me and I respected his learning, I took it upon myself to argue with him at every session. Drucker listened patiently. He was the kind of intellectual opponent who conveys the impression that, for all his seeming openness, it is only a matter of time before you give in to his superior reason. He was stubborn; I was, too. The difference was that when it came to Judaism, he knew what he was talking about and I didn't.

"Mr. Drucker, maybe the grown-ups in Sodom and Gomorrah were bad, but I don't think God should have destroyed the babies or the little children, when they were just copying their parents."

"You are saying that environment influences behavior," said Drucker. "But does that excuse it?"

"Well, if you come from a long line of family members who see evil as normal, you probably act evil, just to fit in. Couldn't God understand that?"

"It is not a question of God's understanding. God understands all. But let us discuss *your* understanding for the moment. Yes, we are shaped by environment, but also we are responsible for our actions. Into each person God puts a *seed*, an awareness of good and evil. We are given free will, which differentiates us from machines, and it is up to each of us to follow the good."

"But doesn't it take a while for that awareness to develop? And in the case of babies or small children, why didn't God give them a decent chance?"

"It is not for us to sit in judgment of God's actions. If God destroyed Sodom and Gomorrah, He must have been convinced that the people in it were past redemption."

"But why does God see people in such black and white terms?" I persisted. "Most people are a combination of good and bad."

"Some people are evil," said Drucker, seeming to speak from experience.

"But God made the world, so He made the evil in it, too. It must have been part of His plan for those Sodom and Gommorahites to be bad in the first place."

"No. He gave them a choice, and they chose to ignore Him. To sin and to blaspheme. You see the difference?"

"But if He left evil around in the world as a temptation, and then made man into a creature who was too weak to refuse, then it was a foregone conclusion that man would fall into the trap."

"You and I are talking about two different things here. I am not discussing how evil came to be in the world, which is an interesting theological problem for some other time, but specifically Sodom and Gomorrah, a place where men and women not only fell into the trap but fell up to their ears. They were extraordinarily evil. And without exception. Let me give you an example closer to home. Your argument reminds me of the Nuremberg trials. After World War II ended, the biggest Nazi criminals were rounded up and put on trial." He paused for effect. I nodded, tired of this analogy: in postwar Jewish Brooklyn, every minor infraction led straight to Buchenwald. "And after they got through pointing fingers at each other, which was a nauseating spectacle in and of itself, they all came up with the same excuse: 'We were just following orders.' They were just conforming to the 'normal,' to use your word, behavior in Nazi Germany. I remember one of them even testified that if there had been protests from the ordinary German people, they might have thought twice—but nobody raised a word of protest. This Nazi officer was trying to say that, in an environment where everyone is guilty, no one is guilty. That is a common misconception. In fact the opposite is true. In an environment where everyone is guilty, *everyone* should be punished!" Here, Drucker turned red in the face and raised his voice. "Only in that way can we have justice. And that is the meaning of God's destruction of Sodom and Gomorrah."

All this time the other post–bar mitzvah boys, who came every week, perhaps because their parents badgered them or because they liked to play basketball afterward in the gym, looked on resentfully at our duel. They thought Drucker was a gimpy wheeze bag, and I a smart-ass show-off. They would have been surprised to know how much it pained me to rip holes in my faith, how much I wished I could have been one of them.

By September, Georgie had become fluent enough at reading Hebrew for me to bring him to synagogue, where he was called to the Torah and read aloud passably for two minutes, during a special Young People's part of the service. His parents were so pleased that they urged me to continue teaching him Hebrew (a language I still insisted I did not know) and, additionally, to help him with spelling, one of his poorer subjects. I was glad for the chance to diversify my pedagogic repertoire.

For an hour each afternoon, after the regular school day, I would enter the Janusches' clean, dust-free apartment. Sometimes Georgie would be hiding, and would leap out at me. Georgie's success at the Torah service had changed him, made him cockier. "It's a snap," he would say when I reproached him for not trying enough, and I let him coast for a while.

With the colder weather, a new craze began: marbles. It started on a rainy day. Punchball being out of the question, Georgie took out his marble set after the lesson, and I fell in with him. I had never gone in for marbles when I was his age, so their charm lay ready to hit me full force. There were black agates, eerie and formal as obsidian, and gray-green combinations the color of cats' eyes, and smoky whites, clouded over like cataracts, and one pure purple.

I loved getting down on my knees with Georgie and matching him shot for shot. The basic idea was to be the first to reach certain destination points—the dining room table leg, the fourth parquet tile, the standing lamp—while knocking out, as in croquet, the opponent's marbles. But we kept making up more elaborate rules. The dining room floor was our playing field, and we spent much of the game under the oak dining table, with whose leaves and brackets I became well-acquainted. The room looked different from this vantage point: we had turned its stuffy order into a shooting range. From sheer rambunctiousness we would send marbles flying under the radiator or even into the bedroom of his parents, which we were expressly forbidden to enter. A sliding door separated the dining room from the bedroom, and when it was left open, a marble would sometimes get stuck in the runner's grooves, or bounce merrily past and roll under the bed. Were we to lose it and should his parents happen to find it there, Georgie warned, "We would be in biiiiiig trouble."

I knew I was forfeiting dignity and moral authority in scrambling around after my tutee on all fours. But perhaps this is why I liked the game: it equalized us. We had marble tournaments that went on for hours, and, once the sport had gotten into my blood, there were days when temptation led me to suspend lessons altogether. This was a serious mistake: I was giving Georgie ammunition for snitching on me. Nor did I like the aftertaste of forgoing my duties and cheating my employers. But the game held such seductive power over me that Georgie knew he had only to propose marbles for my will to buckle. That fall I lived for marbles, their neutral temperature and lightness in my hand, the skill involved in controlling length and curve of flight with a finger flick, their resemblance to cut diamonds or other colorful jewel stones, the hilarious way they kept rolling and ending up in unforeseen places, their momentum and resilience, like a cartoon character falling off a cliff and dusting himself off, seemingly indestructible, all the more curious in that they were made of glass.

I sensed myself entering a morally confused zone where the rules were becoming too flexible, and might ultimately undermine my ability to control my student. What complicated the issue of discipline was that Georgie's behavior seemed to be undergoing a change for the worse. Every day his speech grew more vulgar and full of TV clichés, perhaps mimicking his schoolmates': he had the immigrant's quick ear for slang, the child's need to adapt socially, and would imitate Porky Pig or Bugs Bunny by the hour, until I wanted to thrash him. If I told him to read a page in Hebrew, his first response was likely to be "Thuffering thuccatash!"

"Come on, be serious," I'd say.

"B-b-b-biya, b-bibiya, bibya. That's all, folks!"

He would latch on to a phrase like "Duck, you sucker!" and use it every minute, the way a small child repeats a potty word just to get on your nerves. He became devoted to pig Latin: everything was "ouyay antcay," and so on. "Shoot, Sarge!" was another of his pet sayings, spoken with a lisp, as a coy way to avoid my teaching demands. If I had a hard time locating the authentic Georgie underneath these robotic pop-culture quotations, I could not help but appreciate his strategy. All this spewing of lines from cartoons and radio jingles was a clever resistance to after-school tutoring, a revenge for my robbing him of his leisure playtime.

I needed to find other incentives to keep him involved. But instead, I began losing patience with him. My hold on his respect was loosening, and the more saucily he behaved, the more I wanted to slap him into line. The first time I hit him, he was quite surprised. So was I. "Well, I told you to pick up the book!" I said hotly, hoping my indignant tone would drown out what I had done. It seemed a momentary aberration, one which need never be repeated.

Yet something about his chunky body and squealing laugh made me want to punch him a few days later, and a few days after that. It wasn't only that he was so provoking; in fact, I don't think I ever got angry enough to really paste him. No, basically I liked Georgie, but I just wanted to plant my fist somewhere in his flesh. I have mentioned already what I took to be the boy's hunger for physical roughhousing with an older male, his propensity to come perilously close to me and then wheel away. Well, I discovered much to my surprise that I had a similar longing: to catch the kid and squeeze him in a tight wrestling hug, to graze his head with a noogie (a playful head knuckle), and finally, quite simply, to hurt him. I wonder if it wasn't some sort of sadomasochistic dance on both our parts: he would taunt, I would punch. The same pattern as I had mastered with my older brother, only this time I was the one dealing out blows. One could say in my defense that my whole "environment," with its imprintings of violence, had taught me to act this way, but what kind of bullshit excuse is that? I was supposed to be the good boy, the smart one. Was this the only way I could attempt to shrug off the premature burdens of grown-up responsibility that had been placed on me, or that I had placed on myself? Another bullshit excuse. Was it my retaliation for Mrs. Janusch stigmatizing me as my mother's favorite? Who knows? Each time I lost control and punched Georgie—usually with a swift blow to the arm—I found myself to be a stranger. I was amazed at the brutality surfacing from inside me.

"Don't tell your mother, okay?" I first threatened, then pleaded. He looked at me with a silent, wounded expression, the dark, superior understanding that the abused has of the abuser.

My hunch was that he would not tell his mother. In the meantime, in the week that followed, I made a vow never to hit him again. I became tolerance itself in our lessons. Georgie seemed placated; inwardly I rejoiced at my narrow escape. "Just let me get away with this one thing, Lord," I prayed to the God of Abraham and Isaac. On Friday, I went down to the Janusch apartment to collect my wages. The Countess had taken off her work clothes, and was sitting at the dining room table in a black slip. Her feet were soaking in a basin of warm water. She looked weary as she counted out the money.

"Georgie tells me that you hit him."

"I . . . did lose my temper with him once, yes—"

"Not once but several times," she cut me off. "I am very disappointed in you." She looked me hard in the face, to let me understand that, in addition to my sins against Georgie, I had personally violated her trust as well.

What could I say? I agreed completely. "I'm sorry."

She nodded. "You cannot work for us anymore."

I had prepared myself for some reproach, yet, oddly enough, I had not expected to be fired; such a total break caught me off-balance. It was on the tip of my tongue to ask for another chance, but there was that in me that recognized the justice of her decision. I got up and left.

This passage of my life, this business of teaching Georgie, was really over. In the days that followed I felt sick to my stomach. It was the squeamish guilty sensation that comes from not only knowing you did wrong but knowing that your true nature has been found out. I would encounter that same sensation at various other times in my adult life, when I had to ask myself: how could I have done or said such a cruel thing? I would cringe, I would laugh disbelievingly, to cushion the feeling, and I would never learn a thing from any of it, except that I should not be surprised when some foulness leaps out of me. Like the people in Sodom and Gomorrah, apparently I was one of the evil ones.

My Brother the Radio Host

My brother, Leonard, is a radio personality, heard every weekday in the New York metropolitan area on a midday, two-hour interview show. Being a generalist and a quick study, he ranges widely, questioning novelists, politicians, scientists, film directors, actresses, car mechanics, chefs. I listen as often as I can, not only because he is my brother but because he has, in my opinion, the best show on radio—the most informative, discerning, entertaining. Even knowing him as I do, I am amazed at how astutely he can shape a fifteen-minute or half-hour interview. Of course, knowing him so well, I also am aware when he is bluffing about a subject he has only vague notions about, and I sometimes catch him making errors. I will yell at the radio, "No no no, Lenny!" when he gets his facts wrong or makes a dubious comment. I am more tolerant of his bad puns; those we love should be permitted their puns.

One of my secret pleasures in listening to him is that I can still hear the unsure but learning-eager adolescent he was at our dinner table, imparting his latest discovery, inside the smooth tones of the all-knowing radio personality. Though he always had a euphonious voice, he has done considerable work on that instrument, shaping its baritone, losing the family's Brooklyn regionalisms. The only aspect of his radio persona that dismays me is when he comes across as dripping with solicitude for some guest, say, who is telling a sob story to flog her memoir; and I sense an insincerity in that momentary delay, that vocal catch (ending questions with "isn't it?") that has become a signature tic in his delivery.

Perhaps because I'm so conscious of how sardonically unsentimental he can be off the air, it is clear to me what a constructed artifact is his radio persona of the patient, empathic listener. It's part of what makes him such a professional.

We are both proud of each other's success—he no less than I. Sometimes as I'm listening to his show I will be brought up short by a reference to his brother the writer. I register that I am in his thoughts as much as he is in mine.

Are we competitive? Of course, as brothers often are. But the roots of our sibling rivalry go far back, and have been overlaid with much self-consciousness on that score. The times I do experience sibling rivalry are when he is not around, and others bring him up. People are constantly pitting us against each other, for either sadistic amusement or experimental curiosity, to see what reactions they can elicit. "Do you and your brother get along?" they will ask, often with the juicy hope of hearing that we don't. But we do. Lenny is far more well-known in the city than I: a radio personality cannot help but have more fans than an essayist. And the bond a radio talk-show host has with his regular listeners is psychologically complex: not seeing the person but only hearing that mellifluous, sympathetic voice each day invites them to fantasize about and idealize the host. Though I understand this hero-worshiping dynamic, I still don't like it when I am giving a reading at a bookstore and someone's first question is about my brother: that seems tactless, at a moment when I am trying to project an outsize authorial persona. I forgive his radio fans their need to connect with celebrity through me. I have a harder time forgiving my fellow authors, who should know better but only want to talk to me about the last time they were on my brother's show or saw him at a party. I have the urge to say to them: Look, I've written a dozen books, why not spare a few words for my work? But typically they are more interested in my brother's ability to publicize their writing; they come to regard him as a flattering, megaphone extension of their egos.

An awkward moment, too, occurs when I am introduced to someone who says, "Oh, I love what you do on the radio!" I should take the ap-

proach John Ford did when complimented on *Red River*; he would thank
them politely and never make the correction that that particular western
was directed by Howard Hawks. My brother tells me many people compliment *him* on the books he has ostensibly written. We laugh at this notion that one could be expected to hold down a demanding daily radio
show while turning out books. It's as if the public could not be bothered
to understand that there are two Lopates, so they keep conflating us.

I also laugh *at* him sometimes, because his renown has given him a
touchy sense of self-importance. He does not like to have to wait in line,
or produce IDs. If we go to a party together and people do not recognize
his name, he will sulk. His way of sulking is to stare high into the middle
distance with a frown.

A trickier side to having a radio personality in the family is that he
is not always able to come down from his public persona. I become instantly wary of him when I sense that he is not talking to *me* so much
as to his listeners, or if I catch him making pronouncements, explaining something he should know I know. (Then again, *I* should talk: after
teaching a seminar or giving several readings on tour, I don't always
succeed in descending from Mount Olympus and attending to my wife
and daughter on their terms.) With Lenny, I often find myself on guard,
cocking my ear for a more private, fraternal tone that should be my due;
and if it is not immediately forthcoming, I take umbrage.

In short, I am jealous of our unique connection and do not like to
see it diluted. I would rather get together with him for a tête-à-tête than
share him with his significant other and friends. Those times when we
do see each other alone, going to either a play or a preview screening to
which he has invited me, we converse with the old rapport.

I should point out that, for all my antennae-alert mistrust of my
brother's outer-directed personality, it is Lenny who shares openly with
me his emotional problems or confusions. I tend to be more reserved in
those matters, being the younger and, historically, the more intimidated;
and I guess I prefer the power of the listener-therapist role, whereas
Lenny is much more given to self-dramatization, even if it means being
seen as the one in crisis.

For all that, we are, I suppose, quite a lot alike. When we were growing up, we indulged in *The Corsican Brothers* fantasy that whatever happened to one, the other would also feel at the same moment, however much geographical distance separated us. These days, if we don't see each other for a while and then reunite and compare notes on movies, books, music, or current events, we find we've almost always come to the same conclusions. In our adolescence Lenny was my mentor, introducing me to Billie Holiday, Brueghel, and the Dadaists; so it is hardly surprising that, my mind having been formed to some extent by his, we continue to have similar tastes. This very overlap is a source of both comfort and chagrin: I sometimes get impatient with that consensus and yearn for more stimulating disagreement.

The narcissism of small differences: he is three years older, yet more ardent, youthful, risk-taking. He still chases happiness. I always act like the older, graver, more prudent one, giving advice. He likes fine wines and gourmet food, is something of an epicurean. I, more of a stoic, can appreciate a well-cooked meal but will not go miles out of my way for one.

He is bolder, even to the point of reckless. When we were kids I would watch how he got into fights or into trouble with teachers, and I'd decide to take a safer path. He still acts, I watch. Bicycling around Europe in his midsixties, he had an accident and fell off his bike and was taken to a hospital, where he received several stitches. After he'd phoned from abroad, asking me to pick him up at the airport and drive him home, I waited for him at the receiving entrance, and he had a dazed look, a bandage on his head, glancing around and not recognizing me at first. It was disturbing to see my older brother so vulnerable, so mortal; yet it gave me pleasure to be entrusted, as the younger sibling, with his care.

When we were teenagers, people would cruelly tell him I was the better-looking. Now, he is the more handsome. He has retained a full head of hair, while I have lost mine, following our father's tendency to baldness. He usually wears a full beard and has a commanding stare (no longer hidden by spectacles, thanks to laser surgery).

One of the ways we differ most is that my brother identifies with our mother, and I with our father. Both our parents have died, but they continue to rule our psyches and orient our moral compasses. Our mother was a flamboyant, lusty, histrionic personality, for whom the term *larger than life* could apply. She had wanted to sing and act, was thwarted for many years by having to work and raise a family, but in the last decades of her life she did perform onstage, acted in TV commercials, sang in supper clubs. Our father was a withdrawn, self-taught intellectual who wanted to be a writer; he lived what Matthew Arnold called "the buried life," toiling as a factory worker and textile clerk. He was the taciturn scapegoat of our family: my mother divorced him in old age and placed him in a nursing home. While they lived together they made an odd couple: Eros and Thanatos. I felt sorry for my father; our fates became permanently entwined when I assumed his literary ambition, not entirely to his pleasure, since it meant both honoring and replacing him. My brother, on the other hand, never got along with our father and retains very little fondness for him. Lenny drew his strength from the example of my mother, who threw herself, with bravado, into the fray as an entertainer.

When we were younger, my brother wanted to be an artist. As a child he painted battleships and self-portraits; he was an excellent draftsman. Inclined always to the more austere, rigorous artists, such as Piero della Francesca and Roger van der Weyden, in his twenties he graduated to abstraction, studying at the university with such luminaries as Ad Reinhardt and Mark Rothko. His paintings tended in a geometric, color-field direction. They were good, I thought. Had he continued, he would certainly have made a go of it. But he claimed he was dissuaded when he saw others doing the same sort of painting as his, only better; he thought he lacked the requisite passion to devote his life to painting.

Each of the four Lopate siblings has had artistic ambitions: my brother wanted to be a painter; I, a writer; Betty Ann, a musician; my youngest sister, Joan, a filmmaker. As it turned out, I was the only one who successfully cobbled a career out of my art. This fact looms large in my mind, and fills me with a dark mix of gloating and survivor's guilt. (I *said* we were competitive.) Regardless of the greater adulation my brother receives, or the argument that radio might be construed as his art form, I continue to feel I hold an edge, based on the idea that my writings have at least a chance of enduring, while his improvised radio chatter disappears into the ether. His is a journalist's way of knowing, facts gathered for the day and ejected once the occasion is over; my writing process, I tell myself, is a deeper, more arduous intellectual pursuit.

One of my greatest flaws is the need to regard myself as superior to those around me, and to position myself in such a way that they will feel it, too. Knowing full well that there are many different kinds of intelligence and that, besides, we are all ultimately dust and atoms under the aspect of eternity, I persist in wanting to view myself as the most intelligent person in social situations. That exaggerated self-regard undoubtedly colors my relationship with my brother in unhelpful ways. I insist on holding the "wisdom" and "maturity" cards, and on considering myself the more "reflective." But he overlooks it, perhaps because he is finally the more ample-spirited.

Together we look forward to sharing all the pleasures of old age: nostalgia, illness, incontinence, senility, abandonment. We will not abandon each other, I hope, because the world is less lonely for me as long as my brother is in it. He has been, if not the most important relationship in my life, certainly one of the most defining. I have made it a point alternately to be like him or not to: either way, he has been my lodestar. I'll say more: he has been my personal metaphor for Life itself, in all its encompassing, onrushing urgency.

Wife or Sister?
Abraham and Sarah in Egypt and Gerar

A border incident. Abraham, like many travelers, is worried about being stopped and detained by customs guards for bringing something problematic into the country—in this case, the beauty of his wife. So he passes off Sarah as his sister, to save his own life, and she is brought to Pharaoh as a playmate, and Pharaoh, well-pleased with her, rewards her "brother" with wealth. Then God intervenes and Sarah is given back to her rightful husband. A scandalous story, one of the most unnerving in the Bible: even if you do not consider Abraham "ignoble" (the word Harold Bloom uses), at the very least he seems dishonest. Later, Abraham repeats the ruse in Gerar, and this time Sarah becomes the consort of King Abimelech.* (The scenario is repeated a third time in Genesis, when copycat son Isaac palms off Rebecca as his sister to this same, incorrigibly gullible Abimelech.)

Taken together, these three episodes are referred to by scholars as "the wife-sister stories." I am no biblical scholar, but the stories intrigue me. My plan for this essay is, first, to examine the ways that experts— rabbis, folklorists, anthropologists, literary critics—have written about the wife-sister narratives; then, to consider the psychological viewpoints of Sigmund Freud and Karen Horney on incest, intimacy, and marriage;

---

* The first episode, in Egypt, occurs before Abram's name has been changed to Abraham, and Sarai's to Sarah; the second incident, in Gerar, takes place after the name change. For convenience's sake, I will refer to the couple throughout this essay as Abraham and Sarah.

and, finally, to tell an episode from my own past which I associate, rightly or wrongly, with the Bible tales. I hope to line up all three perspectives like images in a stereopticon, superimposing one over the other over the other to produce a more three-dimensional sense of quandariness.

1. Abraham and Sarah

Rabbinical commentators have labored to put a positive spin on Abraham's deceptions. The customary approach in the Middle Ages was to vilify the other nations as barbarians, accentuating their bloodthirsty and lecherous tendencies, thereby justifying Abraham's fears. These commentators were not above racism, as when one elucidating legend, or *midrash*, has Abraham warn Sarah, " 'now we are about to enter a country whose inhabitants are black-skinned, and therefore your beauty will be all the more conspicuous.' Compared to Sarah's beauty, all other women were as monkeys."* The contrasting modern tendency is to downplay the husband's apprehensions, as when Harold Bloom writes that Abraham "oddly fears that his wife's beauty will expose him to danger"—the word *oddly* making him sound almost paranoid.

One classic *midrash* imagines Abraham going much further to protect Sarah than the terse account in Genesis. In this version, the tax collectors ask Abraham about the contents of his casket, and Abraham answers: barley. No, it must be wheat, they say. Okay, I'll pay the tax on wheat, answers Abraham. The exchange keeps escalating, until he volunteers to pay the taxes for precious jewels and gold, at which point they demand the casket be opened, and they see the ravishing Sarah.

Not all the classic rabbis exonerate Abraham, however. The great Ramban (Nachmanides) unequivocally says: "Know that Abraham our father unintentionally committed a great sin by bringing his righteous wife to a stumbling-block of sin on account of his fear for his life. He should have trusted that G-d would save him and his wife and all his belongings for G-d surely has the power to help and save."

---

* *The Midrash Says*, selected by Rabbi Moshe Weissman.

Somewhere between Ramban and the vindicators lies the analysis of Radak (in Nahum Sarna's paraphrase)

> that Abram was confronted with a moral dilemma, forced to make a choice between two evils. If he discloses the truth he will be killed, and his wife, beautiful and unprotected in an alien society of low morality, will assuredly be condemned to a life of shame and abuse. If, however, he resorts to subterfuge, she may be violated by some Egyptian, but at least husband and wife would both survive. It would have been improper, then, to have relied on a miracle as an excuse for inaction.

Even if we grant Radak's defense, why the need to repeat the story? Surely, if a patriarch's actions look dubious the first time around, our uneasiness can only increase when the story is told twice more. The formalist, literary-critical answer is that reiteration was a "desirable and characteristic feature of the epic tradition" (Sarna). We are still left with fitting this strange piece of behavior into Abraham's overall biography.

Let us take a closer look at our protagonist. A nonconformist, God-haunted man, he leaves the safety of his home at a word from the Deity, wanders like a "discontent" (Bloom's term) here and there, temporarily relinquishes his wife by pretending she is his sister, shows reluctance to send away his second wife, Hagar, makes land deals and grows wealthy, unsuccessfully tries to stop God from destroying Sodom, yet comes close to sacrificing his own beloved son Isaac because God told him to, grieves when his wife Sarah dies, and remarries (according to one *midrash*, going back to Hagar). Vacillating one moment, zealously rigid the next, cowardly and brave, the quintessential father figure (as his name change from Abram to Abraham indicates) who nevertheless takes eighty years to sire a child, he merits our sympathy precisely because of his inconsistencies.

It is tempting to compare Abraham to Odysseus. Both are wily survivors, but it is hard to imagine Odysseus hiding behind a woman, or loaning Penelope to a foreign potentate. Odysseus is a man of action and physical prowess, the classic hero, whereas Abraham is "aheroic" and "belongs to the paradigm of the fool" (to use Peter Pitzele's terms).

Still, as Pitzele notes in *Our Fathers' Wells*, Abraham is a visionary, with a power of spiritual obedience and inward listening which Odysseus utterly lacks. Odysseus would never wander the globe at so vague an instigation as the call of God. And nothing Odysseus does is as noble as Abraham's expostulating with God to save the people of Sodom, trying to bargain the Almighty Himself into compassion.

The folklorists see the wife-sister stories as variants of popular tales about the hero's beautiful wife who risks being kidnapped by a rival prince, and who proves faithful or unfaithful (Helen of Troy, for instance) in the process. One difference between the Greek epics and Genesis, however, is that often the Bible characters are made to appear less heroic, the better to demonstrate God's power. It is God alone, not her husband, who can protect Sarah, by inflicting plagues and boils (read: sexual dysfunction) on Pharaoh, and by sewing up the wombs of the Gerarites so that no one in the land can get pregnant, much less Sarah.

The wife-sister stories also allow the biblical authors to crow about the beauty of the Jewish matriarch (all the more remarkable when you consider that she is well past eighty!). I like the *midrash* that says Abraham was so discreet (or unobservant) he had never before observed how lovely Sarah was. But, says Ramban, "Wading through a stream, he saw the reflection of her beauty in the water," which has the delicacy of a Japanese haiku. After which, he became Sarah's booking agent, you might say.

When Pharaoh, after being afflicted by God to prevent intercourse, bombards Abraham with rhetorical questions ("What is this you have done to me! Why did you not tell me that she was your wife? Why did you say, 'She is my sister,' so that I took her as my wife?"), the patriarch makes no reply. A modern reader might think Pharaoh has a point. He acted in good faith, showing generosity toward this sojourner; it seems unjust for God to punish the Egyptians when Abraham misled them. Later, in the story's Gerar reprise, King Abimelech addresses Abraham in wounded tones similar to Pharaoh's: " 'What have you done to us? What wrong have I done that you should bring so great a guilt upon me and my kingdom? You have done to me things that ought not to be done. What, then,' Abimelech demanded of Abraham, 'was your purpose in doing this thing?' "

It is worth wondering what the biblical authors had in mind by putting such rhetorically persuasive passages into the mouths of the heathens. Abimelech's questions are too direct to be avoided; this time Abraham must speak up, and he does. Source analysts, in fact, argue that one of the reasons the E writer repeats the story that J has already written is precisely to give Abraham a chance to defend himself the second time. The E writer's variant also takes much greater pains to show that Sarah's virtue was untainted—that Abimelech never got a chance to sleep with her—while the earlier, Egyptian episode by the J writer had been less reassuring on that score. In *The Book of J*, Harold Bloom sees such distinctions as proof that J was the more terse, irreverent storyteller ("J has no particular affection for her patriarchs"), while E is "characteristically . . . prissier."

The only problem with this reading is that Abraham comes off looking worse, in some ways, in the Gerar episode by E than in the Egyptian episode. The first time he may be excused by fear; the second time begins to look like cynical realpolitik. Abraham's motivation in going to Gerar was initially weaker, argues Devora Steinmetz in *From Father to Son*: this time there was no famine, and Abraham was putting more at stake the second time by letting Sarah become another man's wife. Since God had already promised Sarah she would become pregnant soon, the paternity of the heir and the whole bloodline might be compromised.

Moreover, Abraham's spoken defense, when it finally comes, is not that impressive. As Devora Steinmetz observes: "He . . . gives more than one explanation, which suggests that no one explanation was good enough." In fact, he gives three explanations: (1) "I thought . . . surely there is no fear of God in this place, and they will kill me because of my wife." We have no way of knowing how reasonable was this apprehension, but we do know that Abimelech demonstrates plenty of fear of God, after the Deity comes to him in a dream and warns him not to touch Sarah. (2) Next, Abraham utters this surprising statement: "And besides, she is in truth my sister, my father's daughter though not my mother's, and she became my wife." No previous genealogies in Genesis suggest so close a kinship between Abraham and Sarah. Either he is improvising a yarn, which would make him a liar, or he is telling the truth that she is his half sister, which would convict him of incest. Some rabbinical commentators believe that he is merely throwing sand in the heathen ruler's eyes. Modern apologists for Abraham have argued that because the Israelites were "underdogs," they had a right to practice deception, as part of a "trickster" culture. Somehow, mendacity justified by minority status does not entirely sit right.

Suppose that Abraham is telling the truth and Sarah is his half sister. One anthropological explanation has it that while incest was certainly taboo in Abraham's day, the prohibition may not have held as strongly between half siblings. There is also the argument advanced by Ephraim Speiser (based on some Nuzi tablet fragments), that Abraham was only following a common practice borrowed from the neighboring Hurrians, to "marry a girl and adopt her at the same time as his sister." Adin Steinsaltz, the renowned Talmudist, takes a similar approach to Speiser in his book *Biblical Images*: "Moreover *sister* was a common term of endearment for a woman in early Eastern culture; for instance, in the Song of Songs, we find 'My sister, my spouse' (5:1) and 'My sister, my love.' . . . The sister-wife as the chief wife, as opposed to the other, secondary wives who were 'outsider.' "

I find this whole line of thought interesting but beside the point. The story's power lies precisely in the fact that Abraham is frightened for his life, and so he asks Sarah to pretend they are brother and sister. If Abraham is not lying when he asks Sarah to do so, but is merely using an honorific, the story loses its guilty tension and is reduced to a lexical misunderstanding. Devora Steinmetz puts it perfectly: "Even if, as some have suggested, Abraham's claim refers to a specific type of aristocratic marriage . . . Sarah is still Abraham's wife, and Abimelech is not free to take her." I also like Ramban's commentary: "Even if it were true that she was his sister and his wife, nevertheless when they wanted to take her as a wife and he told them, *She is my sister*, in order to lead them astray, he already committed a sin towards them by bringing upon them a *great sin*, and it no longer mattered at all whether the thing was true or false!"

Which brings us to Abraham's final excuse: (3) "So when God made me wander from my father's house, I said to her, 'Let his be the kindness that you shall do me: whatever place we come to, say there of me: He is my brother.' " If the first part of Abraham's statement suggests an attempt to shift the blame onto God, the second part gets to the crux of the matter: he admits that not only did this deception occur in Egypt and Gerar but it was their regular arrangement. They were like scam artists using the same brother-sister masquerade in each town.

What of Sarah's feelings in all this? Ilona Rashkow, in her feminist critique, *The Phallacy of Genesis*, views the wife-sister story cycle as a paradigm of "powerful male/powerless female/uninvited sex." She points to Sarah's "silence" as evidence of her being treated as chattel (although elsewhere, I must say, Sarah has no problem opening her mouth: she objects loudly to her rival Hagar's presence, and scoffs at God's promise that she will conceive). Rashkow, not unreasonably, indicts the biblical tale as sexist: "The irony is that Pharaoh, Abimelech, and I as a reader understand the immorality of adultery, and the crime of female sexual sacrifice, more readily than Abraham."

Adin Steinsaltz sees it very differently, reading into Sarah's silence a noble, group-oriented spirit:

> This silence did not arise from passivity or surrender, nor from a wish to be taken by another man, nor because Sarah was a mere tool of her husband: her acquiescence was obviously prearranged with Abraham, with whom she worked as a team on the basis of decisions jointly made. Here, they had decided, despite the shame and humiliation involved, that it was preferable to preserve the wholeness of Abraham's camp—representing, as it did, the new ideal—even at the cost of Sarah's honor. This willingness to sacrifice her personal well-being for the common cause is surely borne out by the fact that Sarah never reproached Abraham for the injury done to her; nor, indeed, did she even mention it.

To Steinsaltz, we may take Sarah's silence for consent; to Rashkow, the opposite. There is no end to the moral interpretations we can extract from these Bible stories, which is why they are so invaluable. I am not in the business of judging Abraham or Sarah. What interests me is the fluid way this couple kept crossing the line between spouse and sibling, and what that might indicate in a larger sense about the situation of marriage.

2. Sigmund and Karen

The first time I registered the story of Abraham passing off Sarah as his sister, I felt a shiver of recognition. I could identify with Abraham's faint-heartedness, since I am not that physically brave a man myself, and might resort to any number of pusillanimous strategies to save my neck. But there was more to the shock of familiarity, something more personal, as though I had once done the same thing but could not remember when. It was the same sensation as when I've dreamed that I'd already killed a man, or already married my mother or slept with my sister, and now, the next morning, must sort out the aftermath of that abomination.

I thought of a passage I'd read in Karen Horney's provocative essay "The Problem of the Monogamous Ideal." One of the reasons people marry, wrote Horney, is to fulfill

> all the old desires arising out of the Oedipal situation in childhood. But the increasing intimacy within marriage leads to a resuscitation of the old incest prohibition—this time in relation to the marriage partner, and the more complete the fulfillment of unconscious wishes, the greater is the danger. The revival of the incest prohibition in marriage is apparently very typical and leads *mutatis mutandis* to the same results as in the relation between child and parent; that is, the direct sexual aims give place to an affectionate attitude in which the sexual aim is inhibited.

The way I'd read this passage was this: even, or especially, in good marriages, where the partners communicate well, there is a tendency to begin as lovers and end up as brother and sister.

Now, perhaps Horney's formulation will seem merely a psychoanalytic restatement of the age-old folk wisdom that marriage is the surest way to kill off sexual passion. The Talmud also tell us: "Since the destruction of the Temple, sexual pleasure has been taken away from those who practice it lawfully and given to sinners, as it is written: 'Stolen waters are sweet, and bread eaten in secret is pleasant.' " What Horney contributes to this sour truism is an explanation: that the decrease of sexual pleasure in marriage comes about not merely by habit but because of a revival of the incest prohibition. It is almost as though one were revirginated by intimacy, which carried within itself the stigma of familial trespass.

Although the incest taboo projected onto the spouse could well be Oedipal, I chose to see it in the light of siblings—wives being rounded into sisters, husbands into brothers. Most likely, this exclusively "sibling" reading of the Horney passage came from the fact that I grew up with two sisters, both younger than I, both very attractive; and each could not help but figure into my erotic imagination. Both my sisters are slender, brunette, and about five foot five, which matches a type I have consistently fallen for. So for me to say that the wife becomes a sister figure is by no means to rob her of a sexual dimension. One difference between the conjugal tie and the brother-sister tie may be that the latter, because unconsummated, never loses its erotic edge.

While parsing what she calls "the affectional attitude in which the sexual aim is inhibited," Horney acknowledges her debt to a well-known paper by Freud, entitled "The Most Prevalent Form of Degradation in Erotic Life," in which he analyzes the tendency of some men (usually of the bourgeoisie) to suffer a polarized split between affection and sexual desire. "Where such men love they have no desire and where they desire they cannot love," declared Freud. Inhibited by the incest taboo, and overesteeming their mothers and sisters, they can only be potent "when the sexual object fulfills the condition of being degraded," either because the woman comes from a lower class or because she has loose morals. Just as important, she "does not know the rest of his life and cannot criticize him" for "perverse" sexual longings. "It is to such a woman that he prefers to devote his sexual potency, even when all the tenderness in him belongs to a higher type."

The modern middle-class male may not have as much Victorian propriety to rebel against, or as developed a courtesan demimonde to turn to, but much of what Freud says holds true, else why the need for the Playboy Channel? He concludes with a sharp, audacious assertion: "Whoever is to be really free and happy in love must have overcome his deference for women and come to terms with the idea of incest with mother or sister."

Coincidentally, Freud refers to Genesis in this essay: "A man shall leave father and mother—according to Biblical precept—and cleave to his wife."

Now, to return to our wife-sister story: Sarah is the mother figure in Genesis, the Matriarch of Israel. Moreover, she is getting on in years—close to ninety, so the text tells us; even if we consider the figure an exaggeration and halve it, she has definitely entered her matronly period. Somehow the shadow of "mother incest" will have to be lifted or diffused for the marriage to revive. Curiously, Sarah is also barren: her greatest anguish is that she is *not* a mother. She urges on Abraham her servant girl, Hagar, and with this "less exalted sexual object," as Freud would put it, he regains his potency—i.e., fathers a child. This, in turn, awakens Sarah's jealousy and her power as a woman.

They have, in a sense, an open marriage: just as Sarah tempts Abraham into infidelity by giving him Hagar, so Abraham hands over his wife to strangers. That their marriage has lost some of its oomph and needs replenishment is suggested by the episode when Sarah laughs scornfully at the promise of childbirth. She does not expect her old codger of a husband to be able to pleasure her. (There is a wonderful commentary on this in the Babylonian Talmud, which Francine Klagsbrun quotes in her *Voices of Wisdom*:

> In the book of Genesis, when God tells Sarah she is to have a son, she laughs and says, "Now that I am withered, am I to have enjoyment—with my husband so old?" When God relates the incident to Abraham, He is recorded as saying, "Shall I in truth bear a child, old as I am?" According to the rabbis, God deliberately changed Sarah's words in telling them to Abraham so as not to reveal that his wife had complained of his old age. At the school of Rabbi Ishmael it was taught: Great is the cause of peace, seeing that for the sake of peace even the Holy One, blessed be He, deviated from the truth and modified a statement.

It seems odd that, at the moment Abraham awakens erotically to his wife's comeliness, he desexualizes her by assigning her the role of sister. But perhaps they are keeping the sexual roots of their marriage alive by playing these taboo roles: you be the sister, I'll be the brother. One could argue, following Freud, that Abraham reinvests Sarah with even more sexual interest by placing her in a compromising situation, where she becomes the potential plaything of other men, thereby whetting his jealousy.

In another essay, "A Special Type of Object Choice Made by Men," Freud wrote that with certain men

> a virtuous and reputable woman never possesses the charm required to exalt her to an object of love; this attraction is exercised only by one who is more or less sexually discredited, where fidelity and loyalty admit of some doubt. . . . Not until they [these men] have some occasion for jealousy does their passion reach its height and the woman acquire her full value to them.

You might say that Abraham forces this most faithful of wives to play the role of a courtesan, a light woman, as a means of recharging the marital spark. By the way, I am not seriously maintaining that this is what happened: for all I know, there may never have been a historical Abraham. I am only suggesting that these undercurrents, when examined, make the story come alive more for me.

Let me turn by comparison to a modern variant of the wife-sister story: Paul Bowles's *The Sheltering Sky*. In this novel, Port and Kit have been married for twelve years and have evolved into a sort of brother-sister pair. (" 'Like two children,' he thought, 'who aren't allowed to go on a picnic with the family.' ") They have long since stopped making love, but they are dependent on each other, and Kit feels convinced that Port could not be interested in any other woman. Actually, he has sex with an Arab prostitute, a "degraded sexual object," in Freud's terminology, unbeknownst to Kit. Port is a wanderer, like Abraham, and he, too, places his wife in danger, by inviting along a very handsome acquaintance of theirs, Tunner. But he rationalizes that she is faithful ("What the hell, he'll never get her"). Actually, Kit does end up sleeping with Tunner. Port is also afraid, like Abraham, of the alien culture through which they are traveling, and this fear motivates a good deal of his behavior: " 'I wonder if after all I'm a coward?' he thought. Fear spoke; he listened and let it persuade—the classical procedure." Port also places Kit (and himself) in danger unthinkingly by traveling to a place without adequate medical facilities, and then falling gravely ill. After he dies, she is ravished by Bedouins and lets herself become their sexual prisoner.

Port and Kit represent the nightmarish turn that might have happened to Abraham and Sarah without God's intervention. As it is, the biblical duo suffers a multitude of troubles—barrenness, separation, wife-mistress tensions, brother-in-law problems—and yet somehow they hold together as a couple. To what extent has their ability to modulate into siblings, as a sort of protective coloration, facilitated this conjugal longevity? Maybe they are only following in the footsteps of their ancestors, for were not Adam and Eve also brother and sister, in a sense, coming as they did from the same parentage?

3. Phillip and Carol

I was married for the first time at twenty; my wife, Carol, was twenty-two, but the two-year difference seemed utterly negligible, or if anything, desirable, so eager was I to catch up with everything older than I. We both felt mature for our age, and our marriage was a way of signaling to the world our eagerness to take on the responsibilities of adulthood. In retrospect, I see I'd grossly overestimated my maturity; I was only bluffing, miming the part of a grown-up.

Shortly after our wedding and my graduation from college (Carol had already been out in "the real world" awhile), we cashed in our wedding presents for a year abroad. We took a Yugoslav freighter, then the cheapest way to cross the Atlantic. I remember the chess-playing, goatish Yugoslav sailors trying to get me drunk on slivovitz so they could make time with Carol. But I had confidence in her loyalty. I had married her not only because she was so brainy and attractive (a sandy-haired anthropology major interested in writing fiction, with sparkling green eyes, a cute figure, and a rueful smile) but because she was so sweetly responsive and dedicated to me. Though I was not surprised to see that many men, like these sailors, were attracted to her, it did not make me particularly jealous because, in the dynamic of our marriage, I was the one treated as the peacock, the visionary, and she, the devotee. She was the daughter of a Viennese psychoanalyst and had been trained to honor men who presumed to think. I was the son of textile workers who had been trained to venerate Viennese psychoanalysts and their progeny.

The freighter touched down in Tangier, where we spent a fascinating week (Arab culture carried for us, as Jews, excitement, fear, and something archaic, ur-Semitic) before traveling on to our real destination, Spain. During the next ten months, we settled into a nesting routine: both of us wrote fiction while we lived on the tightest of budgets. To give ourselves one final treat before flying back to the States, we decided to return to Morocco for a month of tourism. Spain had proven somewhat disappointing—too much like America, perhaps—but Morocco had seemed genuinely different or, as we say now, Other.

Carol was the perfect traveling companion: good-humored, curious about everything, willing to match my stride mile for mile. As we walked, we would compare observations and dissect characters we had met on the road. We enjoyed imagining that we thought as much alike as any two people could, and part of our conversation was devoted to ensuring that accord (even if it meant my not noticing the degree to which she was yielding her own position to my more dogmatically asserted one). Young couples traveling often like to fantasize that their thoughts and feelings are in harmony, that they hold no secrets from each other—that they are two halves of the same psyche. Perhaps it comes from the anxiety of journeying into a threatening world: the "Orphans of the Storm" syndrome. We were two young people somewhat frightened of life, and we clung to each other like brother and sister. I've seen many graduate student couples take on that sibling quality, gladly sacrificing youth's sexiness for the comforts of a more stoop-shouldered, reasonable companionship. At least temporarily: sometimes they wake up five years later and decide they've missed out on the Zeitgeist, the sexual revolution of the moment. That is more or less what happened to us. But even after I'd kicked against the constrictions of having married too young, I would often think: if only I'd met her when we were both older, in our sixties, say, we could have been the happiest pair, the perfect middle-aged couple, traveling in retirement, going to museums, comparing impressions after dinner parties.

In any event, there we were in Morocco, on our way from Marrakech to the next big city, Casablanca, which would be our last stop before taking the plane back to New York. We had boarded a bus for a ride that began at dawn and was scheduled to last twelve to fifteen hours. I don't know what Moroccan buses are like now, but in 1965 the roads were primitive, the bus driver inexperienced if not new on the job, and each mountain curve he took threatened to plunge us into the ravine below. I also had a throbbing headache and a nauseous, carsick feeling—probably occasioned by the couscous I had eaten in the marketplace the night before, though Carol seemed to be showing no ill effects from it. My only consolation was that the bus would be stopping for an hour in a hill town called Béni Mellal, roughly at the midway point of the journey.

Béni Mellal was a town that seemed to exist solely for the purpose of letting travelers stretch their legs. It may have also been a trading and agricultural center, but what I noticed chiefly on deboarding were the beggar kids with hands outstretched, the teenagers offering or threatening to take your luggage, the flies, the chewing gum vendors—all of which might have struck me as diverting on another day, but with the hard-boiled egg I'd gobbled at dawn still squatting on my chest, and my bowels making ominous pincer movements, I felt an urgent need to sit down and close my eyes. The Moroccan heat and sun seemed especially oppressive, and there was no shade in sight.

"What's wrong?" Carol asked. I told her I needed a john fast and was not sure I was fit to continue. If Béni Mellal had an inn of some sort, it might be good to spend the night there, and catch another bus to Casablanca tomorrow.

We were in luck: Béni Mellal had a more than adequate, even pleasant hotel at the top of the hill, run by ex-colonials. It was an obstinately Parisian oasis, with onion soup at lunch and French sports papers arriving six weeks late.

After visiting the w.c., I took a nap, and Carol went to reconnoiter the town. An hour later she returned to say that Béni Mellal was more interesting than it had at first appeared. With her anthropologist's training, she was always scrutinizing hill towns on our travels, with an eye to what sort of study she might do if she had a grant and a year or two to stay put there. This time she had met a man on her walk who told her that that very night Béni Mellal was to host a Moroccan music festival. There would be folk music scattered throughout the village. "What a shame you feel so rotten!" she said. "Oh well, maybe you'll recover in a few hours and we can both go out and hear music. Everyone says it's going to be great."

I was too sick to care. My plans were to stay close to the toilet: if Blind Lemon Jefferson or Leroy Carr had risen from the grave to sing at the local hall, I would have passed him up. "You can go if you want to," I assured her. Actually, I wanted her to stay back and take care of me, and I even half-assumed she would, as she was usually such a good nurse in those situations. But she surprised me by accepting my offer. She may have said, "Are you sure it's okay for me to go?" but by this time I was too locked into my noble-martyr pose to abandon it. I did not like to seem one of those boorish husbands restricting their wives' fun. It was a test: I wanted her to choose to stay at my side, without my asking her to. Always a mistake to say the opposite of what you mean. So she left.

I began shivering in bed, unable to get warm, and the insides of my stomach swirled until I thought it might be a good idea to vomit, and from that thought came the instant realization that I could not *not* vomit, which I did with my head over the bowl. I felt like a child again, unable to control my involuntary reflexes. A run of diarrhea followed that lasted for several hours. A maid came in to mop up the excess vomit on the floor. She helped me back to my bed, asking: "Where is your wife?" Where, indeed.

It was ten or eleven at night before I could finally stop running to the bathroom. My mood had shifted, from self-pity at being abandoned to worry about Carol: Why hadn't she come home yet? What if something bad had happened to her? I waited a quarter hour more, then got dressed to look for her. I was not in the best shape to go searching, but I had no choice. I needed to go out into the Moroccan night, into a strange, pitch-black town I knew not at all, and—protect my wife.

I headed down the hill toward some music that was issuing out of a square white shack. I had made up my mind to signal from the door-way, if she was inside: she could get up, apologizing to her guide, and we would walk home together, not without a lecture from me. Or maybe I would skip the lecture. I opened the door and saw fifty men sitting in burnooses and embroidered caps, with hashish pipes at their feet. No sign of Carol. I forced my eyes to move row by row over the dark faces, in case I had overlooked her. The eyes that met mine were imperturbably grave, telling me I had no business intruding on their ceremony. The plangent, trancelike, bluesy music, a cousin to Coltrane, appealed to me deeply, but I was not there to play the concertgoer. I moved on.

In the distant hills, I saw scattered cottages with lights on, and moved toward each, backtracking across the town in this way for the next hour. I passed more than once the all-night café where truckers sat hunched over stools, passed the bus stop where poor Moroccan women patiently waited with string-tied parcels, passed the boarded-up market stalls. Each time I entered a music hut I would see men crouched on the floor, listening stolidly to the instrumentalists. There were no women in these audiences. What could Carol have been thinking?

Around 1:00 a.m. I met a sympathetic-looking young man in a djel-laba, who asked me in French whether I needed help. I replied in French that I was looking for my wife, she had gone to hear some music. He in-sisted on accompanying me and, with that persistent hospitality toward lost strangers one encounters abroad, never left my side. I was glad for the company, but not for the way he kept questioning me: "Why is your wife not with you?"

"She wanted to hear the music."

"And you were sick? And she left you?" He shook his head: incomprehensible. Proof that the decadent West no longer had any values. Even more incomprehensible was that I had entrusted my wife to a man whose last name I didn't even know.

He stopped by his fiancée's house to tell her what he was up to, and she, a spirited young woman from what I could make out through her veil, joined us. Though they conversed freely, she walked a step or two behind him. I could not have been given a sharper demonstration of the proper respect a woman in that part of the world is expected to show her man. Not that I had any desire to embrace a reactionary, chauvinistic system that kept women in chador, but I was ashamed of myself for not having been able, in this place, to look and behave more like their idea of a man. It now felt cowardly on my part to have let Carol take off by herself, not only because I really wanted her to stay behind with me when I wasn't feeling well but because I had put her at risk by letting her go. For the sake of appearing liberal-minded, I had made her subject to God knows what dangers. I promised God and myself I would never do that again, if only she would materialize at the next corner.

By two-thirty in the morning we were ready to try the police. We decided to check back at the hotel one more time. I was overjoyed to discover from the hotel clerk that my wife had returned. I could not thank the young Moroccan couple enough; they, for their part, were happy that everything had turned out well, and tactfully left without insisting on meeting her.

In the room Carol seemed chastened. Reluctant to talk. She said that the man and his friend had driven her to the outskirts of town, ostensibly to hear music. They were obsessed with American movies, Doris Day movies in particular. They had obviously cast her in a Doris Day mold, which made them avid and resentful. They craved everything they saw in these movies, the Frigidaires, the swimming pools. They tried to rape her, but she managed to fend them off and make her way back into town. I held her: she clearly needed comforting; the lecture would have to wait.

We stayed for five days longer in Béni Mellal, while I regained my health. During that time I tried to learn, without much success, a little more about what had happened to Carol that night. While I took her word for it that she had not been raped—I think she would have been more distraught if she had—a part of me continued to wonder if more had happened than she was letting on. In any case, our two minds no longer seemed utterly in sync. How had it happened? I kept brooding. How had I so misjudged her? She had always seemed the most reliable, prudent woman imaginable: perhaps because she was two years older than I, I had projected onto her a maternal–big sister solicitude. What I had failed to notice was that she was still a young woman herself, struggling to sort out her desires, a side of her probably resisting the "good wife" role. On the other hand, maybe I was making too much of it: what had she done after all that was so culpable, except to exercise some poor judgment?

Béni Mellal produced the first fracture of trust between us. I had an urge to get revenge. In time to come there would be other infractions, mutual betrayals. I pondered my own complicity, using the memory of Béni Mellal to worry feelings of unmanliness. Had I been too much a brother with her, not enough a husband? Was I what Hemingway called an "American boy-man," a Francis Macomber? Had I tempted her into neglecting me, to satisfy some atavistic scenario of disappointment?

Freud teaches that every love object is but a surrogate for the original one, and must disappoint because of that. Had I known what I know now, I might still be married to Carol. No, scratch that. Abraham and Sarah could forgive each other again and again for their ambiguous adventures; but perhaps that's the difference between an older man's wisdom and a younger man's bluff at intelligence. "All things can be replaced," says the Talmud, "except the wife of one's youth."

The Limits of Empathy

I am thinking a lot about empathy these days—defensively, I might add—because my wife keeps accusing me of lacking this quality in relation to her. Of course, I readily agree. I sympathize with Cheryl's pain but stop short of empathizing with it. My saying this infuriates her even more, and she is the kind of person who has no shyness about retaliating. Her retaliation makes me even more disinclined to oblige. I explain that what feeble mechanism I might have for empathy is nullified when I'm being attacked: I cannot identify with a person who wishes to cut me to ribbons. That is my imaginative limitation.

At what point, I wonder, did the word *empathy* begin to displace *sympathy*? *Empathy* isn't even in my 1971 *Oxford English Dictionary*, which may reflect the more reserved character of the British: one assumes the rage for empathy began on this side of the Atlantic. (See Bill Clinton's famous assertion, "I feel your pain.") A recent edition of *The American Heritage Dictionary* tells us that while sympathy "denotes the act or capacity for sharing in the sorrows or troubles of another," empathy "is a vicarious identification with and understanding of another's situations, feelings, and motives."

To me, *sympathy* suggests a humane concern for others' positions or plights, based partly on a general ethic of compassion for all living things. *Empathy* conveys, to my mind, a stickier, more ghoulish shadowing that stems from the delusion that one can actually take on oneself, or fuse with, another's feelings.

It is possible that my wife wants to recapture that sense of romantic communion we had at the beginning, which is usually strongest during the infatuation phase, when lovers' hearts are said to beat as one. But I can't help suspecting she got this empathy bug after a few sessions with her therapist, Barry.

Since then, as a result of our frequent bickering and my wife's conviction that her therapist is a marvelous human being, we have entered into couples counseling with Barry. To my surprise, he is a marvelous human being. Wise, reasonable, scrupulously evenhanded, and empathic—perhaps to a fault. Sometimes, when he commiserates about the pressures we are operating under—raising a three-year-old with health problems while juggling our careers—I begin to wonder about this warm compassion, the depth of which, it seems to me, should be reserved for Romanian coal miners, not yuppies like us.

In one session, we were recounting a disagreement we had had the night before. As it happened, about sex. We had been going through a dry spell, mostly because of my wife's preoccupations with our baby daughter and her mistrust of my capacity to empathize with her. Now she said she was getting ready to consider doing it again, and I replied, like an idiot, something to the effect that I'll believe it when I see it.

Barry offered an alternative script, giving us the lines that, in his view, we might more profitably have spoken. I was to compliment her on making this overture to an advance, and if I still needed to express skepticism, she was to show that she understood my "vulnerability" because I'd been starved for sexual affection. Barry then asked what I thought would have happened if she had replied that way. Feeling the old obligation to speak the truth in therapy, I took a deep breath and said that his suggestions had nothing to do with life as it is lived, that he was trying to indoctrinate us into the new, totalitarian Empathy Speak.

"Are you really against empathy?" he asked, somewhat incredulously.

"I am, yes—"

"You see?" said my wife. "You see what I have to put up with?"

I went on to say that I was for sympathy, that old-fashioned term. The people I admire most, like two friends of mine both in their seventies, operate out of a moral code older than empathy that acknowledges that the gap between two souls can never be entirely bridged. I thought of my old professor Lionel Trilling, who questioned in class D. H. Lawrence's hunger for total honesty in a love relationship by saying: "Why should two people have no secrets from each other?" On the other hand, there is much in the present culture that promotes an exaggerated or false sympathy, like the figure of the talk-show host, the Great Listener, Oprah or Geraldo, whom I consider spurious.

As you might imagine, this did not go over well. I saw that my attempts to explain myself were perceived as inappropriately "academic," therefore cold, therefore removed from emotions and the business at hand. (Interesting: that therapy today has that anti-intellectual quality. This is no place to start *thinking*.)

When people start speaking of reason as a "defense," I get nervous, considering where the irrational has gotten us in the last hundred years. And, grateful as I am for Barry's willingness to help straighten out our problems, I can't help watching my tongue now in counseling sessions. I have a lingering suspicion that many couples therapists train you to say not what you genuinely feel but what is less confrontational, all the while telling you that they want you to be in touch with your feelings. No, they want you to make nice.

I suspect I will never be able to empathize with the panic and depression my wife sometimes feels—for the simple reason that they both terrify me too much. I grew up far too close to such emotions in my parents, and it took all my strength to distance myself from their debilitating pull so as to form a workable, reasonably cheerful self. Where does that leave the marriage? My wife still hungers for a more empathetic soul mate, while I am equally convinced that I am realistically offering something else that is of value. Call it an understanding of limits, based on the intractability of human nature and the intensely problematic—not to say tragic—dilemma of modern marriage.

Given my empathy-challenged nature, I am faced with the choice of trying to fake an empathy orgasm—a distasteful proposition—or waiting out my wife's rage, hoping that in the end she will come to accept my defects, as I hope and pray to accept hers. Forbearance, resignation, and stoicism still seem to me the only way to go. Someone (Buffon or Goethe?) once said, "Genius is a long patience." I don't know about genius, but I would maintain that marriage certainly is—at least when you're committed to making the marriage last.

The Lake of Suffering

About a week and a half after my baby daughter, Lily, was born, she began to throw up. Usually a gentle gush of whitish stuff would flow down her chin, and a minute later she would seem peaceful, no worse than before. Sometimes, however, the vomiting was harsher. Since Cheryl was breast-feeding Lily, she wondered whether something was wrong with her technique (the angle of tilt, the pillow arrangement) or with the consistency of her milk.

We had been told that all babies "spit up." Part of our problem was that, Lily being our first child, we did not know how to distinguish between normal postnatal events and symptoms that should indeed alarm us. For instance, we rushed Lily to our amiable neighborhood pediatrician, Dr. Rhonda, because blood seemed to be collecting in the umbilical area. It turned out this was a natural result of the umbilical plug falling out. Or when Lily got the hiccups (another benign occurrence), Cheryl had me read aloud all the "hiccups" entries in the child-care manuals on our nightstand, to see what we could do to stop it. (Nothing.) As the books' entries did not alter when left unattended, I didn't see why I needed to read every word aloud each time Lily started hiccuping, but doing so was indicative of how everything that first week made us nervous.

We had amassed a shelf full of baby books in the time between the start of Cheryl's pregnancy and Lily's arrival. My intellectualized response to any unknown situation is to buy a book; and since Cheryl designs books for a living, she also finds security in them. So we immersed ourselves in Dr. Spock, Penelope Leach, and the What to Expect series, among others.

I could write a whole essay about these infant-care books as a peculiar literary subcategory, the antithesis of the horror genre. Suffice to say that a butterscotch of reassurance covers them: they address new parents as a set of middle-class worrywarts, counseling you that your fears are natural, even your ambivalences are natural (Leach goes so far as to empathize with the husband who resents ceding oral monopoly of his wife's breast), but that underneath, you have nothing to worry about. Spinal taps, chronic illness, oncology, and death are not listed in their indexes. They are addressed to *well*-baby care. As soon as the reality sank in that we had an ill baby on our hands, we closed these volumes, never to consult them again.

But I am getting ahead of myself. Before plunging into the story of that first cruel year in the hospital, I need to pause and consider why we had so wanted a child.

During my first marriage, my wife, Carol, and I were in our twenties, young and poor and ambitious to become writers and in no hurry to take on parental responsibilities. Our fertility seemed more a curse than a blessing, necessitating as it did two abortions. By the second abortion, the marriage was already tottering. I left it to embark on twenty-one years of bachelorhood. However staunch my political support may be for abortion rights, I eventually began to regret the two chances for fathering I had personally let slip up and to feel, at times keenly, the absence of those children who might have been mine. This feeling was accentuated by ten years of working with schoolkids from kindergarten to sixth grade, teaching them writing, theater, and filmmaking. I had stumbled into the teaching profession as a way to support my own writing habit. Not expecting to be good with kids, to my surprise I seemed to be, enjoying their odd, unpredictable ways, and I drew on these experiences for my book *Being with Children*. When parents came to pick up their kids after school, I'd gush about how much fun I'd had with their

Johnny or Jill during the day, and they would invariably say, "Yeah, that's because you don't have to take care of them after three o'clock." I wasn't sure that was true: their remarks became a challenge I was eager to accept. I certainly liked being around children, listening in on their chatter and keeping up with their quirky behaviors. Why wouldn't I respond fairly well to my own?

By my late thirties, I was sold on having a child. The problem was I first had to find a wife. By no means had I worked through the neurotic patterns of mistrust, hostility, and abandonment that my mother and father had passed down to us as masculine-feminine relations. So I continued to stumble from one woman to the next until, at forty-seven, I met Cheryl. Widowed young, she had a deep understanding of what matters. She was formerly a painter and now an award-winning book designer, creative, intelligent, irresistibly attractive, humane, kind, and thirty-four. That last point was important: I wanted a wife of childbearing age.

Everything else seemed to be in place. I had established myself as a writer, had a full professorship at a local university, and felt an expansive willingness to take on this new work of bringing up baby. To be honest, my professional life had gone somewhat on automatic pilot: I could no longer be motivated by fear of failure, as in my younger years; I had written eight books, taught for over twenty years, and anticipated more of the same. I wanted something else, some new adventure to engross me—a child.

My wife was at first hesitant. She worried about what might happen to her career; she feared, legitimately, that much of the burden of child rearing would fall on her, and that she might get lost in the process. Moreover, having been widowed the first time and wanting to make sure the new relationship would survive, she preferred to spend our first years of married life together, just as a couple. A reasonable request, I thought. I could wait. Not indefinitely, but . . . When she had asked, before the wedding, "What if I *never* want to have children? Would you still want to marry me?" I had swallowed hard, and said yes, though in the back of my mind I'd gambled that she would come around eventually.

Which she did. A few years into the marriage, she told me she was ready. She hoped to get pregnant in time for my fiftieth birthday party, giving me what she knew I wanted most in the world. As soon as she made up her mind, her eagerness for a child outstripped my own. It took us nine months to conceive—not long as these things go, but long enough to plunge us into high anxiety. Two months after I turned fifty, we received the happy news that Cheryl was pregnant, and on September 16, 1994, she gave birth to Lily.

That first week home with the baby, the shock of eighteen hours in the delivery room and an episiotomy fresh in our minds, we had no chance to catch our breaths before jumping onto the roller coaster. I am well aware that every new parent feels overwhelmed. How much of the initial hysteria would have occurred anyway, even in optimal conditions? This is another form of the question that would later haunt us: What would the experience of parenting have been like if nothing had gone wrong?

Already, by the end of the first week, Cheryl seemed a confident and placid mother. Twelve days into our parenthood, Lily began vomiting. We took her to Dr. Rhonda to be weighed, and found she had lost over a pound since birth. "Failure to thrive," those creepy, accusing words, were spoken for the first time, but only as a distant possibility. Dr. Rhonda thought it might be gastroesophageal reflux; a fan of alternative medicine, she recommended trying chamomile tea, which an Andean tribe fed their babies to calm their stomachs. She also had us supplement breast-feeding with a soy formula twice a day, and Pedialyte, to prevent dehydration.

So I began feeding a bottle to Lily. Cheryl was critical of my first efforts: "I can't believe how tensely you're holding her!" she would say, or "Talk to her—no, not in that dead monotone voice!" I'm sure my technique left much to be desired, but it seemed to me adequate to the purpose; underneath Cheryl's criticisms was the real fear that, unless we fed Lily in a letter-perfect manner, she would vomit. (As we later learned, she was regurgitating not because of something so preventable as the wrong bottle angle but because her system couldn't process protein correctly, a far more serious problem.)

One Saturday, toward the end of the second week, I offered to watch the baby while Cheryl made herself breakfast. After giving Lily a feeding, I held her upright for about forty minutes, as I had been instructed, then let her sleep on the bed. Lily was napping peacefully, when suddenly she woke up and began choking. She turned bright red. I lifted her in my arms to get her upright, but she arched her head rigidly away—choking, spewing, gasping for breath. It was the most frightening thing I'd ever seen. She's going to die, I thought, right in front of me, and I can't do anything. I was also terrified that this was a seizure and began thinking epilepsy, brain damage. "Cheryl," I yelled. I placed my hand under Lily's head for support but was amazed at the strength of her arching away. Cheryl ran up the stairs and entered the room shouting, "Don't let her arch back so, that's the worst thing in the world, she'll choke on her own vomit!" I started to explain that I'd been trying to support her head, but she cut me off, shouting, "You're killing my baby!" I completely understood her accusatory panic, but could not stop myself from feebly defending my child-caring skills. A part of me was prepared to believe that I *had* caused the whole problem, and shrank back, letting Cheryl take over. But the attack seemed to have an involuntary dynamic all its own. (Later, the doctors confirmed that head arching during projectile vomiting is a reflex in some infants: nothing you can do but let it run its course.)

In retrospect, that red, choking baby reminded me of the creature from *Alien*. I wonder how much horror imagery comes from our terror of the crying newborn. The theory that Mary Shelley wrote *Frankenstein* after losing her baby makes sense to me.

I called Dr. Rhonda, but she was away all weekend. In desperation I phoned Dr. Lou Monti, a pediatrician connected to Mount Sinai Hospital, where Lily had been delivered. He suggested we take her off the breast milk and soy and give her nothing but Pedialyte, and if she couldn't hold that down, to bring her into the hospital for observation. Lily threw up the Pedialyte; we drove to Mount Sinai, turning her over—with relief, I confess—to the high-tech medical team of pediatric gastroenterologists led by Dr. Neal LeLeiko. Dr. Monti was retained as Lily's pediatrician. Dr. Rhonda, with her holistic, soothing chamomile, was off the case.

*   *   *

The initial diagnosis at Mount Sinai was that Lily had a severe milk-soy allergy. Perhaps the little bit of soy-based formula we had fed her (it only takes a drop) had led to the stripping of her intestinal villi, the hairy coating that aids digestion. The analogy the doctors used was it was making a carpet into linoleum. I believe Lily's physical problem or condition was in place before any of this happened, but giving her the soy milk formula was like feeding her poison.

It is not easy for an unscientific layman like myself to explain, even now, the exact nature of her medical problem—especially since it baffled all her doctors for so long. In the first two years of Lily's life, a good deal of effort was spent in eliminating the possibility that she had some known condition (which, however dire, they would have known how to treat), such as pyloric stenosis, cystic fibrosis, lymphatic dysfunction, Crohn's disease, or some autoimmune disorder. They never really did come up with a clear diagnosis: the closest one was "protein-losing enteropathy," a vague way of saying that she had a gastrointestinal problem with the transport and absorption of protein. This would cause some of the protein she ingested to "spill" into her bloodstream, instead of being absorbed by her cells as nutrition. Testing the blood for albumin was the only way to measure the degree of protein absorption in the body. We began to live or die by two numbers: Lily's weight and her albumin level.

As soon as Lily was admitted to the hospital, my wife made a remarkably heroic and, I think, correct decision, that one of us would stay with the baby at all times. This meant, as it turned out, that Cheryl spent a few years off and on in the hospital, putting her own professional life on hold, though she still managed, amazingly, in retrospect, to produce freelance book designs for Soho Press from the hospital room. She would sleep (or try to, in the interruptive nocturne of clinics) on an army-style cot next to Lily's crib. Some nights I or my mother-in-law, Doris, would spell her. But for the most part Cheryl was there, to see that the erratic night staff did not make a mistake with Lily's meds or the machinery. (It happened once that a night nurse was about to administer meds intended for a different patient when Cheryl caught it and stopped her.) Just as important was the guarantee that Lily would receive as much stimulation as possible, keeping her mentally sharp. We had seen some ward babies, left to the check-and-run care of nurses and attendants, who would stare listlessly up at the ceiling for hours or keep wailing until someone had a moment to look in on them. Cheryl's vigilance paid off for Lily, though the sleep deprivation, worry, and fear took a toll on her, leaving her exhausted and despairing.

If the arrival of children routinely places a couple under pressure, nothing can put more stress on a marriage than a child's illness or life-threatening disease. In our case, each of us had a different way of handling stress. Cheryl's took the form of mastering all the physical procedures involved with Lily's care, so that she could assist and, in effect, stand in for the night nurse. She became so adept that she probably could have passed a nursing examination—and the nurses would often let her do their jobs. But she got furious with any bungling: a tigress protecting her cub, she would throw nurses out of the room if they were about to make a mistake, or dismiss interns if they took too long finding a vein to draw Lily's blood, or forbid anyone, even surgeons, from approaching the crib without washing their hands first. She was not afraid of antagonizing the staff.

My way of facing the crisis was to stay stoically calm, pleasant, diplomatic, offending no one in authority; to remain upbeat and hopeful. I also tried to play the supportive husband, though whenever Cheryl's anxiety led her to lace irritably into me, I withdrew a good deal of my support. But mostly I struggled just to hang on.

Before Lily's hospitalization, I'd had my share of childhood traumas, betrayals, unhappy love affairs, and deaths of friends. But in a sense I'd led a charmed life, in that I always felt strong enough for the circumstances that presented themselves. In fact, I had often felt stronger than my circumstances, fantasizing a reserve tank of energy and courage that I might tap into if, suddenly, I found myself in a grueling or dangerous situation. Faced with the experience of Lily's illness, I quickly went through my reserve tank. My Superman fantasies were ended. I was discovering the irregular nature of courage: two days of heroic pluck, two days of blank despair. Besides, our heroism seemed beside the point; what was needed was patience, a different, more demanding virtue. Now we were In It. I understood what it meant to suffer, really suffer, night and day: to be up to our necks in the lake of suffering.

I was commuting in a triangle between Hofstra (my teaching job at the time) on Long Island, Mount Sinai Hospital on the Upper East Side of Manhattan, and our home in Brooklyn, where I fed the cats, looked at the mail, and crashed. Often I would drive to Mount Sinai directly from work, taking the Long Island Expressway to the Midtown Tunnel, then driving up the FDR Drive to Ninety-Sixth Street, relinquishing any residue of work solace and professorial dignity the closer I approached the hospital.

The neighborhood around Mount Sinai, how well I came to know it! Those sad take-out delis, those bleak bagel sandwich places, the bar and grill restaurants, the florist shop, the five-story tenements with fire escapes along Madison Avenue, the vertical parking garage, the whole borderline gestalt. It seemed fitting that Mount Sinai nestled in a no-man's-land between the posh apartment buildings below Ninety-Sixth Street and the East Harlem public housing projects, which started above 100th Street, because as soon as I entered the hospital complex, I had the feeling that I was nowhere, in a liminal no-time zone along with all the other marked creatures, crawling past the soda machines in the underground tunnels that connected the various wings and pavilions, a whole planet of illness, a leper colony. I would take the elevator up to the fourth floor (Friday nights and Saturdays, to honor the Sabbath, it stopped automatically on every floor), making way for the gurneys in the elevator, and prepare to hold my breath for six, seven, eight hours. The hospital was like a spaceship: no gravity, no up or down, white, weightless.

After you had spent a time-crawling morning and afternoon etherized with small talk, inedible meals, and diaper changes, putting up with the painted clowns, social workers, and clergy who came by on their mercy missions to the children's ward, checking out the art therapy–storytelling room for the twentieth time, the doctor would arrive around four, on his rounds, and everyone would snap to attention: the day would acquire a shape, good or bad, depending on the words he let drop or his tone of voice.

A hundred years ago, a baby with Lily's condition would likely have died. Then came the invention of the Broviac catheter: a device surgically attached to a main artery, which transmitted a slow, steady stream of nutrients to the bloodstream, bypassing the digestive tract entirely. With a catheter inside her, Lily would gain weight regardless; it was like riding an escalator, up up and up. No more anxiety about failure to thrive. The catheter was a godsend, but it had a tendency to become infected at the entry site after a while, and when that happened it had to be removed and another artery found. (The body has a limited number of arteries for this purpose, a scary thought when considering the future.) Catheters also require a sterile environment, extensive tubing, and a semistationary pump that has to be monitored regularly, making a patient less portable, and a baby more awkward to hold.

Cumbersome and daunting as this was, we also disliked the less surgically invasive nasogastric tube, which went down Lily's nose. Not only did it mar the perfection of her face and give her skin rashes, but it required a nasty insertion procedure: you had to stick a thin NG tube down her nostril and keep pushing until it came to rest in her stomach, all the while with her flailing, screaming, and twisting her head to avoid that unpleasant gagging sensation. She soon figured out how to yank the tube out of her nose: flick a fingernail under the surgical tape and rip it loose, triumphantly. Then we would have to hold her down, ignoring her wails, and reinsert it.

The hospital universe preoccupied us. Though I still craved the outside world, it began to recede in reality and color, partly as a consequence of our isolation: no one on the outside knew what we were going through, and we couldn't explain it to them. I would get home some nights and find messages on the answering machine from friends and relatives: "Tell us what's happening, we can't stand the suspense." They wanted to hear that everything was all right. It wasn't. Some people still didn't know about Lily's illness and would leave messages saying: "Congratulations! You must be on Cloud Nine!" I would try to get through all these calls as speedily as possible. Cheryl had designated me the one to stay in touch with and debrief our circle of friends and relatives. But after several such conversations, relaying the same information, I felt awful.

I began to suspect people's motives (idle curiosity? Schadenfreude?). Sometimes little things that were said seemed so insensitive: a friend bragging about how much her child was eating, another forever mentioning news items about medical breakthroughs that had nothing to do with Lily's illness, or telling some anecdote about a second cousin who was born with stomach problems and now played tackle for his high school football team; another saying that if we just fed Lily mashed bananas, all would be well. Yet I knew if they didn't call, I would also have felt slighted. I came to realize that there was nothing anyone on the outside could say or do that would be right. The only person I could talk to without feeling wounded was my friend Max, who had a little girl with problems even more severe than Lily's: her disabilities had resulted from a botched delivery, and now she could not speak, or walk, or eat without assistance. When she was first born, I thought their situation unimaginably pitiable. Now we shared the same vocabulary: Broviac catheters, endoscopies, Mic-Keys . . . Max was my reality check. He told me that, when it first happened, he refused to talk on the phone and hated everyone. Now he just hated most people.

Friends and relatives, unable to grasp the nature of Lily's difficulty, wanted me to go over and over the details, which I hated to do. When her problems didn't get solved with dispatch, they told me to change doctors, though we knew we had the best. Lily's chief physician, Dr. LeLeiko, is one of the top men in pediatric gastroenterology, a brilliant analyst of the facts and a humane, wise practitioner, a cultivated savant such as one might encounter in a Balzac novel. He listened to my exasperation with the outside world and said: "The problem is a social one.

In America, babies are not supposed to be sick. If they're sick, people expect one of two outcomes: one, the baby dies; two, she gets all better. Americans don't know how to deal with chronic illness."

Of course, Lily was not just a medical rarity but an increasingly defined, plucky little person whom you couldn't help but fall in love with—a charmer, who "lured people in," as one doctor put it. First (I say this as a completely unbiased father), she was the most startlingly beautiful baby, with porcelain skin, flashing dark eyes, long eyelashes, masses of black hair, cupid lips. "Like a porcelain doll," everyone said, and her mother dressed her in outfits accentuating that old-fashioned Victorian look. Second, she had remarkable interpersonal skills: from the moment her eyes could focus, she would fix you with an interested gaze, follow you around the room, react with pleasure or laughter if any opportunity offered, allow herself to be held and hugged by visitors, and generally flatter them with her attention. It is conceivable that babies or small children who undergo, like Lily, the pain of needles, splints, CT scans, and spinal taps, may develop survival skills that enable them to mature faster in order to attract the love of adults. Lily was the pet, the darling of the ward: sometimes she would be brought up to the nursing station, catheter pump and all, and hang out amid the residents and nurses as they were having conferences, ordering meds or take-out food, answering the phones. Her three male physicians competed for her love. The best attendants on the floor—Aloma and Averill from the West Indies, and Norma from Chile—were all devoted to Lily: bathed her, changed her, sang to her, helped her stand, encouraged her to take her first steps around the crib. One hospital study, I was told, confirmed that babies perceived as "cute" received more care than those seen as homely. Lily's beauty and winning ways seemed at times a Lamarckian compensation.

In March, Lily looked healthier, and there was talk about going home in a few weeks. Then the lab test came back, showing her albumin level had plummeted to 2.1 (3.0 or above was considered healthy). No one knew the reason for this setback: maybe they were pushing her too fast, maybe it was a lab error.

I remember vividly an occasion around that time when, to cheer us up, one of the best nurses, Suzanne, came in with two gifts: pearl earrings for Cheryl, and a tape of Disney's *The Lion King*, which had just gone on sale that day. Suzanne wheeled the fourth floor's VCR and TV into our room so that Cheryl, Lily, and I could watch the movie in bed. (Cheryl had this specific hopeful vision that we would all be home someday, nestling on the bed together like three little bears.) *The Lion King* opens with scenes of rejoicing over a newborn, which struck us with bittersweet poignancy. I dozed through the middle: I was so tired those days that I would nod out as soon as you put me in front of a TV. Lily and Cheryl napped, too. When the film was over, Lily seemed restless, so Cheryl decided to feed her. I prepared the bottle. Lily was crying and agitated as the bottle approached. I thought, Something's wrong, let's not do this. But we went ahead anyway, because we felt it important to keep up the habit of oral feeding, in preparation for that day when Lily would be taken off catheters or gastric tubes. Cheryl brought the bottle to Lily's lips, and Lily puked up everything, all over her mother's blouse. For mesmerizing spectacle, there was still nothing like Lily throwing up: I was frozen in watcher mode. "Get some cloth diapers, get a wet washcloth, do something!" cried Cheryl. I bustled about, trying not to gag from the sour milk smell of her formula vomited up, and castigating myself: Why didn't I say anything? Warn her not to feed Lily? Well, Cheryl was the one in charge, I rationalized, I didn't feel I had the authority. But we were always looking to blame each other for Lily's vomiting, as though it were simply a matter of human error. Would that it had been.

Shortly after the *Lion King* episode, we agreed to Dr. LeLeiko's recommendation that we suspend oral feedings. LeLeiko wanted to regulate strictly the quantities Lily was receiving and did not like these random extra feeds; he also feared that they might exacerbate Lily's reflex tendency to vomit, since liquid was being introduced from the bottle at a faster rate than drips through the tube. Cheryl had been resisting his advice, afraid, as it turned out rightly, that, if we suspended bottle feedings, it might be more difficult to get Lily to take food through her mouth later on. Perhaps something else was behind her resistance: she felt bad enough that she could no longer breast-feed Lily; at least she could give her a bottle from time to time and fulfill some of the maternal role of feeding her baby. But we acceded in the end to the doctor's request: no more oral feedings, for the time being.

Seven months into this ordeal, we wanted desperately to get Lily released from the hospital: that became our main focus. For one thing, she did not seem as sick as many children on the ward, some of whom had leukemia or equally serious diseases. One boy, the child of Hasidic parents, passed away, then a little Hispanic girl, and we did not want to have to witness any more deaths. In plain English, we had had it with the hospital; however kind the staff had been, we wanted out. Lily kept catching colds and getting infections, which set back her progress. In a children's hospital, you pick up every retrovirus and infectious bug. Then she started to do well; her albumin level had even risen up to 4. We had battled with the insurance company for months and finally got it to agree that we were entitled to night nursing if and when we went home. (Since Lily was still on a Broviac catheter, she would require constant nursing care during her nocturnal feeds.) Finally the word came down: we could leave. The nursing staff threw us a going-away party, we drank champagne with funny hats on, packed up the room, and said good-bye to Mount Sinai.

I was surprised that Cheryl did not seem happier. Here, a difference between our characters, or between fathers and mothers, asserted itself. As soon as I ascertained that Lily was not in mortal danger, I breathed a huge sigh of relief, whereas Cheryl continued to be distraught because there was still no clear explanation of what was wrong with her baby. Feeding a child is so basic a part of a mother's functioning that she could not sit still and wait for some far-off improvement. "Will this kid ever eat normally?" she kept worrying. She fretted if Lily's bowel movements started becoming looser, and was as attentive to her stools as the old soothsayers to Pharaoh's. She worried if Lily's skin looked blotchy. At the time I thought her pessimistic, but now I must admit it was Cheryl's acute maternal observation that made her quickly pick up danger signals. Two weeks after we came home, she voiced what I had been thinking but dared not say: that Lily was starting to look puffy. The medical term was *edematous,* an indication of not absorbing protein well. "I'll bet her albumin's fallen," Cheryl predicted grimly.

"Oh, not necessarily," I said. "It could be just a cold."

A month later we were back on the ward. All the symptoms had returned, one by one. Her albumin had shrunk to 1.9, which only confirmed the external signs: throwing up, diarrhea, swelling in the face and fingers, distended stomach, lethargy. Jane, the able chief nurse, and our favorite attendants—Aloma, Averill, and Norma—were sorry to see us return but helped us settle into our old room. We were living a recurring nightmare, back in the trenches. The first day on returning to the hospital, I felt a powerful desire to write the whole story of Lily's illness; the words were marching through my head, and writing seemed the only way of releasing the emotions within me. The next day I felt devastated, had no desire to write, wanted to lie in a fetal position and be fed intravenously myself.

Cheryl this time took it better than I, acted calmly, perhaps because she *was* at this point a pessimist. I had directed all my energy to getting out of the hospital: we'd done it, I was happy, I felt we had put the whole sorry story behind us. And then to go back inside made me crazy. I didn't know what to live for. A healthy Lily, of course. But how?

Cheryl admitted to me in private that she was fighting off a major depression. She would do her weeping in the bathroom. She had just enough energy to attend to Lily and the medical professionals but not to the outside world. Seeing mothers feeding their normal children or pushing strollers in the street would scald her. She had stopped returning friends' phone calls. Other people couldn't give her what she wanted, so she had no interest in them.

"What do you want from them?" I asked.

"An answer. Make the problem go away. I know it's irrational, but I have so much anger against the world. And so much guilt, for having borne a sick child."

"Why guilt? You've nothing to feel guilty for. That's wacky."

"You're not a mother, you wouldn't understand. I feel guilty, that's all. And then people tell me I need *distractions*. I should get out more, jog around Central Park, see friends for coffee, go to a movie. What a joke! I'm not interested."

More setbacks, other recoveries. A little over a year after she was born, Lily came home again. There had been fears that she might have developmental or intellectual delays, as is common with babies institutionalized the first year, but for the most part she tested on track for her age. We still requested physical and occupational therapy, so a couple of these therapists came to our house to work with her. I would usually accompany the physical therapist to the local park, where we would help Lily climb the jungle gym or go down the sliding pond. Lily began speaking early, forming complex sentences and making jokes, flashing a large vocabulary. By three years old, she was quite the chatterbox, and continued to be unusually perceptive and alert to others. At four she would engage the neighbors in long conversations. She was taken off the catheter but remained fed by a gastric tube, which was now inserted in her stomach. The line led behind her into a knapsack, which contained the pump and her formula, hidden from strangers' sight; Lily herself could forget about its existence, which meant we no longer had to guard every second against her tearing it out, as we had with the nasal tube. She got forty-five-minute feedings five times a day and for much of the time when she slept at night. The rest of the day we could take her off the feeding and she could run free, more or less, though within our anxious sight.

Without getting saccharine, I would like to describe at least some of the journey by which we came to a healthier, happier time.

Cheryl and I, with the invaluable aid of my mother-in-law, Doris, made an enormous effort to normalize our situation. When strangers encountered Lily for the first time, we uttered no allusion to her condition, feeling it was none of their business. The only obvious anomaly was that she was small for her age (the euphemism the household favored was "petite"): at seven, she might be mistaken for a five-year-old, at nine for a seven-year-old. But if someone commented on her lack of height, we said nothing about her first years in and out of hospitals. I think we were ashamed, as parents often are when their children are not completely "normal," though the way we framed it was that we simply did not want to advertise Lily's condition because it might turn her into an object of pity. A crossroads occurred when Lily had a setback in first grade, and had to miss several weeks of school during a return sojourn in the hospital. When she came home, we no longer had the option of taking her off her tube feeding all day: she needed continuous, slow-drip infusion. There was some debate in the family that she might be stigmatized if she went to school with the feeding pack in plain sight, and homeschooling was discussed as a temporary option. I decided it was more important to send her to school every day, to let her make friends and be socialized, even with the feeding pack attached. Fortunately, her classmates took it in stride and embraced her. Children at that tender age can seem blessedly tolerant.

Lily's constitution remained very fragile through ages six to ten: she still vomited too often and had diarrhea. A new symptom arose: she would sometimes get the shivers, and need hot tea and piles of blankets to arrest them. She would neither eat nor drink by mouth, though there was nothing anatomically preventing her from swallowing. It was more a psychological problem: having missed the earlier milestones, she was afraid of gagging and vomiting, and had to learn painstakingly from point zero how to eat—a seemingly natural act for a younger child. It would have been too risky a gamble to cut off her feeding and see if hunger might prompt her to learn more quickly. She was very small for her age and needed every calorie to count.

We went through a troop of feeding therapists, all of whom practiced some variant of behavioral modification. I remember one of them crooning and zooming the spoon like an airplane into (or onto) her clenched mouth. Another counseled our leaving the room, abandoning her, so to speak, if she refused a morsel. A third boasted a 100 percent success rate, but nevertheless gave up on us. Lily resisted eating by mouth for the longest time: she was not the best candidate for a rewards-and-punishment system, being stubborn and independent; and, it must be said, neither Cheryl nor I ever cottoned to behavioral modification, so perhaps she was picking up on our skepticism. Nor were we, snobs and loners that we were, willing to join the various parent support groups that might swap stories about their own children's eating struggles, or place Lily in a hospital for a month of strict supervision and tough love. Dr. LeLeiko, too, was dubious about these approaches, and thought we were wasting our time.

"When she's ready to eat, she'll learn," he said. He was increasingly sanguine that her malabsorption problems would resolve and her body learn to make adaptations. In fact that is what happened. Her organs adjusted to whatever enzyme or endocrinal imbalance might have caused this illness in the first place. I don't remember exactly how or when, but she began eating normally, with a healthy appetite and a preference for Asian cuisine. After careful monitoring indicated that she could gain weight normally through regular ingestion, my wife decided to remove the feeding tube. All this while Lily was getting taller: our goal was to see her one day reach five feet, and now, at seventeen, she stands at five foot three. She is, for all intents and purposes, a healthy teenager, which means she is snappish, moody, dictatorial, and self-absorbed; but she also has a warm sense of humor, writes poetry, acts in plays, makes beautiful ceramics, dotes on her cats, and tolerates her parents reasonably well. Mother and daughter continue to enjoy, and at times endure, a semiumbilical attachment: the more Lily's health has improved, the happier, lighter in spirit, and more easygoing Cheryl has become.

The transformation in Cheryl is equally remarkable. Lily's sturdiness gives her great satisfaction and, I hope, a deserved sense of accomplishment, since it is mostly due to her efforts and years of sacrifice. We still watch Lily microscopically whenever our only child, about to enter college, comes down with the flu, or is simply under the weather for a day—I watch with held breath for some downward spiral that, fortunately, never recurs. Fatherhood has brought me all that I had hoped. If I do not love Lily "unconditionally" (whatever *that* means), I do love her to distraction. If because of her I was obliged to enter the Kingdom of Anxiety, such is the lot of all parents, and a small price to pay for the plenitude of her being.

Lily's illness has been the most intense, challenging experience of my life. I have my doubts that the pain I underwent taught me a valuable lesson, or made me a better person; and certainly the pain Lily underwent seems to me entirely undeserved and unnecessary. But I now know what it means to suffer—I have a set of memory images from that time that will never go away. The curious part is that I have no desire to relinquish them: I sometimes summon these memories (such as Lily getting prepped for an endoscopy or passing under the spaceship dome of a CT scan) and fan them out like a deck of cards, just for the fright of it, just for the knowledge that that time is now past. Lily, though she writes engaging personal essays, has never written a word about her hospital time. Perhaps as a residue of our years of circling the wagons and putting up a normal façade, she sees no need to revisit those trials; she has put them behind her, like childish toys. Cheryl may have held on longer to her sense of grievance against a world that would not cut her enough slack, given the complexity of her caring for Lily, but eventually she, too, has put it to rest. It is only I—to their eyes the one who was the least involved, and hence the least entitled to claim the experience—who cannot seem to let it go. Is it because it shook me to my very core? Or is it because I am too proud of having survived that ordeal to stop dwelling on it? All I know is that a part of me continues to haunt those wards, those corridors, those nurses' stations, while seeming to attend to my ordinary daily life.

II

THE CONSOLATIONS
OF DAILY LIFE

Memoirs of a Wishy-Washy Left-Liberal

I t is bad enough to have to read in the paper each morning some political setback to the progressive cause, some reactionary nonsense put forward to maintain unnecessary tax breaks for the rich or subsidies to the banks and oil corporations, some further protection of those who would despoil the planet. What makes it even worse is that I cannot take much pleasure in the responses of my own kind, because I know too well what they are going to say before they say it, and because there is something disagreeable to me in any political party line, which too often commits the espouser to tit-for-tat distortions and petty vituperations.

A friend phoned the other day in an outrage, because of some conservatively skewed article in *The New York Times* by a foreign correspondent whom he knew to be "on the Right," having gone to school with the fellow. "We have to do something about it," my friend insisted. "We have to counter this nauseating reactionary propaganda." He used the word *we* with some justification, knowing that I held the same left-liberal views, more or less, that he did. But I had no intention of dashing off an angry letter to the *Times*, or whipping up a satire of the offending journalist for *The Nation*. Newspapers would always be filled with opinions that ran counter to mine, and if I were to retort to each one, I would be worn to a nub, like a fastidious fourth grader's eraser. This inaction on my part may sound like quietism or submission to the policy of "Resist not evil," but it is more an economizing of energies, which I find myself, in middle age, increasingly obliged to do.

When I was younger, I had energy to burn. I could go on protest marches, dash off political statements, and still write poems, essays, and novellas. I didn't yet know who I was or what my limits were—I thought I might yet turn into both a writer and a cabinet minister, someone like Lamartine or Malraux or Havel. I had a slight tendency in that direction: in 1968, for instance, my peers elected me president of Alumni for a New Columbia, a left-leaning group formed during the campus strike as an alternative to the official alumni organization. We were sufficiently naïve to think that world revolution was around the corner, and that everyone who wanted to change society needed to get organized by joining some group. Alumni for a New Columbia's main tasks were to support the student strike by raising bail, providing medical assistance in the event of a police bust, and filing amicus curiae briefs in court for the arrested student leaders. It was, truth be told, a rather small organization: two hundred names on our mailing list, and a hard core of twenty working members, which included a few lawyers, a few old CP organizers from the Maritime Union who had scurried out of the woodwork, a few militant shrinks, and a bunch of writers like myself, who had graduated only a few years earlier and envied the students their rebellion. We writers tried to make the group sound larger than it was by issuing one statement after another to the press, protesting how "shocked and appalled" we were by the university administration's "insensitivity."

I ended up a group spokesman, going on radio talk shows to debate the more conservative alumni or administration representative, inveighing against the university's "complicity in racism, sexism, and the war machine." My grasp of the facts was shallower than I would have liked, but I could be briefed quickly and was an adequate bluffer, and, besides, neither side was listening to the other anyway: it was an exercise in what a psychologist friend calls "synchronous narcissism." I was certainly against the Vietnam War, I liked the attention I was receiving and the challenge of thinking on my feet, but I could never get over some queasiness from indulging in strident public rhetoric which took me further and further away from my own interior musing, in which skepticism, ambivalence, and uncertainty play large parts.

I remember being interviewed once by a Pacifica-WBAI reporter in a live hookup before a campus rally. We were standing in front of Butler Library, facing the Columbia quadrangle, looking out at the lawn, and the interviewer asked me a question about strategy. As I started to frame the answer a blue jay hopped about, twittering nearby. It so mesmerized me, that bird, that I forgot to speak, and the interviewer began sweating, since nothing is more verboten to radio people than dead airtime. Finally I brought myself to utter the requisite clichés, but I couldn't forget that a part of me was truer to watching the blue jay than to caring about the impact that a new university gymnasium proposed for Morningside Park might or might not have on the adjoining Harlem community.

I was in over my head, in short. I had started reading Marx and going to classes in the SDS Liberation School, where I encountered the dazzling rigidity of left-wing sectarian thinking. It was here that I first encountered the scary slogan "The struggle against revisionism is the struggle to the death!" It was here I first heard that we must cast out of the canon Dostoevsky ("reactionary"), Fromm and Niebuhr ("liberal"), Nabokov ("elitist"), and Hamsun and Céline ("fascists"). I had no intention of boycotting these estimable writers, and even at the time thought that grading writers by standards of political correctness was nearsighted. But I confess I was intrigued by the very sound of such clangorous, dismissive conviction.

It was here, too, I first heard human rights and civil liberties contemptuously referred to as "bourgeois freedoms." Could it really be said that these noble humanist ideals were nothing but a smoke screen, as Fanon maintained, by the ruling class for domination of people of color? And could a revolutionary situation truly justify the suppression of free speech, assembly, and religion—or the mass execution of class enemies? These were chilling thoughts.

The lesson I learned most from that era was that the truth was being distorted and manipulated by both sides. Of course the United States government lied massively and daily; its misdeeds in Vietnam and neglect of our urban and rural poor were inexcusable. But we left-liberal foot soldiers were also being shamelessly deceived: told, for instance, that the People's Republic of China had no capital punishment, only re-education, as later we would be assured about Cambodia's Pol Pot that he was a good guy and don't pay attention to the lies being spread about him by the capitalist media.

Mao's China was the standard of purity, the wind from the east; Fidel Castro's Cuba, the other model held up for imitation. How well I remember a German graduate student named Fritz who had come to New York City to study what he called the "exemplary model" of the Young Lords, a Puerto Rican ex–street gang turned political. Personally, I got a little nervous whenever the Young Lords appeared in public, with their para-military red berets and macho display of military discipline. This was the period when the student Left fantasized making a political alliance with street gangs like the Blackstone Rangers of Chicago—a prospect that scared the shit out of me. Maybe I saw it differently because most student radicals were disaffected middle- to upper-middle-class kids of suburban privilege, whereas I had grown up in the Brooklyn ghettos of Williamsburg and Fort Greene/Bedford-Stuyvesant, had experienced street gangs close up, and wanted no part of them.

Most exemplary of all exemplaries, of course, were the Black Panthers. That some police actions against the Panthers turned out to have been triggered by shoot-outs between rival street gangs is a part of history we on the Left still have trouble accepting. At the time, the rationalization was put forward that crimes were essentially revolutionary actions against the State. Huey Newton, who it later came out was something of a psychopathic thug, a pimp who killed prostitutes, dealt drugs, robbed warehouses—was our movement's prince and poster boy, by virtue of looking as beautiful as Paul Newman in a rattan chair while bedecked with guns; for his ambiguous, cherubic smile, even more compelling than Che's martyred scowl, we granted him all our love.

I don't mean to say that I swallowed the Black Panther rhetoric entirely back then, but I certainly felt a kinship with their "struggle" (as we loved to say) and on one occasion even went out of the way to demonstrate my solidarity. It was during the winter of 1969, when the police were making brutal raids on Black Panther headquarters. The raids always came in the early-morning hours. Fred Hampton was shot to death in his bed during one of them, and hundreds of rounds of ammunition were traded in a Los Angeles shoot-out. Everyone I knew had the same reaction: stunned anger. A call went out to supporters to *protect the Panthers* by assembling in front of the Oakland national headquarters. The assumption seemed to be that the police would not dare to storm Panther headquarters in front of a racially integrated crowd of witnesses.

I was living in Berkeley at the time, a runaway from my early marriage, and felt that I had to "do something." I arrived around 10:00 p.m. at the Black Panther storefront, which was on Shattuck Avenue near the border between Oakland and Berkeley. Strangely enough, everyone who had come to demonstrate was white. We looked at each other, and our eyes snapped away in embarrassment. I could understand that no top-level Panther, no Bobby Seale or David Hilliard, had bothered to show and address the crowd of supporters, but at least they could have sent down the Minister of Fund-Raising or the Chair of the Anti-Fascist Alliance! Two black high school boys had alone been left behind the counter, to accept donations and sell the Panther newspaper; and the Berkeley ideologues, hoping to raise the teenage kids' political consciousness or at least rustle up a sympathetic discussion with them about repression, found them ill-informed. It was going to be a long night.

There was nothing to do but leaf through police brutality literature and wait. A framed portrait of Joseph Stalin hung above the counter. Not one of my favorite leaders. *What am I doing here?* I asked myself. If the police do stage a raid, we'll all be massacred. If they don't come, we'll be disappointed.

Eventually, the group formed a "presence" in front of the storefront, moving in a slow circle, talking about everyday matters: teaching loads, landlords. A stiff wind blew across Shattuck Avenue. Cars whizzed past on their way to the freeway without braking for a closer look. There were so many traffic lanes separating us from the other side of Shattuck that we could only make out a fuzzy pink and green of bungalows and trees across the street. Occasionally a person on foot approached us, usually a sympathizer who would be immediately pressed into our circle.

If only the newcomer had not joined us but had stayed looking at us, say, from the median, our demonstration would have felt less pointless. Without an audience, we were walking in circles for the benefit of a lone streetlamp. We might as well have been protesting the coolness of the night, or the unapproachable distance of the stars.

After midnight the temperature dropped further and we tried to keep warm by walking faster or rubbing our arms. Someone went inside to make a cup of hot Postum, and brought out several additional cups for demonstrators. I was lucky enough to get one. We were suddenly in high spirits—who knows why? Maybe it was simply that the absurdity of the situation had been acknowledged and accepted. If the police *should* come, we had nothing but this hot Postum with which to arm ourselves. We must remember to throw it in their eyes.

Why I Remain a Baseball Fan

I sometimes encounter ex–baseball fans (invariably middle-aged men) who tell me they have given up following the sport because of the steroid scandal, the huge salaries of the players, the duplicity of the owners, "it's all become just a big business," or some such explanation, which they deliver in a tone of principled disgust. I listen with feigned sympathy, but of course I don't share their feelings, either because I have many fewer principles or because the ones I have lie in other directions, and I would not dream of relinquishing the pleasure (and pain) of a new baseball season. I anticipate being a baseball fan until I lose all my marbles, and possibly beyond that.

The fact is I have never been a particularly good athlete, and I can no more begrudge baseball superstars getting hundred-million-dollar contracts for doing what I could never do than I would resent well-paid Hollywood actors who manage to radiate aching beauty and charisma on-screen. I have noticed that most of the men who object to the so-called inflated salaries of ballplayers have larger bank accounts than my own. If they had grown up poor, as I did, they might not have figured it was any of their business to identify with and assess the remunerative levels of ballplayers, but simply assumed these idols would always be incomparably above them.

I grew up in the 1940s in working-class Brooklyn, both my parents were factory workers, and of course I rooted for the Brooklyn Dodgers. My father took me to Ebbets Field for a Sunday doubleheader with St.

Louis: the first game was a duel between the Cards' ace Robin Roberts and the Dodgers' Don Newcombe, my favorite pitcher (I liked his gigantic jaw and the way he grinned) and went to extra innings, before the Cards took it in the tenth, 1–0. Stan Musial hit a homer in the second game: what a thrill to watch a great player like Musial connect, even if he was on the opposing team. Most of all I liked to watch Jackie Robinson dancing off third base, taunting the pitcher. He and Carl Furillo, Gil Hodges, Duke Snider, et al. have been celebrated in retrospect as archetypical "lunch pail" ballplayers, who lived in the neighborhood and rode the trolleys or subways to Ebbets Field. Supposedly they were "like us," a nice fairy tale, but in the neighborhood we experienced them as demigods, not blue-collar workers like our fathers. Besides, baseball players are not cops or civil servants: I see no reason why they should be expected to live within the city limits of the locality named on their uniforms. It's true that Ebbets Field had an intimacy, you felt as though you could touch the center fielder, but maybe that's why attendance and profits started to drop near the end. In any case, one good thing about rooting for the Dodgers was that, when their owner, Walter O'Malley, broke our hearts by moving the team out to Los Angeles, in 1958, for the most logically mercenary of reasons, I lost my innocence in one fell swoop, and never had to be shocked to that extent again. I was inured to owner shenanigans, having learned once and for all that baseball is indeed a business.

In a sense, the Dodgers' move away from us was anticlimactic, because they had already won their first World Series, which was what mainly counted to me as a kid. It was such an important event that the principal of our public school allowed the final innings of the final game to be broadcast over the PA system, only the second time that had happened (the other time was the fall of Dien Bien Phu, the French losing in Vietnam!). So the Dodgers won, they were no longer losers, Dem Bums, and were free to go off to sunny California. For a while I rooted for the L.A. team, not able to stop caring about Sandy Koufax and Don Drysdale (I cheered this pair of aces on during their salary sit-down strike). But then when the New York Mets got started up, I, like millions of other ex–Dodger fans, switched my allegiance to them. Part of the reason was geographical: the Mets played in Queens, which was adjacent to Brooklyn (the same long island). Also, both Mets and Dodgers were National League teams, and it seemed as inconceivable to root for the other league as to switch from being left-handed to right-handed. We could have turned into Yankees fans, but we didn't: the Yankees were associated in our minds with Republicans and Big Business, the Dodgers (the first team to integrate) with liberalism and labor. I now consider such characterizations nonsense, since all baseball teams are millionaires' playthings. And so, let the games begin.

It is sometimes posited as an enigma that anyone can continue to root for the same team after its star players have been traded away, or the players themselves have allegedly betrayed their loyal fans by signing for more money elsewhere as free agents—in other words, after the roster has been completely reshaped. I find this no mystery: after all, the cells in one's body are replaced every seven years, and yet one continues to retain the same individuality. One may continue to love one's country, in spite of its misbegotten wars and scurvy domestic policies. If consumers remain loyal to brands, and continue to buy Toyotas, say, despite corporate changes in design, why not a baseball team, which has a shared history, tradition, and even style of play? Some ballparks with deep outfield dimensions promote pitching; others, power hitters or base stealers. The essence of a team's identity, its tendency to choke or rise to the occasion—its karma, if you will—is felt to be a reality by its fans, however delusional or superstitious those expectations may be. The Cubs show promise at the beginning of the season and fade at the end, the Mets, give or take a few illustrious seasons, are a .500 team, and the Yankees are champions, though both play in the same big-money market.

Part of becoming a grown-up is accepting one's limitations. I am not nor ever will be a good athlete, though my tennis game has lately improved; I am something of a klutz, but I have moments of surprising grace. So it is with my team.

Becoming a baseball fan means learning to absorb failure and be on a friendly footing with defeat. It is a truism that the hardest thing to do in sports is hit a baseball; a hitter who makes an out seven out of ten times is having an excellent season. Your team, considered as a whole, will not win year after year: if it gets to two World Series in a decade, it is doing phenomenally well. Every baseball fan knows this. When blowhard owners like the late George Steinbrenner make speeches about there being no excuse for coming in second, the only thing that counts is winning, the true fan yawns at this gasconade. If, as Montaigne wrote, "to philosophize is to learn how to die," then to be a baseball fan is to learn how to lose. Ivan Morris once wrote a fine book called *The Nobility of Failure*, in which he argued that the heroic tradition in Japanese history and narrative culture was built around the general who fails, the samurai who, surrounded and outnumbered, falls on his sword. It is not surprising that the Japanese have taken to baseball.

I can still see in my mind's eye the Mets' former star outfielder Carlos Beltrán, with the tying run in scoring position and two men out and the count full, frozen by Adam Wainwright's curveball—the pitch that ended the Mets' season. I still ask myself: Why can't Mets hitters learn to foul off more of those borderline pitches? Why are they so one-dimensional? And wasn't that pitch a little outside? A team's key defeats stay so much fresher in the mind—in my mind, at least—than do their victories. We all know how to triumph; we need no schooling in that department. Baseball teaches us bitter wisdom.

Speaking of Beltrán, that so gifted, likable, oft-injured player can still smack the ball out of the park or chase down a long fly ball, but he limps slightly when he runs. The older I get, the more fascinated I am with watching the aging process in my favorite baseball players, who point the way to my own diminished, arthritic future. The Mets used to make a habit of signing aging sluggers, like George Foster, Eddie Murray, or Gary Carter, who would then demonstrate "warning track" power, no longer able to hit home runs but specializing in deep fly-ball outs.

Of course being a baseball fan is not all about accustoming oneself to decline and defeat: there are those remarkable debuts, like the rookie seasons of Ken Griffey, Jr., or José Reyes, when blazing young talents happily revel in their speed and power and joy of living; or the sophomore years of talented players who begin to put it all together. Part of the pleasure in baseball is matching expectation to outcome: the hard-working, nondescript-looking Dustin Pedroia accomplishes more than larger, more muscled players and wins the MVP award. A runt like short-stop Bucky Dent, not one of their dangerous sluggers, hits the home run that salvages the Yankees' season. Those dramatic reversals of character, when adrenaline propels the shrimp to excel in postseason while the stud goes into an 0-for-20 slump, are like passages out of Homer: the gods or goddesses whimsically lend support to someone on the field, infusing him with their celestial spirit while abandoning their usual beneficiary.

Here we come to the most essential reason I cling to baseball: its ability to generate narrative. The baseball season is like a long, complicated, novelistic drama series on television—*The Wire, The Sopranos,* or *Mad Men*—where you follow various quirky characters and become invested in their fates. That the craven yes-man should act in such an atypically bold manner, or the cold-blooded killer suddenly show prudence, is part of these television series' appeal. I would not expect a viewer to come upon an episode of *The Wire* in the middle of the second season and make sense of what was happening, any more than I would expect the same of my wife when she idly watches a baseball game behind me for five minutes without knowing the players and their past histories or potential. I fully appreciate why she finds the mere spectacle of baseball insufficient. Without knowing the individual players as a cast of characters, it is a pretty dull, abstract ballet. But once they are known, every at-bat turns into a little story, with the pitcher moving the ball around, trying to hit his spots, and the batter trying to second-guess what's coming next. And if you know in addition that the new relief pitcher just arrived the day before from the minor leagues because another relief pitcher was injured, and he is facing the most fearsome hitter in baseball, the David-and-Goliath narrative wheels start turning automatically.

Then there is the family-lineage dimension—the father-and-son duos that both made it to the big leagues, or the many sets of brothers who play against each other for different teams. There are the baseball scouts who traditionally sign up players of a certain skill set, or from a specific group of colleges, or from a particular Dominican or Puerto Rican town, and that becomes another kind of dynastic network. All of this intriguing if finally petty historical knowledge, which probably takes a lifetime of following baseball to acquire, makes the sport seem like a small Southern town where everyone knows everyone's kin. Dave Magadan is Lou Piniella's godson, that kind of thing. It adds to the game's novelistic texture.

Baseball has always attracted serious writers, a mixed blessing. I am not one of those authors tempted to gush about the April zephyrs lifting opening day banners, the verdant velvet swards, the elegant geometry of the bases. . . . Yeah, we know, baseball has a poetic side, but it's been overemphasized. I did not remain a lifelong baseball fan because of the smell of peanuts and hot dogs. I mostly watch the game on television, so that sensual aspect is beside the point: the color of the grass merely the best green my HDTV can conjure at the moment. I watch for the story line: what's going to happen next.

With such powerful inducement to keep me engaged, perhaps you understand why I was not put off baseball forever by learning that some of the players doped themselves with steroids. Yes, it was unfortunate, and tarnishes in our minds many records broken at the height of steroid use. But I view it as one more impurity to accept in this life. The old ballplayers drank; my childhood idol Don Newcombe was often stewed on the days he started. Dock Ellis pitched a no-hitter on acid. Granted, alcohol or LSD offers less physical advantage than steroids. But I still think it took incredible hand-eye coordination and skill to hit homers the way Barry Bonds did. For every Barry Bonds or Sammy Sosa or Rafael Palmeiro, who went from being all-stars to being superstars with the aid of steroids, there were dozens of journeymen who shot themselves with juice constantly but didn't improve much. Look, I am glad steroid use is monitored and has abated, but I wouldn't be surprised if some other advantageous substances or technologies were employed in the future. Baseball players are always looking for an edge, be it pine tar or spy cameras; it is part of the evolution of the game.

Nor do I buy the idea that baseball players must behave like role models for youth and therefore shouldn't drink, gamble, or fornicate outside of marriage. Sports media today contain precious little illuminating analysis of the way the game is played, physically or mentally; but they are filled with stories of ballplayers' misdeeds off field. Every sports columnist sets up as a pontificating Savonarola. Baseball players, whether active or retired, are indeed sinners like the rest of us, and out of curiosity I am as happy as the next man to read about their barroom brawls, speeding tickets, holing up with strippers, getting caught with illegal drugs; committing suicide, murder, rape, statutory rape, negligent homicide while driving; their filing for bankruptcy, embezzling luxury cars, and shoplifting, beating girlfriends, being stabbed by girlfriends, swapping wives, getting run in by the local police for lying naked and asleep with a prostitute in a car on Main Street, Florida, during exhibition baseball season, et cetera and so forth. But none of this misbehavior will ever make me inclined to give up watching baseball.

I have no idea how the peccadilloes or felonies of baseball players statistically compare with those of a similar sampling of the population, like dentists or politicians. We rarely hear the other side of the story, how some ballplayer put his child to bed by reading a story, or helped his wife through a difficult situation with her parents. Not that I would want the sports pages to be clogged with such goody-goody anecdotes either. The point I am making is that all of these peeks into the private lives and moral frailties of players (or owners, whose messy divorces and susceptibility to Ponzi schemes have become headline fodder of late—wait, even the longtime clubhouse manager of the Mets was just arrested for stealing equipment and uniforms) have no bearing whatsoever on why I remain a loyal baseball fan. It's a game that I simply like to watch, pitch by pitch.

Novels and Films:
A Comedy of Remarriage

The Plot So Far

In 1926 Virginia Woolf wrote an amusing if snooty essay called "The Cinema," in which she decried the way that movies were adopting literature.

All the famous novels of the world, with their well-known characters and their famous scenes, only asked, it seemed, to be put on the films. What could be easier and simpler? The cinema fell upon its prey with immense rapacity, and to the moment largely subsists upon the body of its unfortunate victim. But the results are disastrous to both. The alliance is unnatural. Eye and brain are torn asunder ruthlessly as they try vainly to work in couples. The eye says "Here is Anna Karenina." A voluptuous lady in black velvet wearing pearls comes before us. But the brain says, "That is no more Anna Karenina than it is Queen Victoria." For the brain knows Anna almost entirely by the inside of her mind—her charm, her passion, her despair. All the emphasis is laid by the cinema upon her teeth, her pearls, and her velvet. Then "Anna falls in love with Vronsky"—that is to say, the lady in black velvet falls into the arms of a gentleman in uniform and they kiss with enormous succulence, great deliberation, and infinite gesticulation, on a sofa in an extremely well-appointed library, while a gardener incidentally mows the lawn. So we lurch and lumber through the most famous novels of the world. So we spell them out in words of one syllable, written, too, in the scrawl of an illiterate schoolboy. A kiss is love. A broken cup is jealousy. A grin is happiness. Death is a hearse. None of these things has the least connexion with the novel that Tolstoy wrote, and it is only when we give up trying to connect the pictures with the book that we guess from some accidental scene—like the gardener mowing the lawn—what the cinema might do if left to its own devices.

In other words, the cinema should keep its cotton-pickin' hands off literature and discover its true, pure essence, which is something apparently more in a documentary vein. Since the medium has not chosen to obey Woolf's advice, scholars and critics have had no recourse but to keep examining the relationship between novels and movies. Let us try to bring some fresh air to this overworked topic, the subject of countless high school and college English courses that dutifully explore film adaptations of novels, hoping to lure a visually besotted generation back to reading, not to mention countless film studies courses approaching it from the other end. At professional conferences, academics present papers singling out the filmic treatment of x or y novel, a comparison usually made to the detriment of the movie, which is seen as more crass—as in the *New Yorker* cartoon Hitchcock recounted to Truffaut that showed two goats eating film cans, one remarking to the other, "Personally, I liked the book better." Film is treated as the trashy blonde corrupting the professor. Sometimes, however, the older medium's stuffiness is viewed as polluting the more innocent, populist art.

First it may be necessary to question received wisdom. One such premise is that it is easier to make a fine film out of a mediocre novel than out of a superior one, because the adapter will feel less reverent toward the source material. (In reality, any screenwriter who has had to adapt a weak novel can tell you that inheriting lousy plots and thin characters does not make the job any easier.) A short list, barely scratching the surface, of beautiful films made from superior fiction might include *Diary of a Country Priest, Mouchette, The Leopard, Berlin Alexanderplatz, The Life of Oharu, Pather Panchali, Greed, Day of Wrath, Floating Clouds, Little Women, The Scarlet Letter, Double Indemnity, How Green Was My Valley, Nana, The House of Mirth, The Heiress, The Magnificent Amber-*

sons, *The Marquise of O, Wise Blood, Les Enfants Terribles, The Key, The Sound of the Mountain, A Tree Grows in Brooklyn, Barry Lyndon, Persuasion, Hard Times, Contempt* . . . Even superlative novels that had seemed unfilmable, because of size, canonic status, or interiority—I am thinking of *Great Expectations, Les Misérables, Remembrance of Things Past, Wuthering Heights, War and Peace, Don Quixote, Madame Bovary*—have yielded creditable versions which succeeded at least partly in bringing these texts alive on-screen.

Another received truth is that the best way to make a vivid movie adaptation is to cut loose from the novel as soon as possible. Some screenwriters boast that they will read the novel once, then never go back to it; and there are directors (such as John Ford with *The Grapes of Wrath*) who claim they never read the original novel. There may be some ego protecting here: Jean-Luc Godard was being a bit disingenuous in dismissing Alberto Moravia's *A Ghost at Noon*, his source for *Contempt*, as a conventional novel to read on a train, thereby downplaying the psychological insights he had borrowed from the author. But for every instance in which a rough, indifferent attitude (or the pretense of one) toward the source material resulted in a successful film, there are others in which the screenwriter and/or director took the original quite seriously, such as Nelson Pereira dos Santos, who used the pages of Graciliano Ramos's book as the shooting script for his superb *Barren Lives* (1963).

One Approach: Hyper-Naturalism

The most famous example of a filmmaker refusing to acknowledge any dividing line between novels and movies, or relinquish devotion to his source material, is Erich von Stroheim. The tragedy of *Greed*—that his nine-and-a-half-hour version of Frank Norris's *McTeague* was whittled down by the studio to roughly two hours and its original negative destroyed—has become the central, cautionary myth regarding film adaptations, like Icarus flying too near the sun. But we could just as easily view Stroheim's *Greed* (even in its butchered form one of the great classics) as an exemplary model of film adaptation. It is generally assumed that Stroheim went about trying to film the novel paragraph by paragraph—and indeed, there are many direct correspondences of that kind—but the truth is more complicated, as the critic Jonathan Rosenbaum usefully notes: "In fact, Stroheim got so far inside the spirit and texture of the original that, like any good Method actor, he was able to generate his own material out of it: almost the first fifth of the published script of *Greed*, nearly sixty pages, describes incidents invented by Stroheim that occur prior to the action at the beginning of the novel."

Anyone who has seen *Greed*—either in its 1924 studio release or in Rick Schmidlin's fascinating 1999 four-hour restoration, which incorporates recently discovered production stills and dialogue cards—can attest to its thick texture of background objects, signs, faces, and clothing, all of which generate a poignantly convincing material atmosphere, brick by brick. Anyone who reads Norris's novel will notice his similar fondness for amassing physical detail. Norris's mentor in naturalist fiction was Emile Zola, who also loved to pile on the details, and to roam, like a tracking camera, over his chosen milieu. (See, for instance, the marvelous department store descriptions in *The Ladies' Delight*, or the open market scenes in *The Belly of Paris*.) If Flaubert, as has frequently been observed, could be said to have anticipated crosscutting in the agricultural fair sequence of *Madame Bovary*, Zola was even more important to the movies as avatar and inspiration. More than sixty adaptations of Zola's novels have been made since 1902, when Ferdinand Zecca adapted *L'Assommoir*. But Zola's usefulness to directors has been more than just as a source. First, his descriptions convey the constant flow of life, that seemingly endless supply of visual information such as has also been suggested in documentaries and city symphonies from Lumière on, and which is the right and privilege of the camera eye. Second, Zola's penchant for deterministic fatalism channeled that flow and gave it narrative point. Jean Renoir, the grand master of insinuating a cinematic river of life which seems to spill out beyond the frame and lap around his fatalistic protagonists (*Toni* [1935], *La Bête Humaine* [1938]), acknowledged his debt to Zola, not only by adapting several of his novels but by stating outright: "I believe that the so-called realist film is a child of the naturalist school." And: "One usually takes Zola as a purely realist author . . . but what interests me in Zola is his poetry."

This filmic discovery of the implicit lyric resources in naturalist fiction, derived from Zola, was so important to 1930s French auteurs such as Renoir, Marcel Carné, Julien Duvivier, Jacques Feyder, Pierre Chenal, and Jean Grémillon that their works were even grouped under the name "poetic realism." Dudley Andrew, in his splendid study of this school, *Mists of Regret: Culture and Sensibility in Classic French Film*, is quick to point out the debt that classic French cinema owes to novelists of the day (for instance, Simenon), when he speaks of "the evasive quality of 'atmosphere' that stands as an intermediate term between literature and cinema. Although atmosphere at one time may have belonged more properly to the poetic and painterly arts rather than to the novel, which was considered the medium of social analysis and intrigue, in the 1930s atmosphere had descended like a cloud on the narrative arts of novel and film."

Another Approach: Avant-Garde Stylization

The bane of many filmed novels is the episodic, that hurrying-along effort to cram in so many scenes from the book that high points get flattened and details blur. One strategy to circumvent that pitfall has been a highly stylized, austere, antinaturalistic approach. In *Not Reconciled* (1965), the first of many rigorous features by the duo Jean-Marie Straub and Danièle Huillet, Heinrich Böll's novel *Billiards at Half-Past Nine* was used as inspiration for a film about a bourgeois German family coping with the period before, during, and after the Nazi regime. Rather than pack in as many sensational incidents as possible to capture a story spanning several decades, the filmmakers slowed down their fifty-five minutes by patiently recapturing unhurried moments of being (such as a man smoking a cigarette on a stairwell or sitting down to his customary breakfast at a hotel). The result is a masterly contemplation of the way daily life goes on in the midst of historical upheaval. The Straub-Huillet team also adapted Kafka's *Amerika* (as *Class Relations* [1984]) and Elio Vittorini's *Conversations in Sicily* (as *Sicilia!* [1999]), and made two features from Cesare Pavese's *Dialogues with Leucò*

(*From the Clouds to the Resistance* [1979] and *These Encounters of Theirs* [2006]), in both cases filming Pavese's elaborate dialogues word for word.

Manoel de Oliveira, in *Doomed Love* (1979), filmed Camilo Castelo Branco's nineteenth-century Portuguese novel more or less in its entirety, by having a narrator speak voluminous voice-over texts when the actors were being quiet. This method imposed an intentionally static rhythm, as the actors were obliged to stand around while the voice-over narration unfurled, though sometimes the camera would go its own way, tracking to a window, for example. The somber delivery of long, formal speeches between the nonprofessional actors violated film adaptation's received wisdom, which states that a novel's dialogue must be recast and abbreviated so as to sound as natural as possible issuing from the actors' mouths. Yet somehow the results are mesmerizing. Oliveira explained that he found himself "making a film from a romantic work—but this work operates on two distinct levels. One is superficial, anecdotal, sentimental and very explicit; the other is much more profound. I didn't wish to remain with the first level. . . . Since I was adapting a work of literature to an audio-visual medium—a work of great beauty, moreover—I thought it would be legitimate to concentrate on the text, the words, and to let the images have a more serene form." Oliveira subsequently refined his filmed-novel technique with *Francisca* (1981); *The Valley of Abraham* (1993), loosely based on *Madame Bovary*; *La Lettre* (1999), based on *La Princesse de Clèves* by Mme de La Fayette; and *Eccentricities of a Blond-Haired Girl* (2009), based on an Eça de Queiroz text. All of these experiments deliciously and stubbornly resist the conventional wisdom which says that, when adapting a novel, avoid at all costs the "literary." In the process, they challenge that quasi-religious dogma of film studies: The visual must take precedence over the verbal.

The Stigma of the Literary

Being story-hungry, as Virginia Woolf noted, the cinema looked from its first, silent days to novels and plays for raw material. At the same time, defenders of this insecure young medium were eager to assert that it had unique qualities, putting forward a program of "pure cinema" and, in so doing, trying to distance it from the older media. The original sin, so to speak, was for film to ape the theater. Gilbert Seldes argued that "not one single essential of the movies has ever been favorably affected by the stage; the stage has contributed nothing lasting to the movies; there isn't a single item of cinema technique which requires the experience of the stage; and every good thing in the movies has been accomplished either in profound indifference to the stage, or against the experience of the stage." The advent of talkies made the theatrical menace more palpable, and there were many highbrow film critics, such as Rudolf Arnheim, who thought that sound would spell the death of cinema as an art form.

As it turns out, they were wrong. Talk, lots of talk, even a theatrically inflected mise-en-scène, led to many extraordinary movies, from Marcel Pagnol, Sasha Guitry, George Cukor, Jean Cocteau, Joseph L. Mankiewicz, Carl Dreyer, and Orson Welles (who confessed he was always more interested in words than images) down to Erich Rohmer, John Cassavetes, Woody Allen, and Alain Resnais, with his recent "film-theater." My point here is that a fear of language tainting the screen's noble essence expanded, from the theater as principal villain to the literary per se, including novels, short stories, and a harder-to-define gestalt. When James Agee, in praising Vittorio De Sica's neorealist *Shoeshine* (1946) to the skies, qualifies his enthusiasm by saying "Such feeling for form as there is, is more literary than cinematic," it is not entirely clear to me what he means by calling the director's approach "literary," but the tone of reproach is unmistakable.

Two forms of snobbism and prestige are involved here: the cinematic and the literary. Novels originally brought cultural prestige to movies. Classics and established novels of the day have always enjoyed the marketing advantage of being presold, familiar names, and the number of novels adapted for high-budget, Oscar-friendly pictures (from *Quo Vadis* to *Gone with the Wind* to *Memoirs of a Geisha*) is much greater than for lower-budgeted ones. It was this built-in prestige attached to novels that raised the hackles of those *Cahiers du Cinéma* critics who would go on to constitute the New Wave. Truffaut's attack on the French "cinema of quality," by which he meant lush, creamy films such as Christian-Jaque's

Charterhouse of Parma (1948) or Claude Autant-Lara's *The Red and the Black* (1954), was also a veiled critique of the whole practice of drawing films from respected novels, which seemed safe and studio-industrial. Of course, this hostility was suspended when, for instance, Robert Bresson, an auteur the *Cahiers* critics admired, adapted Georges Bernanos. And Truffaut went on to reverse himself in his own directorial career by making many loving pictures drawn from novels, such as *Jules and Jim* (1962) and *Two English Girls* (1971). But some of the bad odor surrounding literary adaptations has remained. Even now, auteur directors such as Otar Iosseliani go on record that they will never engage in such a "stinking practice" as filming a novel.* To be a true auteur, in their eyes, is to write and film an original screenplay.

In line with this antiliterary sentiment is a mistrust of two other devices frequently used in adaptations: voice-over and flashback. Screenwriting teachers tag these as forms of cheating, or caving in to the uncinematic. (This in spite of the many visually virtuosic films, from *Citizen Kane* to *GoodFellas* to *Kill Bill*, that employ one or both techniques.) Sarah Kozloff, in her excellent book *Invisible Storytellers*, analyzed the prejudice: "Obviously it is this emotional legacy of aversion to sound in general that provides the bedrock for all complaints against a particular use of the sound-track—voice-over narration. If one believes that all true film art lies in the images, then verbal narration is automatically illegitimate." Kozloff also connects this aversion with another prejudice, this one derived from Henry James's craft advice, and so dear to writing workshops: Show, don't tell. She writes:

> As we know, during the first half of this [the twentieth] century, the followers of Henry James waged a battle against "intrusive" narrators speaking in their own voices, and in favor of the dramatization of the action in scenes devoid of overt narratorial mediation, claiming that this al-

---

* In an article he wrote celebrating Boris Barnet, Iosseliani made a long list of traits a film artist must have to be deemed admirable, concluding: "Above all, he must show imagination and a sense of fantasy by refusing, for example, to adapt famous literary works or film the biographies of famous people. That is also a moral position."

lows readers a closer, more objective relation to the action represented and the privilege of drawing their own interpretations. . . . Granted that voice-over narration adds a certain slant, or even definite bias, to a film—why is this bad? Where are the laws saying that films have to be realistic, objective, or impersonal to begin with?

When an adaptation is criticized for being "literary," the real objection may be to its sets, costumes, and air of smugness. Film buffs of my generation learned to scoff at PBS's *Masterpiece Theatre* or the Merchant-Ivory adaptations of classic novels. We denigrated them as overstuffed—meaning visually uninventive. There can indeed be something dreary and mechanical about the way each scene from an Austen or Forster novel gets broken down into establishing shot, two-shot, and sneering or teary reaction shot—as blatantly coded in its emotional underlining as soap opera. On the other hand, Merchant-Ivory made some subtle, astringent film adaptations, such as *Mr. & Mrs. Bridge* (1990) and *A Soldier's Daughter Never Cries* (1998), and British television rises above its own cozy-adaptation formula occasionally, as in the BBC's 2005 *Bleak House* or its *Twenty Thousand Streets Under the Sky* (also 2005).

To go from film to television may seem a jump, but these days so many projects start in one medium and end up in the other that the distinction becomes almost academic. Generally, I look to television more and more for the transposition of a novelistic mind-set to the moving image. I first realized this with a shock when, some years ago, I saw a multievening televised series, *From Here to Eternity*, with Natalie Wood, that came much closer to the feeling of the James Jones novel, thanks to its relaxed unfolding, than had the overheated, Oscar-winning movie version directed by Fred Zinnemann in 1953. Edgar Reitz's remarkable *Heimat* series, made for German TV in 1984, has all the qualities of a great thousand-page novel, and Rainer Werner Fassbinder's monumental *Berlin Alexanderplatz* (1980) is another stunning model in this regard. For that matter, any television series with a developing story, be it *The Sopranos*, *The Wire*, or *Gilmore Girls*, allows more scope for the novelistically shaded, progress-and-regress evolution of its characters than a feature film, where the main character is expected to undergo change and be "transformed" in one way only, usually positively. Television drama allows the writer to slip the noose of the three-act structure or all those Robert McKee–Syd Field prescriptions for plot points, and to invite a more leisurely, discursive, novelistic sense of time.

Some filmmakers persistently exhibit a novelistic temperament. Visconti, after adapting Giovanni Verga, James M. Cain, Thomas Mann, and Giuseppe di Lampedusa, had plans before he died to film Mann's *Buddenbrooks* as well as Proust. Stanley Kubrick seemed always to require a novel to get his cinematic juices going. Not only did Mikio Naruse turn again and again to Fumiko Hayashi and Yasunari Kawabata for source material but even his original screenplays continued to deemphasize the dramatic in favor of novelistic atmosphere and the patient accumulation of behavioral patterns. Of course, the influence flows the other way, too: hardly a major novelist in the last hundred years has not been profoundly influenced by the movies. The newsreel montage style of Dos Passos's *U.S.A.*, the hard-boiled concisions of Dashiell Hammett and Raymond Chandler, the hyperconcreteness of Alain Robbe-Grillet's *nouveau roman*, the camera eye of Don DeLillo are but a few examples of the ways that novels have been cinematized.

The Plot Thickens: Infidelities

George Bluestone's *Novels into Film*, which first appeared in 1957, is the ur-text of film adaptation studies, and the source of many of its received truths. Though dated (it was drawn from American movies between 1930 and 1950, when the Production Code still exerted a puritanical influence), it did raise key questions, and I have to admire the thoroughness with which Bluestone drew the parameters of a then-new field. He summarized the difference between the production of novels and films as follows: "The reputable novel, generally speaking, has been supported by a small, literate audience, has been produced by an individual writer, and has remained relatively free of rigid censorship. The film, on the other hand, has been supported by a mass audience, produced co-operatively under industrial conditions, and restricted by a self-imposed Production Code."

Bluestone's method is "to assess the key additions, deletions, and alterations revealed in the film and center on certain significant implications which seemed to follow from the remnants of, and deviations from, the novel." This plodding, back-and-forth, comparative approach had at least the merit of clarity, and it led him to some conclusions that are still valid, up to a point: that movies privilege plot at the expense of character; that they deemphasize anticlerical, sexually experimental, and politically activist elements to ensure the largest mass audience; and that they gravitate toward happy, triumphal, or redemptive endings. Bluestone quoted a study showing that 43 percent of the film adaptations sampled were altered to give them romantic, happy endings. Whether or not the figure would be that high today, studio executives remain in thrall to the falsely redemptive. Still, many scholars have since argued that a happy ending tacked on at the last minute to a feature film does not negate the feelings of anxiety and pessimism that preceded it. Audiences know how to take the "good news" with a grain of salt.

Bluestone comes down hard on Vincente Minnelli's *Madame Bovary* (1949) for its overly moralizing frame story of Flaubert's trial. Today, our interest in auteurs might incline us to give more leeway to Minnelli (or Renoir, also lambasted for his 1933 *Madame Bovary*) and find intriguing their separate treatments of the Flaubert novel. There are also dividends in the way of individual performances: Both *Anna Karenina* adaptations made with Greta Garbo, in 1927 and 1935, dropped the Kitty-Levin story, as Bluestone charged, but Garbo brings something new to our understanding of Tolstoy's heroine, a weary forbearance, perhaps, just as Jennifer Jones's ardent, dreamy, self-righteous Emma Bovary (still dewy from her *Song of Bernadette* triumph) captures a piece of that moral sleepwalker's ambiguous unconsciousness in the Minnelli version. In short, it is possible for a film adaptation to "betray" its source and at the same time contain elements that augment our appreciation of the original.

Why even speak of betrayal when we can view these deviations as alternate paths that the novel might have taken—other lives it might have lived? The novelist pauses indecisively to consider whether to deal the heroine a happy or unhappy fate and chooses in the end, say, a miserable one, but the alternative, joyful, romantic one is inscribed like a shadow buried in the body of the text; and the film adaptation helpfully uncovers it. The same holds for vulgarizing the source material. As a sometime novelist, I have often fantasized that one of my novels would be adapted to the screen and made much tawdrier, in ways that my refined good taste had regrettably prevented me from allowing.

We cannot avoid raising the issue of faithfulness when novels are made into films: Is it a foolish expectation or a valid one? Over twenty years ago, the film scholar Dudley Andrew sensibly called for a moratorium on criticism that narrowly applies "the discourse of fidelity." And yet, after we have mouthed for the hundredth time those platitudes about how each film needs to function as an autonomous artwork, how fidelity to the spirit rather than to the letter is what counts, how inevitable and even necessary are changes from one medium to another, how a film adaptation is perforce no more than a digest appropriating some of the characters and plotlines for its own ends, might there still not be something unstoppably human in the hope that beloved novels be rendered faithfully on-screen, or at least not distorted beyond recognition?

I am of two minds here. On the one hand, I think it silly to regard novels as a frail endangered species that must be protected from the brute movie producer's predatory knife. I agree with André Bazin's questioning what he calls the historically recent notion of "the untouchability of a work of art." Every screenplay, after all, is an adaptation of something or other, a pastiche of experience and quotation. If a film delights audiences, maybe that should be the end of the matter. Many stimulating movie adaptations, such as *I Walked with a Zombie* (from *Jane Eyre*), *Apocalypse Now* (from *Heart of Darkness*), *Clueless* (from *Emma*), *A Cock & Bull Story* (from *The Life and Opinions of Tristram Shandy, Gentleman*), and *Pola X* (from *Pierre*), have used some classic novel merely as a point of departure, radically updating the plot.

On the other hand, the problem of fidelity seems more acute when the film adaptation presents itself as intentionally following the book. In such cases, I admit, I have been personally appalled by certain adaptations. What bothered me about the 1963 movie version of *Tom Jones* (a favorite novel of mine) was not that Tony Richardson tried to find modern analogies for Fielding's parodic humor but that his silent-comedy speedups were cheap and patronizing. Jane Campion's *Portrait of a Lady* (1996) drifted so far from the spirit of its model that I could not help agreeing with Cynthia Ozick that it "perverts" James, even as I told myself that it was perfectly valid for Campion, an auteur in her own right, to make the story more relevant by turning it into a Generation X erotic thriller. In sum, I do not think we can ever wholly discard concerns about fidelity, but we need a more sophisticated approach.

Two recent collections of essays, *Film Adaptation*, edited by James Naremore, and *Literature and Film*, edited by Robert Stam and Alessandra Raengo, attempt just that. The good part is that the various film scholars and critics who contributed to these volumes are much more open and receptive to experimental, nonindustry product, and they challenge the old literary-cinematic dichotomy; the discouraging part is that they tend to do this by putting everything through the theoretical strainer of Barthes, Foucault, Derrida, Bakhtin, and Genette. Adaptation studies are freed from the onus of fidelity, only to be chained to the wagons of dialogism and intertextuality. Fassbinder is quoted as saying that his novel adaptations constitute "an unequivocal and single-minded questioning of the piece of literature and its language." In other words, a film adaptation should be the filmmaker's critique of the novel. So we have evolved from the notion of the filmmaker as barbarian at the gates of fiction to that of the filmmaker as postmodernist critic deconstructing it. I'm not sure this is an improvement.

Film adaptations are like biographies, in that even if the writer starts out admiring the subject, a time may come when deference turns to hostility, by having to live in such close subservient contact with another intelligence. Welles's 1962 version of Kafka's *The Trial* is both a superb spatial recasting of the novel and an insouciant repudiation of a kind of spiritual anguish with which the filmmaker seems to have been fundamentally at odds from the beginning.

When judging film adaptations, we must first place them in their historical contexts and in the light of changing fashions. John Ford's *The Grapes of Wrath*, which seemed revolutionary when it initially appeared because of its sympathy for the common man, now looks rhetorically inflated, almost like a piece of socialist realism, with its camera shots tilting to the clouded sky. (Also, there are so many better Fords that we don't need to protect this one.) Roger Vadim's *Les Liaisons Dangereuses* (1959), which transposed Laclos's classic to contemporary France, seemed the height of raciness when it first appeared; now it is memorable mostly for its Thelonious Monk score. *Greed* and *Doomed Love* still have the freshness of their lunatic integrity.

As for recent adaptations, they, too, are affected by historical considerations. *The Painted Veil*, directed by John Curran in 2006 from a W. Somerset Maugham novel, was a competent, mildly affecting picture, with a strong performance by Naomi Watts as the beautiful, shallow wife of an idealistic doctor who is transformed by her husband's death. Many film critics found it "old-fashioned," and indeed it was, not only because the adultery in the East and theme of sacrifice seem dated today, the filmmaker having taken seriously a now-dusty Maugham novel of the British colonies that was all the rage in the 1920s, but because the adaptation was executed with an unobtrusive craft that seems almost archaic. I am more willing to forgive period distortions or quaint sentiments in a film placed as far back as the 1920s because for me it is all part of the Distant Past. But I am old enough to have lived through the 1950s, the period in which Richard Yates set his cherished novel of suburban anomie, *Revolutionary Road*, and perhaps for that reason was put off by Sam Mendes's 2009 adaptation: not only did the film render the fifties as a fashion magazine layout, but by siding so strenuously with the wife and turning her into an idealized heroine, it made a mishmash of the novel's sorrowful complexity, violating the delicate balance of error Yates had established between the husband and wife. Again, fidelity seems to be more of an issue when the adaptation touches on the viewer's personal history or literary preferences.

Last Shot: Can Movies Think?

Bluestone stated that "the cinema exhibits a stubborn antipathy to novels"—a claim I resist. I think that what lies at the bottom of this statement is his idea that movies cannot think. "Or rather," writes Bluestone, "the film, having only arrangements of space to work with, cannot render thought, for the moment thought is externalized it is no longer thought." That is a very curious assertion. Leaving aside the exception of the essay-film, which assuredly and overtly does think, I have to say that when I am in thrall to a sublime film masterpiece, such as Ophüls's *The Earrings of Mme de . . .* or Mizoguchi's *Ugetsu* (both, by the way, literary adaptations), I experience it as a continuous flow of consciousness—observant, melancholy, detached, worldly, commenting—and as such, in essence, thought. Perhaps I am being simpleminded here, and missing some subtle nuance. Bluestone argues that film "can show us characters thinking, feeling, and speaking, but it cannot show us their thoughts and feelings. A film is not thought; it is perceived." His confident assurance that film "is incapable of depicting consciousness" is partly based on his claim that metaphors cannot be rendered on-screen, because the camera supposedly turns all phenomena into fact. I consider this an overly literalist understanding of the way metaphor operates.

I would also take exception to the French aesthetician Étienne Souriau when he argues that films are incapable of inhabiting one character's point of view, the way novels can, and that they therefore lack interiority. There are many examples of films that feature unreliable narrators or cleave to a more claustrophobic subjective interiority than these theorists will allow.[*] Even Siegfried Kracauer, who in *Theory of Film: The Redemption of Physical Reality* peddles the old malarkey about language being the enemy of the cinematic, allows that "inwardness" *is* possible in films, concluding: "In general, the differences between the formal properties of film and novel are only differences in degrees."

---

[*] Off the top of my head: Claude Chabrol's *The Third Lover*, Robert Bresson's *A Man Escaped*, Lodge Kerrigan's *Keane*, parts of Béla Tarr's *Sátántangó* . . . I'm sure there are many more.

But Bluestone would have it that they are fundamentally at odds, impossible to cross-pollinate, like "apples and oranges." He writes: "What is peculiarly filmic and what is peculiarly novelistic cannot be converted without destroying an integral part of each. That is why Proust and Joyce would seem as absurd on film as Chaplin would in print." I don't know about Joyce (although John Huston's *The Dead* is a rather good film adaptation), or Chaplin (who wrote a pretty decent autobiography), but Proust has actually been fairly well-served in recent years. I am thinking of the producer Paolo Branco's commissioning of various filmmakers to adapt different volumes of Proust, which led to Raul Ruiz's amazing *Time Regained* (1999) and Chantal Akerman's superb *La Captive* (2000). What Ruiz does is to take soundings of the Proust novel and reorganize them into a symphonic whole. He also boldly challenges the Bluestone assertion that "the novel has three tenses; the film has only one" by transporting a seated Marcel, as spectator, into his own re-created memories. Proust mixed up past and present, dream self and real self, and this is what Ruiz does, too, with his thoughtful cross sections or samplings of Proust's text.

I have been arguing that novels and films have more in common than is generally asserted. Perhaps they are like one of those screwball-comedy couples, analyzed in Stanley Cavell's *Pursuits of Happiness*, who marry and get divorced and then, understanding that despite past infidelities they are better off together, submit to the comedy of remarriage. Kracauer's maxim is suggestive: "Like film, the novel aspires to endlessness." Once we understand that there is no limit to a film's intellectual or artistic complexity, we will be in a better position to appreciate the past relations and future symbiosis between novels and the cinema.

On Changing One's Mind About a Movie

For anybody who has ever tried to palm himself or herself off as a film critic, or even to assert confident judgments about movies in social gatherings, the nagging awareness of just how unstable and fluid these judgments can be is a secret embarrassment, a threat, possibly a stimulus. You feel sure you like or dislike a particular movie, and then, over the years, that certainty begins to waver.

I am not talking here about exhibiting a taste for the campy or the obviously awful. *Film Comment* would occasionally run a column called "Guilty Pleasures," inviting critics and filmmakers to confess the outré pictures they loved. The problem with that category is that, for the film buff, either everything is in a sense a guilty pleasure, or nothing. Once the film buff has accepted the guilt for wasting a good part of life chasing eroticized shadows and filling in gaps with encyclopedic pedantry, there are no true sinful pleasures anymore: cinephilia is a collecting avarice, drawn to marginal, half-good/half-bad finds as much as if not more than to unarguable classics.

I had once thought of compiling a list of Guilty Displeasures, consisting of revered, paradigm-shifting movies I didn't much care for (such as *The Graduate* or *Bonnie and Clyde*), but this gambit too seemed questionable, since, however much I personally found them overrated, I could still appreciate their contribution. A more valid category might be the movies about which I have changed my mind.

Pauline Kael asserted that she never went back to a movie twice because she wanted to trust her first, gut impression. Andrew Sarris took the opposite critical approach, re-viewing, mulling over, and altering his opinions about certain movies over a lifetime. He admitted, for instance, that he had been quite taken with *Sunset Boulevard* when it first opened but had shifted his view after some critics he respected sniffed at it, and he subsequently downgraded Billy Wilder, its director, in his chart of American directors for being too cynical, only to reopen the case years later and revise his estimation of Wilder upward. In that respect I am much more a Sarrisite than a Paulette, since my own tastes seem to fluctuate inadvertently, whether or not I am paying attention.

To give an example: A few years ago I was channel-surfing on a Sunday afternoon with my daughter, Lily, then aged thirteen, when I discovered that IFC would be showing Jacques Demy's *Young Girls of Rochefort* in fifteen minutes. I got very excited. I hadn't seen it in since it had opened, in 1967, and I had somehow missed the restoration print rerelease, though I recall thinking at the time about taking Lily (whose first exposure to a subtitled film, when she was ten or eleven, had been *The Umbrellas of Cherbourg*). "This is by the same director who made *Umbrellas of Cherbourg*. You liked that, remember?" I said to her. She got that patient, forbearing, resistance-gathering look that appears whenever I try to foist an older, sometimes black-and-white, or even black-and-white, silent movie on her. I told her it was very pretty—and in Technicolor! "What's it about?" she demanded, which I recognized as a sensible question for a normal viewer, if not a die-hard auteurist cinephile like myself, to ask.

"It's beautiful. The camera work, the costumes . . ."

"Yes, but what's it about?"

"Love," I said, appealing to her taste for romantic comedies. "I don't remember. I saw it a long time ago."

Because she is essentially a kind daughter, she agreed to watch the beginning with me, and then, if it proved not to her taste, she would peel off into the other room and read her book.

I'd already decided that, even if she didn't like it, I would watch it from beginning to end. I felt sure I was about to be enthralled. What I didn't tell her was that the first time I'd seen *The Young Girls of Rochefort*, the movie had left me cold. It had seemed as thin and insubstantial as cotton candy, precious yet overworked, the effort to retrieve the insouciant elegance of MGM musicals dooming it to taxidermy. The French New Wave's slumming adoration of Hollywood, the film's use of an over-the-hill, toupee-wearing Gene Kelly to give it American authenticity, had struck me (in my young man's severity) as misguided. How could I be so certain, then, that I would love it this time?

Before I can answer, let me backtrack. In my teens and twenties I counted myself a Jacques Demy partisan, having reveled in the bittersweet inventiveness of *Lola* and the mordant *Bay of Angels*. I had even fallen for *The Umbrellas of Cherbourg*, which I found enormously moving, bucking the taste of my peers, who regarded it as retrograde corn. But *The Young Girls of Rochefort* seemed to foreground all of Demy's self-indulgences. I swore off him for a while. Later I was charmed by the fairy-tale *Donkey Skin*, and was puzzled by but able to find some peripheral merit in *Model Shop* and more in *A Room in Town*. In short, I climbed back on the Demy bandwagon.

The film began with a title in French, crediting Demy's widow, Agnès Varda, and various funding agents for the restoration. "This is boring!" Lily announced.

"Give it a chance."

"What's it about?" she demanded and hit the TV guide remote button, to see if that might provide some plot information. Shocked, I grabbed the remote away from her, afraid I might have missed the first shot.

"Hey, calm down, Dad!"

We proceeded to watch the opening dance number.

"Is it a musical?"

"Yes, it's a musical. Lots of singing and dancing."

"Subtitles—ick!"

But I had faith that the women's outfits would win her over; and soon she was watching it with engrossment. "See, it's like *Funny Face*," I murmured, bridging to a movie I knew she loved, meaning that it too was stylized in its color scheme. I explained that the twins were played by sisters in real life, Catherine Deneuve and Françoise Dorléac, and that the redheaded one died shortly after making this movie.

"How?"

"In a car crash, I think." I was entranced watching every second of their duet. It struck me that Dorléac did look a little pale, like someone who foresaw she had not long to live. Part of what I appreciated this second time was seeing it all through the lens of death. Its very archness seemed tenderly endearing, alluding to a voluptuous, liberating, self-conscious "movie love" moment in cinema that was gone forever. Knowing as I now did that Jacques Demy was gay, or bisexual, that he had died of AIDS, I saw the telltale pink and mauve sweaters assigned to the male dancers as a defiant confession; and all those arias about finding the Ideal Woman came across as much more poignant, retrospectively. My emotional response was affected by the many friends and acquaintances I had lost to AIDS. Nevertheless, it would be wrong to think that I was giving the film only extracinematic credit. On the contrary, everything that had once seemed artistically weak to me had been turned on its head and appeared as a virtue. Artifice, serendipity, the fragile transience of happiness—I was seeing it the way Demy had intended, as a painful fairy tale about yearning and the improbable search for true love. This time I got the references to his earlier films and to those still to come. Demy was like a spider situated in the middle of his life, weaving a connecting web between recollection and prescient fate which only now I could begin to understand.

If I attempt to isolate which factors contribute to changing my mind about a movie, they come down to the following: my particular stage of life, my overarching aesthetic, auteurist reconsiderations, public response, and peer pressure.

In adolescence I, like many teenage boys, cherished grotesquery: I delighted in seeing the gruesome wedding party scene of *Freaks*, with its dismemberment, or the beggars' violation of their benefactress in *Viridiana*.

Now that I am middle-aged, the grotesque refuses to engage me as much, the siren song of the edgy sounds obvious and shrill, and extreme violence disgusts me. When my undergraduates loan me DVDs of their favorite Miike Yakuza films, I have to turn them off at the first facial razor slice.

Big changes in one's life may also alter one's viewing tolerance. After I became a parent, I could no longer watch with equanimity any movie in which a child was kidnapped, endangered, or physically harmed.

I am more interested now in movies that reflect wisdom and compassion, rather than mere sensation, at their core. This is not to say that I've become wiser with age. Youth has its own wisdom. I think I was right to react, as a young man, against what had seemed cloying in *The Young Girls of Rochefort*, but now I see that preciosity from a different perspective and cherish it. I was too young then to embrace the film's underlying romantic pessimism; I had plenty of yearning, but it was not yet infused with regret. The ultimate question may not be, What is the correct critical judgment to make of a particular film? but, What are our different needs and understandings at various stages in life?

In my teens and twenties I ate up everything Jean-Luc Godard did, while disliking Ingmar Bergman's spiritual heaviness, his seemingly middle-aged, middlebrow gravitas. Though I still love much of Godard, a trifle like *A Woman Is a Woman* strikes me now as *only* playful, and even *Two or Three Things I Know About Her*, reseen recently, seems underbaked. Conversely, Bergman's *Winter Light*, which looked to be so ridiculously strained and cosmically stodgy that I gave it a pass when it opened, I now regard it as magnificent, approaching *King Lear* in its courage to contemplate harsh truths. I seem no longer as threatened by serious, unresolvable anguish.

Film magazines are infused with a bias toward youth culture. They are ever on the lookout for the "cutting edge," which curiously suits academic discourse to a T. The film which draws attention to itself *as* film is doted on, because, we are told, it punctures the complacent illusions of realism. Do we really need to keep having the fact that film is an artificial construct pointed out? To my mind, self-reflexive cinematic jokes have become old hat; they have lost much of the daring they had for me in my youth.

When I was younger you could have me in the palm of your hand with a 180-degree camera movement. I have since seen many film school graduates circling their actors vertiginously to no discernible point, but well-written dialogue has come to seem rare. In my youth, I found Samuel Fuller the most refreshing filmmaker alive, exuding as he did a pulp gusto that looked to reinvent movies and upend prevailing pieties. But recently, when I watched *House of Bamboo* for the third or fourth time, the stilted dialogue and over-the-top performances made me wince. I hesitate to revisit all those beloved Fullers, given my lesser enthusiasm for shock edits and my enhanced regard for literate dialogue. I would probably now opt for Joseph Mankiewicz's talky *Letter to Three Wives* over Fuller's hyperkinetic *Shock Corridor* (though I still prefer Fuller's *Pickup on South Street* to any Mankiewicz: that much of a boy film buff I remain).

Then there is the matter of overarching aesthetic. Regardless of further tweaks that may occur along the way, I have retained my loyalty to a formalist style that first won me over in adolescence: this Bazinian preference for long takes, flowing use of space, incorporation of the full body and the surrounding environment, implying a more detached sympathy toward human drama and, on the other hand, an avoidance of zooms, rapid-fire editing, tons of close-up reaction shots or slow motion, has had the effect of limiting my taste options. There are certain films I can never change my mind about, because I so embrace their worldview. I know, going into a Renoir, Mizoguchi, Ophüls, Naruse, Minnelli, Ozu, Satyajit Ray, Nicholas Ray, Rossellini, Cukor, or Borzage for the first time that I will probably like it a lot, and I almost always do; and if I see it a second or third time I still like it. To not like it would be to reject my own aesthetic DNA.

No, it is those filmmakers who run counter to this overarching aesthetic who cause me initial confusion, and force me to reverse my judgments later. Robert Altman, for instance, whose technical gifts are unquestioned, has sometimes struck me as smart-ass: the first time I saw *Nashville* I found its satire of America too easy and patronizing. Having worked through my initial distaste, I am able in subsequent viewings to enjoy *Nashville*'s many terrific performances and fascinating digressions.

Stanley Kubrick, a magisterial formalist, often puts me off with his su-perior scorn. To my shame, I walked out of *Barry Lyndon* for that very reason the first time I saw it; now I watch it with eager absorption and it seems to me a brilliant masterpiece, though I must admit I still cannot warm to *A Clockwork Orange* or the self-pleased *Dr. Strangelove.*

A nonformalist director on the order of Sidney Lumet took me a long time to appreciate, because his camera setups seemed muzzy and insuffi-ciently rigorous. *Serpico*, the first time I saw it, looked ragged, slapped to-gether; now I find it bursting with life, with an unrivaled feeling for 1970s New York City. Later Lumets, such as *Prince of the City*, helped me dig back into *Dog Day Afternoon* and *Serpico* and discover their considerable merits. Similarly, I was repelled, in my first exposures to John Cassavetes's *Husbands* and *A Woman Under the Influence*, by what I took to be an overly operatic, boozy, hysterical approach to character, too many laughing jags and Method-indulgent performances. It was only when I saw *The Killing of a Chinese Bookie* that I revised my opinion about Cassavetes, and de-tected the patient method underneath the seeming pandemonium. (But a part of me still wonders if I wasn't partly right the first time.)

I also find myself giving way to peer pressure. Much as you would like to believe yourself an independent-minded critic, you inevitably adapt. I would be blind not to have noticed the reverential status accorded Cas-savetes by my peers: he went from being scoffed at, a marginalized indie figure, to one of the key seminal figures in world cinema.

With each passing decade, the canon keeps readjusting itself. Hot newcomers who had seemed like sure bets run aground, while once-mistrusted filmmakers stay the course, and their accrued quality begins to register as something unique and irreplaceable. The steady release of utterly worthless, forgettable product, year after year, cannot help but make you feel more benign and tolerant toward anyone with a spark of originality. In death, their corpus complete, Altman, Kubrick, Cassa-vetes, Lumet look like giants compared to the mediocre cinematic land-scape that has come to surround them.

Some movies I resist, I'll admit, because they are simply so popular on release that I associate their appeal with pandering to the audience

(*The Graduate, American Beauty, Titanic,* or *Avatar*). Though I enjoyed Woody Allen's early slapdash comedies, I had problems with his best-received films, such as *Annie Hall, Manhattan,* and *Hannah and Her Sisters,* because they struck me on first viewing as falsifying New York and smugly self-congratulatory. Since then, I have come to regard Woody more as an American master, who goes his own way regardless of trends, and can appreciate *Annie Hall* and *Manhattan* for what they are, without gritting my teeth. But perhaps I like him better now because he is no longer so popular.

Peer pressure certainly plays a part in forcing critical revisions. However dogmatically I may speak out about a movie, I don't always completely trust my own opinion. Though I had very much liked Terrence Malick in the past, *The New World* struck me as a self-indulgent mess on first viewing, and I walked out before the last hour, telling myself that life was too short for such turgid neoprimitivism. Younger critic friends who adored the Malick film said I had missed the point, which resided in the final hour, and convinced me to give it a second chance. So I saw it again and virtually willed, almost hypnotized myself, to admire it. But in recent years I have sometimes parted ways with the enthusiasms of younger critics for art-crowd pleasers such as *Moulin Rouge, Lost in Translation, 2046,* and nothing could drag me back to them for a second viewing. I suspect this clash in tastes has something to do with the generation gap (a gorgeous sensual surface or a hip, pop-music sound track mattering less to me than to them), though I'm not sure. I may change my mind even about these films. It depends how much the internal quarrel between my critical selves and my own perversity might tip me toward the opposite pole, and partly on the offerings of a slow afternoon's TV schedule.

There are certain movies I can see over and over without worrying that I will lose my affection for them, precisely because they embody an enjoyable combination of shallow and deep, and the demands they make on me are minimal. Hitchcock's *Notorious* and *North by Northwest* are such movies; if I stumble upon one of them while channel-surfing, I can watch it happily from that point on when I have nothing better to do. But I need to steel myself for something like Bergman's *Persona* or Bresson's

Au Hasard Balthazar; I do not always feel adequate to dipping into these great, exigent movies.

Some movies invoke in me a perpetually fluid, uncertain state of judgment. I've gone back and forth between thinking Charles Laughton's *Night of the Hunter* is an exciting one-off masterwork or a clumsy, semiamateurish academic pastiche. With Max Ophüls's *Lola Montès*, at times I can embrace the weak central performance of Martine Carol's Lola as uncannily essential to its elegiac charm, and at other times I resist it as stultifying waxworks. Much as I revere Carl Dreyer, the first time I saw *Ordet*, at twenty, I found it interminably slow-going, a big letdown after *Day of Wrath*. Then I saw it again years later, in my forties, and had one of those transformative spiritual-cinematic experiences during the miraculous reviving of the dead woman; I was ready to believe in God, almost. The third time I watched *Ordet* I respected its craft but found the spiritual atmosphere a bit too morbid, hokey, even unhealthy, you might say. Maybe when Lily turns eighteen I'll show her *Ordet* if she'll let me, and perhaps I'll discover what I finally feel about the film. One argument for having children is that you get to revisit the cultural landmarks of your past, with the option of allowing your kids' presence and their response to help change your mind.

You can wear out any film's magic if you see it too many times. That is pretty much what happened to me about the eighth time I watched *The Third Man*—this seemingly irresistible, marvelous cuckoo clock suddenly struck me as tinny and calculating. I always think about what Chabrol said after he had seen *Vertigo* for something like the thirty-fifth time; he came to the conclusion it was really a rather silly movie. To me, *Vertigo* is still sublime; but then, I sense where the cracks in my admiration may run, and so I am determined to ration my viewings of it in the future.

Laws of Attraction

1.

I confess I have always been attracted to women with affections. It scarcely matters whether the mannerism is that of a coquette or a school-marm, so long as she projects some theatricality. Why should artifice put me so at ease? I think because affectation implies playfulness and ironic distance from a single, integrated core of being, which promises more tolerance of my own self-mistrust. Since I don't always feel I am being authentic, or on the up-and-up, by all means let my companion be not afraid of masks. The natural, wholesome type stifles me by her solemn placidity; she seems so lacking in perverse mischief that I feel apologetically Mephistophelian beside her.

I also appreciate gestures of adornment that go beyond the natural. I like lipstick, for instance. Of course it serves no useful purpose, fades quickly, and requires constant reapplication. But it represents a festive ideal, through exaggeration, of the redness of a woman's lips. There is that suggestion that she has just eaten a cherry ice or bitten someone's skin bloody. I like the glistening sheen, the taste (if I am allowed to taste it), and the telltale evidence it leaves on the collar or cheek. It is hard for a woman to kiss you without spoiling her lipstick, but that is part of the fun. For a man of my generation, who grew up on Cyd Charisse movies, lipstick will always connote the worldly and sexy. If it has no other function than to signal that the woman wearing it has taken the trouble to prettify herself for the public, that is enough to gain my gratitude.

It seems a pity that just as I was coming into my own romantically, in the 1960s, many women started abandoning lipstick, eye shadow, and a dozen other tactics in the armamentarium of arousal. In California, where I lived for part of the sixties, I witnessed the enthronement of the no-fuss, "natural" aesthetic. Guys would boast that their girlfriends looked much more beautiful without that gunk on their faces. The natural look seemed to be about youth: the creamy, dewy skin of a seventeen-year-old, during that optimum moment when a peachy complexion (for those lucky enough to escape acne) provides all the glow that is required. It so happens I've always been attracted to a more experienced, worn-soulful look, so I resent this privileging of youthful sincerity.

Later, cosmetics companies took to marketing "the natural look," which required quite a lot of product, applying and then removing layers of powder, blush, eye shadow. It probably takes longer to achieve the no-makeup look than it did the older, artificial one. I agree that the no-makeup look can be very pretty; I am not fanatically antinatural. But I regard the "natural look" as just another stylistic option.

Living as we do in a postmodern era when all historical, ethnic, and environmental styles are available to us like frozen packages in a super-market bin, it is understandable that we contemporary Marie Antoinettes might wish to play at the pastoral, simple life. Hence the fashion in high-rise apartments for country decor, baskets and patchwork quilts and distressed furniture, everything rough-textured and naïve. Meanwhile we want our beds to be nice and comfortable, with a humidifier on the night table. Well, why not? So long as we understand that "natural" is at best an unattainable ideal; myself, I prefer the urban, the human, and the artificial.

Art teaches us that the naturalistic effect is a cunningly arranged fabrication. Degas was fond of saying that, to draw realistically, you must distort. The natural-sounding dialogue in an Elmore Leonard story is the product of laborious sweat; actual conversation, transcribed from tapes, reads as something vague and unconvincing. When we venture into Nature, even trekking to a place with no other humans or manufactured objects, we bring our conditioned responses to the experience. We visit the Grand Canyon and see an Ansel Adams photograph. For most of us, there is no possibility of entering through the doors of perception unaffected. The natural is beyond us. We need to embrace impurity, the mixture of nature and artifice, and stop feeling guilty about it.

To return to female costume: Take the elevation of blue jeans from a grubby if utilitarian work garment to the unaffected look in leisure wear. Blue jeans are made by petrochemical processes; so much for their naturalness. Anne Hollander, in her book *Seeing Through Clothes*, wisely summed up the contradictions: "To justify and explain their adoption of various modes of nonfashion, women have often invoked the concept of comfort. . . . Jeans worn so tight that the labia majora are clearly molded, and the wearer has to lie down to get the zipper closed, cannot exactly be called physically comfortable; it is the image of comfort that is desirable, the look of wearing something sanctioned by the fashionable ideal of comfort. Trousers are actually no more physically comfortable than skirts, with a few exceptions."

One argument against skirts, lipstick, and other signs of stylized femininity is that they degrade a woman by turning her into an object of desire for the male gaze. While jeans may ultimately be no more comfortable than skirts, the fact that jeans are unisex means that women who wear them may feel less gender-stereotyped, less frilly, more free to act boldly in the world. On the other hand, how is it possible with a tight T-shirt and jeans to deflect the libidinous male gaze? Such a costume packages a woman's anatomy as explicitly as possible while stripping away her glamour.

I draw a distinction between glamour and physique: glamour is the allure produced by the intersection of comeliness and artifice. It requires the proper setting, good lighting, elegant clothes, and a suitable companion. It is a hard-won sophistication, not for teenagers. The ability to re-create oneself as a mystery, you would think, is an empowerment, not a diminution, of the female.

I admit that it is intensely flattering for a man to be on the receiving end of that effort. But I am willing to go to considerable bother in return, as is only fair. Nothing could be more artificial than to put on a tuxedo with button studs, cummerbund, satin bow tie. However, I have grown to like the ritual of squeezing into a monkey suit, just as I like the old-fashioned exactitude of a suit and tie. A poet I know would attend formal parties wearing a tuxedo jacket and blue jeans, to show off his independence. All he was showing was his dependence on the approval of his absent bohemian pals. Embrace formality, affectation, artifice, I say. What have you really got to lose? Besides which, the propriety of formal wear can be an aphrodisiac once you get home from the gala. There is nothing more fun than the crumpling of her gown and the wrinkling of your boiled shirt, now that sartorial perfection no longer matters. Let the dry cleaners deal with it tomorrow. Such are the joys of artifice, mixed in with a little nature.

2.

Most men have certain ideal notions of femaleness derived from movies they saw in their youth. No matter how cockeyed some of these archetypes are, and no matter how manfully I struggle to assimilate the truth that women are as variable, real, and complex as men are, a part of me continues to want to match up the actual women in my life with the celluloid temptresses and saints in my imagination.

I grew up in the postwar era of dangerous brunettes and redheads, like Rita Hayworth, Yvonne De Carlo, Jane Greer, and Jean Simmons, who would no sooner look at a Robert Mitchum or a Glenn Ford than they would begin to seduce him and stab him in the back. Double-crossing came as easily to these femmes fatales as smoking a cigarette. Yet you had to sympathize with this survival tactic of what we were told was the "weaker sex." It was a mystery to me how this supposedly frailer sex could rise not only to a tortuously complicated duplicity but also to a level of selfless heroism that seemed outside the compass or capacity of masculine experience.

I am particularly fascinated with one convention of older melodramatic films that seems to have disappeared: the woman who stops a bullet for her man. She was usually, in classic-triangle terms, the redundant woman—say, the native mistress of a man stationed in the Orient, a rival of the newly met, supposedly more suitable white lady. The mistress is beautiful. She is faithful, she loves her man, and she has a deeper understanding of life than the white lady. So, the audience wonders restlessly, how can the hero reject her?

But because her love for her man is so deep, it transcends self-preservation, as maternal love is often alleged to do. Maybe such passionate romantic devotion exists only in the backwaters of civilization, among colonial or underworld women who have gone beyond the ladylike. Did I mention that sometimes vice takes the place of race? A gangster's moll or bar girl with a tarnished past, an Ida Lupino/Gloria Grahame type, may also administer the reproachful lesson about how far a woman's love may go for her man.

Now, just try to imagine a love so powerful that it would cause a woman to hurl herself in front of gunshots, when most of us would hit the ground. Such love no longer exists, you say; we live in a more calculating age or, to put the matter optimistically, a more progressive age, in which women are less dependent on men, less masochistic. Am I sorry to see the convention disappear? To be frank, I don't know whether to pray for such a love or to be terrified by it.

I try to imagine a man pointing a gun at me. As he starts to pull the trigger, my Chinese girlfriend blankets me with her body. She takes the bullet. As grateful as I am, I cannot help feeling there is a certain presumptuousness in someone's stealing the death that was meant for me. I am so stunned by her act that I forget to knock the gun from the killer's hands. Now he is pointing it at me again, and she has already given her life for me. Would it be cowardly to prop her in front of me, or would that be a way of honoring her original intention?

In any case, how will I shove her limp body forward at the precise moment the gun is fired? My respect for this woman is growing, not only because stopping the bullet was a noble thing to do but because it required incredible athletic timing, like a basketball player's leaping to block a shot. My own reflexes are rustier. Even if I was quick enough to stop the next two bullets with her as a shield, the gunman—always assuming he had six bullets to begin with—might get angry at the waste of ammunition. He might change his tactics, rush behind me, and shoot me in the back. How awful, to be shot in the back!

Why doesn't my other girlfriend arrive? Isn't she supposed to bring the policeman who will knock down the door and save me? All my life I have trusted in the Eternal Feminine to save me from disaster, which does not keep me in the least from suspecting all women of being betrayers. So it is inevitable that I start to think that my fiancée, my other girlfriend, may be in league with the killer. But why does she want me dead? I would have bowed out if she had asked me to. It dawns on me that she is an avenger, and that I am about to be punished for my unfaithfulness to the good mistress, she who gave her life for me.

Of course it is idiotic to expect women to die for me. The very idea must be a ghost remnant of the child's wholly unrealistic expectation that his mother will love him unconditionally, no matter how meanly he tests her or how sadly he disappoints her. And yet, when I look over at my wife playing with our orange Abyssinian cat, Newman, on the couch, I can't help wondering to what lengths she would go to protect me in a fusillade. I hope she would have the good sense to duck. I *know* she would. Nevertheless, these movie fantasies of Oriental mistresses die hard. I now begin to understand why I bought my wife, on a recent trip to China, a red silk brocade robe with dragon couchant, and why I keep pestering her to wear it.

Duration, or, Going Long

Fornicating is like parenting: no matter how you do it, you have the guilty sense that somewhere other people are doing it more correctly. Myself, I wonder if I am lasting long enough. With all due attention to foreplay, penetration, and the bliss that follows, it is still usually over in half an hour, so that if my wife and I start going at it by 10:30, even with the reverential postcoital snuggle and love-you exchange, one of us still has time to say, "You wanna watch the news?"

Of course, a marriage going on fifteen years with a little one sleeping down the hall may hardly be optimal conditions for sustaining the heights of lust. Still, I can't help wondering: if making love a half hour is pleasurable, wouldn't making love two hours be four times as pleasurable? And then there is the "all night long" boast that Casanova and so many rhythm-and-blues singers have claimed. I have never done it all night long: with the best intentions, even in my youth, when I was more inclined to show off by going at it more than once, afterward I would feel woozily satiated, preferring to drift off or talk rather than keep banging away.

Whenever I've watched pornography, I've been amazed at the variety and duration of these partners as they rotate front to back, top to bottom, with one orgasm after another. I take my hat off to their appetites as much as their stamina. Even knowing that filmmaking is a fragmented process, with time off for camera repositioning, I can't resist the belief that pornography constitutes the norm for humans of another, sturdier disposition. As for me, if I am stroking intently for fifteen minutes, there comes a point when I begin to think, Okay I've got the message, I've had my fun, it's time to bring this to conclusion.

What is wrong with me?

Henry Miller wrote in one novel that he kept a bowl of ice by his bedside so that he could withdraw when he felt close to ejaculation and plunge his balls into it. That strikes me as so . . . *industrious*! O. J. Simpson was widely reported to have contracted a hugely expensive coke habit in order to fuck longer. Not that either of these worthy gentlemen is my role model in other respects, but I cannot help wondering if they were onto something—if their almost puritanically conscientious focus on sexual duration may have brought them closer to a spiritual truth than I, with my laissez-faire approach.

I recently asked a few women friends what they thought of the question of duration. One woman said: "I get bladder infections, so I really wouldn't want to be pounded for more than ten or fifteen minutes." Good: I can do that. Another woman offered: "Great sex tends to be quick or long. Most sex is medium-length. Obviously, most sex is not great sex." Women characteristically say that what matters to them is the quality of connection, not longevity. In the sixties, the feminist Germaine Greer wrote that she preferred genuine passion in a male, however short-lived, to the calculated marathons that seemed to arise from performance anxiety, and that suggested the man was dulling his brain by remembering train schedules in order not to come. Indeed, though the *Kama Sutra* and other Eastern sex manuals stress the importance of learning to defer ejaculation for the woman's sake, it often seems that a man's desire to go long has little to do with a woman's pleasure, and more with his own competition to better his personal best.

In my own experience, sometimes when I've tried to be my partner's selfless servant in foreplay, she might say impatiently, "I want you inside me," just as when I try to prolong the actual stroking so that she can reach orgasm first, she is apt to whisper in my ear, "I want you to come!" Some women's orgasms are only brought on by a man's ejaculation. In other cases, I don't doubt it's because the man is not touching or stroking her sensitively enough, so she may feel: let's get this over with.

It's fair to assume that emotions affect a man's capacity to sustain himself in the sex act. But rarely is love the determining factor. First-time excitement and romantic ardor frequently shorten the act. Tenderness, from long familiarity, often results in medium-length coition. A disengaged, blasé mood may enable you to feel you can continue indefinitely. Similarly, anger: there was one lover who made me frequently enraged, whom I used to screw for a long, long time. On the other hand, unacknowledged hostility or alienation can make it difficult to keep an erection.

Clearly, Viagra and other potency-ensuring drugs have thrown a wrench into that old suspense about whether or how long you will be able to keep it up. For the very reason that they rob the sex act of one of its most interesting dimensions, anxiety, and pump up the performances of ordinary *schlubs*, who come to have a distorted idea of their amatory capacities, they should be avoided whenever possible.

I remember one woman I dated who stretched me to the limits in bed. She was a petite, pretty, rather reserved graduate student in architecture named Nina. I was teaching at the time in Houston: Nina was not my student or even in my field, but an advantage of a city like Houston is that even minor writers can acquire an aura of celebrity. Nina let it be known through mutual friends that she had a crush on me. I took her on a date and thought her winsome and very appealing in her cashmere sweater, though conversation did not exactly flow. She seemed too frightened around me to do anything more than ask an endless series of questions; I felt almost like I was being interviewed by the press.

There was no question but that we would go back to her house that first night. In bed, she lost her shyness and became the one in charge, the *metteuse-en-scène*. Everything had to be done in a certain manner. She first asked me to help put her diaphragm into her. She had very definite ideas about sexual procedure, most of which I've forgotten, except I recall that in the middle of our doing it she had me pull out, so that we could repair to the living room. There she brought me a dish of raspberry sherbet and sat on my lap. She had a wonderfully curvaceous body, and in my lap the difference between our heights (I am fairly tall) was minimized. After what seemed to her the proper amount of eating, fondling, and kissing, she let me back into her bedroom and we went at it again. Each time I showed signs of starting to come, however, she would ask me to pull out to defer ejaculation. I tried to assure her that, even if I came, I could get hard again, but she seemed not to trust that, or else somehow felt only my first ejaculation counted, and she was determined to put that off as long as possible. Hours passed this way, I increasingly baffled, though glad for the experience of having sex with a self-styled expert—until finally, rebelliously, and, I must say, more than a little bored with the old in-and-out, I let myself come. She didn't.

Which is not surprising: many women don't feel comfortable enough to have an orgasm with a man the first time. But over our next several dates, for all my efforts, hand, mouth, and member, she still didn't come. Obviously she could have orgasms and had in the past—just not with me. I remember she would vary the setups, the positions, the entr'actes. She also carefully planned a picnic, with oysters, red wine, and other aphrodisiac fare. Everything related to the art of love had a ritual character for Nina: sensuality was her religion, and she took it very seriously, even solemnly. I wondered how this shy, thirty-year-old woman from rural Louisiana had acquired such sophisticated carnal notions. It was her hidden life.

Meanwhile, we had only gotten slightly better at talking with each other, and the lack of conversational rapport added to my claustrophobic sense that the ever-stimulating, beckoning world was shrinking to this one hothouse cube of her bedroom.

I went away for the summer, to New York City, and broke up with her like a coward by mail. At the time I told myself that I had not wanted to string her along, and that it should be obvious ours was a short-term, doomed experiment in lust. Or so it seemed to me. Maybe not to her. A year later, I received a phone call from Nina, inviting me to a popular upscale cafeteria, Butera's, near the Houston art museum. I gratefully accepted. It was a beautiful day, I was on spring break. I'd been misusing my vacation, and thought how wonderful it would be to have an adventure—maybe we'd even go back to her house after lunch and make love in the afternoon.

She was already sitting at an outdoor table on the terrace when I arrived. She looked diminutive from a distance, but as I approached I saw again how voluptuous her body was. Why had I been so stupid as to break up with her? I reviewed the various reasons, the problems and incompatibilities, but still, her face looked so pretty! Especially in the sunlight, her green eyes sparkled in the most enchanting way. We selected our food and settled in. The conversation bubbled along for an hour: this time she spoke amusingly and articulately, as we both caught up with each other's lives. I took off my jacket, rolled up my sleeves—was in fact demonstrating for her a kind of projected undressing, when she looked at her watch. She said she had to return to the university library, as she was in the middle of a research project.

I felt disappointed, but intrigued: Why had she asked me to lunch? Though I could not bring myself to inquire outright, I provided a helpful silence, and she took it. She said she had called because the last time we had seen each other she had been left with an unresolved, unsettled feeling and that she "needed a sense of closure." I now realized that, with unintentional gallantry, I had been sitting here all this time, helping to erase myself from her troubled heart. She confessed that it had been difficult for her to make the phone call inviting me to lunch, but that it had worked out surprisingly well.

"And," I asked, trying to keep the irony out of my voice, "do you feel—closure?"

"Yes, I feel much better." She went on to explain blithely that she no longer had a crush on me. Since one of our problems in the past had been her being tongue-tied, you might say she was now giving me a chance to see what a fun gal I had passed up, what a resourceful conversationalist, once her infatuated feelings for me were extinguished.

She seemed really happy to have brought off this pleasant hour. I, for my part, was burning to make love to her one more time, but was not entirely discontented to have performed my part so well. I had deactivated my charm, had provided "closure." I had finally gone long enough.

Warren Sonbert:
Friend and Filmmaker

Until complications from AIDS claimed him in 1995 at forty-seven, the avant-garde filmmaker Warren Sonbert was the picture of robust health. Tall, with curly hair kept trim, a triangular mustache that extended from a strong nose, warm, often ironically amused eyes, and a lank, tanned physique toned from regular workouts at the gym, he looked remarkably consistent from decade to decade. Warren exuded a nonchalant, burnished vitality, and seemed never to tire, however overstuffed his schedule. He was fully *present*, whether at work or play (which, in his case, seemed an almost meaningless distinction, since each fed the other so relentlessly), driven by inner discipline. On the one hand the most sociable person I have ever known; on the other, by his own cheerful admission, a solitary. "I just follow my own needs and wants and desires," he once told an interviewer. "Do I sound too megalomaniacal? Well, I think all artists have to be very solipsistic, very exclusive."

I first met Warren around 1967; we were introduced by our mutual friend, Jim Stoller, who noticed Warren at a distance, leaning back in his chair in an outdoor café on Lincoln Center's plaza on a perfect summer day in June. He looked bronzed, worldlier than his eighteen years. He was wearing a brown velvet tie and a shirt with subtle tan and yellow stripes. I searched for years for such a shirt, and never found one. It's funny to think that, long before we became friends, Warren was my sartorial model on the basis of that one fleeting encounter, since, in later years, I became more of a clotheshorse, and he pared his wardrobe down to lumberjack red flannel shirts and jeans (plus the occasional tux for opera nights). In any event, I projected onto him an air of gilded youth.

Sonbert was already celebrated in underground film circles, and in Jonas Mekas's *Village Voice* column, as a post-Godard wunderkind. Curious what his films might be like, I took in a one-man screening in the basement of the Wurlitzer Building on Forty-Second Street, where Mekas's underground screenings were then held. I was very impressed. In two years, 1966 and 1967, he had made eight short films: *Amphetamine, Where Did Our Love Go?, Hall of Mirrors, The Tenth Legion, Truth Serum, Connection, The Bad and the Beautiful, Ted and Jessica.* They were an explosion of wry, electric imagery, each one a roller-coaster ride: you just hung on and followed.

The venerable underground filmmaker Rudy Burckhardt, himself a master of the collage-diary film, wrote about this work: "What first attracted me to Warren Sonbert's films in the Sixties was their easy elegance of moving among beautiful people. In one scene the camera circled completely around a handsome young couple in Gramercy Park, in another fashionable models flitted by, then you could get lost deliciously in Lucas Samaras's room of mirrors. The movement seemed more sensuous and relaxed than Brakhage, and up-to-date rock music added excitement." It was the world of sixties urban chic: boutiques and discos and art openings, Andy Warhol and Henry Geldzahler. But these fashionable subjects were not photographed as they'd been in *Vogue.* We saw both their scarlet silk blouses unbuttoned and their pimples and postnocturnal eye bags, and they were filmed in context, in their East Village apartments or on the street. His *Bad and the Beautiful* consisted of several portraits of couples edited in the camera, showing their tenderness, horsing around, relaxing with friends, clinging to each other. Someone would be lying on a bed, waiting for a lover to return from the other room. Sonbert already had the knack of creating an intensely elegiac mood about the present, as though he knew how quickly these sixties costumes and attitudes would fade. Even his

Motown song choices ("Where Did Our Love Go?") accentuated the anticipated loss, as much as did the haunting tracking shots, which seemed to be searching for the separated lover.

After that first brief encounter I did not see Warren Sonbert for several years, until around 1974, when we bumped into each other, again, in the Lincoln Center area—this time at a bar after a New York Film Festival screening of Fassbinder's *Fox and His Friends*. I was with my girlfriend at the time, a poet named Kay, and I remember Warren entering with a loud group. I went up to tell him how much I had enjoyed his films, and he, in friendly response, detached himself from his entourage and sat at the table with Kay and me. He was drawn to writers, especially New York School or Language Poets. We had friends in common, and this time we hit it off immediately. I also recall Warren flirting with Kay, who was much taken with him, that night and thereafter. Kay, a Southerner, knew how to flirt with gay or bisexual men. Warren, for his part, was good at befriending both halves of a couple, and remaining loyal to each (much to my chagrin), long after they split up.

We discussed the Fassbinder film, which I (a huge fan of the German filmmaker) liked very much, and he liked less. He found its class analysis of the gay scene heavy-handed. Odd that this particular film should have been the occasion of our reunion. Kay, I think, assumed from the start that Warren was gay, whereas I tabled the question. He and I exchanged phone numbers, vowed to stay in touch, and (a New York rarity) actually did.

In the formation phase of friendship, usually one person feels he is making more of the overtures, but the advances between Warren and me seemed equally distributed. We were both men-about-town, though he was certainly more in demand; he was devoted to the punctilio of popularity, the duty not to give offense. We would meet twice a month or so for dinner, talk for hours about movies, books, work, the people we knew. I found Warren wonderfully discriminating and sympathetic. He had a way of taking your side in any dispute you recounted, while leavening his response with just enough humor to permit you to laugh at yourself.

Every time we parted, no matter how gossipy or frivolous the conversation had been, he would produce this leave-taking look, his eyes liquid from the pleasure of your company and regret at its imminent removal, his voice velvety with promise: till next time. Even if he did this with everyone, I was pleased at the effort: part of his courtly manners, from which I, who rarely modulated the abruptness of my exits, could well afford to learn.

The question of his sexual orientation did not clarify, strangely, in the first few months. For one thing, Warren never spoke, acted, or gestured effeminately; that was not his style. For another, he had the uncanny ability, like many socially gifted people, to mirror the person with whom he happened to be. Too, he may have kept back that information, leaving pronouns vague, while figuring out just how shallow or deep my homophobia ran. Perhaps *homophobia* is too strident a term: certainly in our liberal-artistic circles, it was assumed everyone was comfortable with homosexuality, and had many gay friends and acquaintances— both assumptions valid, in my case. Yet I had my moments of bitchily overgeneralizing about gays: at the very least, the novelist in me was always looking to interpret an individual's behavior as an extension of tribal or group patterns, and the gay life provided abundant material for such speculation. To give an example: once I knew that Warren was gay, I began to interpret his velvety, throaty vocal tone as the product of a constricted larynx that suddenly seemed typically gay. My thinking went something like this: gay men were often choking back considerable rage in their determination to be nice, which tightened up the vocal cords.

What complicated the issue of sexual preference was that Warren let me know, even boasted, that he'd been sleeping with a female ex-student of his at Bard, where he taught film. Though his primary sexual identity was gay, he was up for the occasional tryst with a woman, especially during this period. At the time, he seemed to be testing his sexual magnetism on everyone. According to his friends, Warren would go into a record store, say, and in less than two minutes would have made eye contact with someone, and the next thing you knew, they would both disappear into the men's room. I never saw him employ this pickup technique when he was around me, but once I realized he was gay (not from any dramatic confession: Warren was genuinely surprised I hadn't known all along), he found ways of showing me less obliquely this part of his life.

One night he took me to an all-male bash of balletomanes near Lincoln Center. It was a small apartment in a brownstone walk-up, and Warren and I got jammed behind the kitchen table with the booze. Some corpulent, red-faced queen accosted Warren with belligerent lust: "Well, where have *you* been hiding out?" he demanded, diving into Warren's shirt and squeezing his chest. Warren took it good-naturedly, looking tolerant and amused. He was the favorite that night, discouraging no one, giving none consent. I stood by his side, for safety's sake, the only straight man there.

Later, giving Warren the opportunity to operate alone, I drifted into the living room, with its exposed brick wall. The men there, most with cropped beards, were either cruising or making out on the couch. That didn't faze me, they were not my friends, but their fierce eye contact, first intense, then hostile and dismissive when they realized I wasn't in the game, as though annoyed I was taking up space, made me uncomfortable. I felt unsure where to stand until David, a film critic and one of Warren's friends, came up to rescue me. We talked film theory: he'd been reading Noël Burch, who claimed we Westerners misread Japanese movies, we thought we grasped their core meaning, but we were being "universalist," deceived by our bourgeois-humanist-hegemonist codes. The conversation grew more abstract the more the scene heated up around us, and for one paranoid moment I even suspected he was speaking in code, as though to say: Just as the Japanese subtexts elude you, so you misperceive the meanings here.

I kept insisting it was possible for a gaijin like me to get Ozu. The conversation went around in circles, but I clung to it, for lack of anything else, until Warren's approaching leather jacket and red flannel shirt caught my eye. He whispered, "Had enough?" his mustache ticking my ear. I said yes, I was ready to go, and we left. Warren started laughing as soon as we hit the street. "What an obnoxious party! Had I known what assholes would be there, I never would have wasted your time or mine."

I was tempted to complain how alienating the whole experience had been—how straight men and gays seemed suddenly antagonists, each mocking the other's desires. But before I could deliver this harangue, I admitted to myself that the party hadn't been all that bizarre. I was exaggerating its off-putting nature to distance myself from it as much as possible. When I was a teenager at an all-male college, I had had what seemed like crushes on classmates, and worried about it. My therapist asked me: "What are you most afraid of? The first thing that comes to mind." I blurted out: "Becoming a homosexual." As it happened I didn't, and Warren did. Friends live the lives we don't have the aptitude for, or taste, or courage. What matters is that they live an alternative to one's own life.

A couple of years into our friendship Warren began dating the famous choreographer Jerome Robbins. They had an on-again-off-again relationship, and during one of the "on" periods, Kay and I were invited to a dinner party at Robbins's town house, just the four of us. I sensed that Robbins had insufficient regard for Warren's stature in the experimental film community—that he was treating Warren like a pretty young thing and not much more; and it may have been my imagination, but I also thought Warren was showing me off that night as a friend of substance. I was determined to engage the maestro with the white Vandyke in stimulating conversation. As it happened, I had recently directed a production of *West Side Story* with elementary schoolchildren at P.S. 75, and I wanted to draw out Robbins's impressions of that show, which had after all been one of his greatest hits. Robbins became animated in his exchanges with me, and I—out of my dubious need to shine—flattered him with interrogative references from the forties and the fifties, which seemed to put us more on the same level, age-wise, and to exclude the other two. Warren and Kay exchanged a knowing smile, and Kay said: "I guess we've been relegated to the wives' section."

Sometime in the late seventies, after his affair with Robbins broke up, Warren moved to San Francisco, a city for which he became an avid booster. He would give *Vertigo* tours to visitors, taking them around to Ernie's and

Coit Tower and other locations that had appeared in Hitchcock's master-piece. But he would always schedule annual visits to New York, timed to coincide with his film screenings or that part of the opera season that most interested him. Over the years, Warren had become a classical music afi-cionado. On these fortnight visits to New York he would sometimes stay in my flat, which was small and musty but close to the Metropolitan Opera.

Warren had a curious habit of keeping a small piece of unlined white paper in his back pocket (I assume he did not use a pocket calendar because it would have made an unsightly bulge and broken the trouser line), on which he would have written his daily schedule hour by hour, from 8:00 a.m. onward. He tried to accommodate all his old friends, new acquaintances, and business associates on these whirlwind visits: breakfast with J, watching a morning rehearsal of the opera (he knew all the ushers, who sneaked him in), lunch with K, checking rushes at the film lab, then tea with L, maybe a quick movie, then a dash to the opera, after which late dinner with M, N, and O, followed by a night-cap with P and Q . . . and perhaps after that, some catting around. On a few nights he did not return to my place at all but showed up the next morning, with an abashed "don't ask" smile, followed by some morsels of gossip about mutual friends to throw me off the scent, then a shower and morning calls. Eavesdropping, I would hear him gather-ing information about the condition of the opera singers ("Tatiana has a sore throat, she may not even go on!"). Tatiana Troyanos was his then favorite: there is a lovely shot of her in one of his movies, tak-ing a bow and receiving a bouquet. Warren was a passionate mission-ary for opera among his more ignorant friends. I tried to learn from him, waited in line to buy a ticket for the Paris Opera's production of *Otello*, with Margaret Price, sets by August Everding, which Warren assured me it would be unthinkable to miss. I certainly liked it, but the transcendent registers of the opera experience eluded me. I would be thrilled beyond measure for the first hour or so, then after two acts would invariably feel I'd sat long enough. But I didn't dare tell Warren that, because once, when he and I were at a *Marriage of Figaro*, before the last act some of the Met's season-ticket holders, elderly businessmen and their begowned wives, started leaving, and he hissed to me scathingly, "Some people would walk out of heaven!"

Warren's film style had changed from the sixties: he had abandoned the Motown beat for a more severe succession of composed shots, projected absolutely silently. His suppression of the sound track had a good deal to do with his love of music, and his desire to give his visuals a "musical" form. As he explained once in a lecture: "In very much the same sense as one hears a series of notes, chords, or tone clusters, one sees a progression of a series of shots . . . to purely watch the images is a much freer, broader experience than any track would add. The film can truly breathe this way—go many more places than it can anchored to sound."

This aesthetic austerity was combined with a much broader social and geographical focus. The first of his films in this manner, *Carriage Trade* (1967–1971), had an ambitious global range, and that Sonbertian knack of framing an anecdote in three seconds, but it also taxed viewers with its lengthy stream of silent images. I like what Jonas Mekas wrote about it in *The Village Voice*:

> What it is, it's a canto on people and places. It's the first canto film I know. Sonbert keeps splicing together, one bit after another (each bit about the same length, not very long and not too short) bits of footage from his journeys in Europe, Africa, India, and the United States. He cuts these pieces in such a way that places and time are completely jumbled together . . . a collage of the world, a world which seems to be the same everywhere. I don't know if there are any lessons to be learned from this film, and I have overheard some people complaining that there is nothing new in Sonbert's footage, no new information is given. Nevertheless, as I sat through these eighty minutes, I felt there was a completely different information being passed to me. . . . Something begins to happen, after ten or twenty minutes, the information is changed by time, by the ever repeating rhythms of places and people, and a new kind of information and form is born.

The eighty-minute version Mekas saw was eventually edited down to sixty-one minutes; and thereafter Warren—as though sensing that, all glories of time accretion aside, there were limits to an audience's patience—settled into a roughly half-hour format for his films. In his next, *Rude Awakening,* Warren imposed a strict conceptual grid on the editing. As he described it in an interview: "It's very much influenced by what I would call 'directional pulls,' where either the composition within the shot, or the camera movement itself, would be going either right-to-left or left-to-right. . . . But I would never have a moment in *Rude Awakening* where a figurative shot would be followed by another figurative shot, or close-up followed by close-up and so on. In other words, it would be close-up, wide angle, movement vs. still, abstract vs. figurative."

It was as though Warren were seeking the cinematic equivalent of Schoenberg's twelve-tone row. The problem is that filmed images, except for the most abstract, are not as neutral as musical notes; they cannot help but convey certain meanings, certain narrative possibilities. You watch two children playing in snowsuits in the park on-screen for three seconds and are immediately plunged back into your own childhood, while wondering about this specific pair (one seems more aggressive, the other more tentative). Depending upon how you feel about childhood (sentimental, repelled, uneasy), you project your own affective baggage onto the fleeting image. Warren was well-aware that each person "read" his shots in a subjective manner, and even exulted in this semantic liberty: in a sense, he wanted to be the detached impresario of the spectacle, without taking a moral position himself. On the other hand, he kept being drawn to certain "loaded" images or shot combinations, whose meaning seemed all too obvious. He flirted with cliché, only to undercut it by further shots.

To give a much-discussed example: In *Divided Loyalties,* he shows shirtless guys embracing in a Gay Pride parade, followed by a shot of a graveyard. It would, on the face of it, appear to be a sardonic commentary on the gay lifestyle. Warren was certainly not averse to taking an ironic distance from any group propaganda, including that of gays; but we also know that Warren was increasingly gay-identified from the time he moved to San Francisco, so we wonder what to make of this juxtaposition. He told an interviewer: "Well, in one sense it may be obvious. You know, 'All is vanity.' Those beautiful bodies will eventually be dust. But what follows after that—you just can't take it from A to B without including C as well. It changes with all the things that are surrounding them. There is a shot of sheep getting clipped and another of sitting ducks on ice. It's people being exploited and not really knowing it. It's both embracing everything and being unbelievably critical at the same time."

Formally, he is arguing for the necessity of looking at the whole film as a montage and connecting any shot to any other shot, regardless of where each falls in the sequence. Sonbert disliked Eisenstein's didactic "dialectical" connections (shot of plutocrat, followed by shot of crowing rooster, means the rich guy is a silly braggart). But he is also a montage filmmaker, like Eisenstein: so how do you keep the audience from drawing its own simpleminded conclusions from the collision of $x + y$ images? To say that later images may complicate or contradict the simplistic equation will not keep the viewer from jumping to glib cause-and-effect conclusions based on reading two successive shots. One way Sonbert tried to evade these links was to separate two potentially narrative-making images with what he called "palate-cleansing shots," usually of a flower or something in nature, filmed so close up as to verge on abstract. This neutral device doesn't really defuse the satiric editorial effect of other individual shots, however.

Warren was, intriguingly, a nonnarrative filmmaker who loved classic Hollywood story-films (Ford, Hitchcock, Sirk, Minnelli), and whose curiosity about human behavior led him to catch people on-screen enacting tiny, three- to five-second narratives. He faced the further challenge of being an experimental filmmaker dedicated to difficulty, abstraction, and ambiguity, who also had strong political and moral points he wanted to make. He qualified his own didacticism by saying: "Usually works are mirrors of what is contained already in the viewer, and it is the role of the creator to 'place' or qualify these reactions. Lead the viewer down one road only to diverge onto another, upset inbred expectations at the same time as exploiting these very clichés." This sounds like having one's

154 / PORTRAIT INSIDE MY HEAD

cake and eating it too. I wonder to what extent his desire to keep things morally ambiguous and multivalent as long as possible, his subversive urge to "upset inbred expectations," was connected to Warren's being gay. Is it part of a gay aesthetic? Of course this subject has been worried by better theoretical minds than mine, in queer studies and elsewhere, so I risk sounding naïve by raising it. But I am trying to convey how, from a heterosexual (i.e., naïve) vantage point, one tries to puzzle out one's gay friends' inner lives, particularly if they are artists.

The paradox of Warren's films, it seems to me, is that they are both sensual and punitive, with ravishing images that add up to futility. This paradox not only is aesthetic but goes to the heart of Warren's personality. He had stunning charm and a core of anger. He may have been angry at straight society for having stigmatized him as a homosexual; he may have been angry that his mother had died early, and his father had also passed away, leaving him orphaned before he had even reached middle age. He was alone in the world—except for a million friends. The resulting bitterness or malice or urge to lash back, in contrast to his seductive, all-embracing public persona, had to emerge somewhere, and it came out, albeit masked, in his art. Note the oxymoronic, prodding nature of his titles: *Rude Awakening, Divided Loyalties, Friendly Witness, Honor and Obey*.

He seemed quite aware of the malice latent in his film method:

Some people are disturbed by the brevity of some of the images—particularly those that one might label "beautiful" or "ecstatic." They are over before one has a chance to barely luxuriate in them, they are taken away before one can nestle and coo and cuddle in the velveteen sheen of it all, so that feelings of deprivation, expectations dissolved, even sadomasochism arise. Very often a cut occurs before an action is complete. This becomes both metaphor of frustration, hopes dashed, and yet of serenity if you like—that perhaps all of this activity has been going on, is going on, will be going on, and even all at the same time. That we are privileged viewers of many sectors of humanity.

Warren loved to have it both ways. On the one hand, admitting to a certain sadomasochistic urge to undercut expectations, pull the plug on beauty; on the other hand, expressing a desire to heal by offering us the solace of an ever-running material stream. It was in the tension between these impulses that he operated, and created a body of work that has earned him an enduring place in American experimental film.

When I visited San Francisco, I would sometimes stay with Warren, who lived just off Castro Street, in the heart of the gay district. He shared a lovely Victorian with bay windows and a wooden stoop leading from the sidewalk to the first floor. I slept on a couch in the front parlor, which had a large piano and a theatrical arrangement of tall orange irises in a vase, and a statue of two men embracing, and a bookcase filled with *Gone with the Wind* editions and paraphernalia (his roommate was a Margaret Mitchell fanatic). Warren blithely dissociated himself from the kitsch decor, blaming it on his roommate. Solicitous of my comfort as a guest, he took me around the district the first night and pointed out which shops and bars catered to straight men as well as gays, and which I would do well to avoid—adding with a laugh that I should have no trouble picking up women. He had a mocking irreverence toward aspects of the gay lifestyle, the sartorial conformity of what he called "Castro Street clones," for instance; at the same time he was proud of the Castro as an international attraction.

He seemed to be dating four, five, six, or seven men at the moment. One of his regulars arrived while I was reading a novel by Trollope on the back porch. I heard him go into Warren's bedroom and, twenty minutes or so later, about the length of a chapter, leave, before I got a chance to introduce myself.

Warren showed me what he called "the playroom," a little cube-space added to the back, just above the basement. The house, located on a steep San Francisco hill, was built on stilts, and the playroom had been tucked under the back porch steps. It was the fashion, Warren explained, for many of these Victorians to have their own playrooms. This one was small, dark, with black walls, black curtains, one naked green lightbulb, a mattress with one black sheet, a Super 8 projector, and a leather harness floating in the center, suspended from the ceiling. The harness looked like some sort of torture device, though Warren assured me it was "actually quite comfortable, or so they tell me," accompanying this statement with a strangled laugh, dismissive hand gesture, and the pleased look of a host offering a tasty tidbit to my compendium of late-twentieth-century manners.

I examined the black executioner's hood, the metal chains on the floor, and the row of shiny silver balls strung on a wire. "What are these balls for?" I asked.

"Oh, those are from Japan. Japanese prostitutes would put them in the man's anus and pull them out one by one to induce a bigger orgasm. As I say, I never use the place myself, though we do put up guests here!" he added wickedly.

My eyes kept returning to the Super 8 projector on the night table, cocked at an angle intended to throw an image against the wall screen, and already threaded though stopped at midreel, under what circumstances one could imagine. Cinephile that I am, I was tempted to watch the film.

The playroom left a somewhat comic impression on me, like a spook house. I was not bothered by it, but I did feel threatened overall by the range of Warren's sexual activity. Not because I feared his getting AIDS—this was before we had heard that deadly acronym—but because I was repelled by that seemingly effortless promiscuity, which mocked the consequential difficulty of life as I understood it, and which felt hollow at the core, though this conclusion could have been envy. If I found in his movies an underlying emptiness, beneath the pleasure-seeking spectacle, it was partly because he put it there—describing one film as "things not working out, things not materializing, people having certain expectations, plans, input, and those *dissolving*"—and partly because I wanted to find it there, as the apt price for his sexual freedom.

But I don't want to belabor the point: after all, I never actually saw Warren having sex, but I saw him plenty of times preoccupied with his art. When Warren was filming, usually with a spring-wound 16 mm Bolex, he did it in a relaxed, unobtrusive manner, his camera a natural extension of his bearing, like a coiled dancer's prop. Once, he came to the public school where I was working and filmed the kids and me from a gym mat, a shot that turned up in *Divided Loyalties*. When he edited there was that same blend of casualness and concentration, a toasted bagel with cream cheese lying precariously close to the slicer, on which two celluloid strips were about to be joined. Warren defied the usual precaution by cutting the original, instead of making a work print first. He relished the whole artisanal, low-tech setup of physically cutting film with a safety blade, scraping off the emulsion, applying glue, and watching the results through a flickering monitor, guided by turning the take-up reel's hand crank.

He knew there was little financial reward for his kind of filmmaking—as little as there is for writing poetry, which may explain why he felt close to poets. I used to wonder how he supported himself. The answer, I think, was partly from a trust fund his parents had left him, and partly from fees earned showing his films, partly from selling prints to archives, or occasional grants, or teaching. Within the limited remunerative constraints of his genre, he was quite successful: hustling showings, networking, cultivating friendships with festival and museum curators, both here and in Europe.

He also began writing movie reviews under the nom de plume Scottie Ferguson (the name of Jimmy Stewart's character in *Vertigo*) for a local Bay Area newspaper. These reviews were always lively, often acerbic. Gone was the gallant, omniappreciative manner of Sonbert in his youth: it had given way to a more jaundiced tone, a dislike of stupidity, as he approached middle age. Warren put it this way: "There's so much junk around, there's so much crap. Webern talked about this—about there's so *much* junk, why not produce *less*, something really scaled down and perfected. A small, contained body, that really says it all."

It seemed to me that Warren was making the same film over and over. He had perfected a form which suited him, and which yielded quality results, even though it did not quite express the full brio and range of its maker. I said as much in a piece I was asked to write in the 1983 issue of *Film Culture*, which contained a special Warren Sonbert tribute section. After praising his movies, I questioned his repetition of certain motifs, such as parades, circuses, elevated trains, car trips, be-ins, airplane wings, divas taking bows, which made each film begin to look like the outtakes of the previous one. (We might consider here the ethics of criticizing a friend in print. I told myself at the time that Warren was so surrounded by admirers, and that avant-garde film in general is so resistant to self-criticism that it was up to me to prod him toward taking up new challenges. I now see more clearly that this response was tied to a certain unconscious hostility and rivalry; I should have kept my doubts to myself. It is always a gamble to critique a friend's art, in public or private, and more often than not a mistake, but one I keep making, and will probably continue to make, driven as it is by vanity and laziness: the vanity is my misguided assumption that it is my job to be honest, and the laziness, that to tell the truth as I see it is easier for me than to modulate into another, more diplomatic if disingenuous way of responding.)

Warren replied to my criticism in the same issue. He bristled at the term *diary-film*, which he thought too suggestive of accidental, unintentional composition, but noted that he relied on the materials of his daily life: "There are certain things that interest me, and that's what I film. People think that when they see new work of mine that I'm using outtakes from past films, things from seven, eight years ago. But I'll always go to the circus during a given period of film-making, or a parade, things that are out there on public display. But at the same time, the opposite of that—private, intimate things with friends, what they'll do at home, leisure, etc."

It was a good answer: How much does anyone's daily life change from year to year? But it didn't answer my underlying reservation, which could have applied to many other experimental filmmakers besides Warren: that the need to assert a recognizable, avant-garde-approved identity led to the too-narrow refinement of a style, and that the general public's indifference toward experimental filmmaking promoted a too-cozy, uncritical appreciation within the beleaguered ranks.

As it happened, Warren did harbor dreams of making other, more ambitious films. He wrote a screenplay which he showed me for a feature film set in Nazi Germany, built around the premiere of Richard Strauss's opera *Capriccio*; but it was so intricate, with a dozen characters and as many locations, that it would have cost millions. Unable to raise the funding for it, he continued working on his self-contained, jewel-cut cantos, which I see in retrospect generously offered more than enough insight and beauty for any reasonable lover of film art. The cineaste in me is perfectly content with Sonbert's oeuvre, especially knowing there will never be any more. At the time I wrote those comments in *Film Culture*, though, I was greedy. What we want from our gifted artist friends is—everything.

A stabilizing force had come into Warren's love life in the form of an older man, Ray. Immensely kind, cultivated, and knowledgeable about art, silver-mustached and rail-thin, securely employed, Ray became the protector, nurturer, devoted partner, and advocate whom Warren had long sought. They moved into another Victorian near Castro Street, which soon became a gathering place for their circle. Ray and Warren liked to entertain and give lavish dinner parties, and I had the privilege of attending a few when I was in the Bay Area. Living with Ray, Warren became more domestic. They traveled together, Ray shepherding Warren to his screenings in foreign cities, Warren indulging Ray's scholarly passion for tracking down Renaissance paintings. They had over ten happy years: in the best of circumstances, they would have grown old together. But Ray came down with AIDS and died.

Warren was bereft. Ray had been his lover, older brother, manager, and guardian angel. "Who's going to take care of me now?" he said, with honest if brazen self-centeredness. In the year after Ray's death, Warren's friends, including myself, began to notice that he was becoming rather irritable and imperious, his temper flaring more readily. One would hear reports of his storming into projection booths and complaining about some technical flaw in the projection. He was acting more like a prima donna, which I see now must have been a side effect of his condition.

Warren began telling his friends that he was suffering from a mysterious disease. He insisted it was not AIDS but some baffling brain problem which eluded the physicians' diagnoses. He described to me episodes of passing out and being taken to the hospital, going through grueling tests, and finally being released. Knowing how Ray had died, I suspected early on that Warren was HIV-positive, but perhaps his pride could not bear admitting that he had been afflicted with the common scourge, rather than some rare, exotic ailment. A mutual friend who was very close to Warren noticed certain medications on his bureau and asked her physician-father about them. He confirmed that they were treatments for AIDS. She confronted Warren with this information, and he, still denying the fact, added testily: "Well, given the fact that I'm gay and the life I've led, it wouldn't be surprising if I *were* suffering from AIDS!" It was classic Warren, wanting it both ways: to tell and not to tell. Perhaps he wanted to resist seeming pitiable in front of his friends. I had another friend who had acted similarly—gone off by himself to die back home in the Midwest, where his sister could nurse him, without telling his New York friends (especially his straight male friends, like me) he had AIDS. Regardless, I kept wishing Warren would trust me enough to tell me; but he stonewalled everyone, until close to the end.

The last few times I saw Warren, he made an effort to keep it light. He had hooked up with a young Hispanic named Ascension, who was looking after him and whom Warren, in turn, was educating in the finer points of life. They were running from one social engagement to another, seeing everyone and catching up with New York's cultural offerings. One day in early October, I got together with Warren for what turned out to be the last time. His speech sounded slurred from the drugs he was taking, and it was hard for him to stay on a subject; his attention kept wandering. He was most looking forward to the opera that night. He was wearing gray lederhosen with the hems rolled up, and he bragged about how he still kept going to the gym and his body looked great, all things considered—"See, I'm unafraid to walk around in shorts in October, when most New Yorkers have already started bundling up." I recalled his long-ago statement explaining the editing together of a Gay Pride parade and a graveyard shot: "You know, 'All is vanity.' Those beautiful bodies will eventually be dust." All is vanity, indeed, I thought: a step away from death, and he still has to show off his muscle tone? I have no doubt a gay man would have more sensitively approved the bravado behind Warren's wearing shorts, and seen it more intuitively as a species of courage.

Warren had to leave to introduce a screening of his films at the Museum of Modern Art. After that, he and Ascension would go to the opera. "Ciao," he said amicably, walking up Fifty-Third Street to meet up with one of MOMA's curators, who would be waiting for him in the museum lobby.

Ciao. It will always seem too short, Warren's last good-bye, like an essay which ends with clumsy abruptness and you turn the page, thinking there must be another page that's missing. He who taught me the value of a gently graduated leave-taking was forced to make his own overly hasty exit from this life. We can stare at photographs of him, marveling at his jaunty presence, vitally bronzed as a movie star, yet detached, contrapposto, head turned away from the torso, away from us, and try to grapple with the paradox that someone can still be so alive to us and yet—gone. It is like one of those cruel facts he alluded to with his titles, *Rude Awakening, Divided Loyalties, Friendly Witness, Honor and Obey*, something he was trying to tell us all along.

III

CITY SPACES

Brooklyn the Unknowable

I sing of Brooklyn, the fruited plain, cradle of literary genius and stand-up comedy, awash in history, relics from Indian mounds, Dutch farms, Revolutionary War battles, breweries, and baseball. In Brooklyn, miles of glorious brownstones, some of the most architecturally rich residential neighborhoods in urban America, coexist not far from slums with some of the highest infant mortality rates in the country. Brooklyn is home to millions of immigrants, many of whom never learn to speak proper English, surrounded as they are by Brooklynese, a curiously hardy dialect. Brooklyn is my hometown.

There must be some mercury in the water that promotes a need to recount, show off, or intimidate. Brooklyn breeds writers, performers, and gangsters: Bernard Malamud and Norman Mailer, Barbara Stanwyck and Barbra Streisand, Woody Allen and Mel Brooks, the Miller Boys (Henry and Arthur), Al Capone and the Amboy Dukes, Red Auerbach and Spike Lee, all came up in the fanatically competitive atmosphere of its school yards. Even more numerous have been the gifted, born elsewhere, who took to the hospitality of Brooklyn: Marianne Moore, Walker Evans, Hart Crane, Richard Wright, Truman Capote, Gypsy Rose Lee, Carson McCullers, Thomas Wolfe, William Styron . . .

Brooklyn is vast and unassimilable. Like the Great Wall of China, it mocks our hankering for finitude. For all its bragging, the place is so diffident and secretive that even a homeboy like me is hard-pressed to characterize it. When you've said that it is the most populous borough in New York City, that some 2.3 million people live here on eighty-one square miles, on the southwestern tip of Long Island, you haven't begun to describe it. When you note that it's a patchwork of neighborhoods, such as Crown Heights, Fort Greene, Williamsburg, Bensonhurst, Bay Ridge, Ditmas Park, Dyker Heights, you're a little closer to its essence, though not much. A friendly place (I knew more about the people on my block two weeks after returning to Brooklyn than I did about the occupants of a Manhattan street where I'd lived for a decade), it can also exhibit a fortress mentality: how to explain the contradiction that Brooklynites can be so inviting to newcomers within the neighborhood enclave, yet so xenophobic and murderously guarded toward strangers. (See the sad episode of Yusuf Hawkins, a black youth killed for straying into the wrong white neighborhood while trying to buy a car.) Pete Hamill recalled this Brooklyn territoriality in an interview: "Where I grew up there were hamlets that were sometimes two blocks wide in which everybody knew everybody. . . . But they didn't know people from the hamlet nine blocks away. Often they fought each other. All these fights that street gangs would have over turf, or girlfriends—they acted as if the people from Eighteenth Street were totally different from the people from Ninth Street."

If, as the song goes, there is a "New York state of mind," what might be a "Brooklyn state of mind"? I would characterize it as combative, stoic, and resilient: troubles are nothing new, but you relish daily life in all its plainness and peculiarity. From General Washington's strategic retreat over the East River to the present, often it consists in making a virtue of setbacks. Brooklyn Dodgers fans were famous for their fortitude and obstinacy: "Wait till next year." It is no accident that when the Dodgers finally won a World Series, they quit the borough almost immediately for the sunnier, celebrity-happy climes of Los Angeles. Brooklyn likes a beautiful loser.

Perhaps the defining loss was municipal identity: in 1898, when Brooklyn was the fourth-largest metropolis in the United States, it amalgamated with spindly Manhattan (and three other boroughs,

Queens, Staten Island, and the Bronx, but that's another story) to form modern New York City. In amalgamating with Brooklyn, Manhattan became the python that swallowed the elephant. I am not one of those who rue consolidation. I rejoice that Brooklyn feeds the greater whole. There are those who will not accept her diminished status, who still speak of Brooklyn as its own city. Perhaps they have in mind a symbolic rivalry along the lines of St. Paul and Minneapolis. I am a realist, I consider it a borough. But what a borough! I will go so far as to say that the spicy character of Brooklyn derives in large part from its "codependent relationship" with Manhattan. Having relinquished its municipal birthright, it haunts Manhattan Island like a doppelgänger conscience. Manhattan is the tower, Brooklyn the garden; Manhattan is Faustian will, Brooklyn, domestic life. Manhattan preens, disseminates opinion; Brooklyn is Uncle Vanya schlepping in the background to support his peacock relative.

For over a century, millions of men and women have commuted every day to make their living in Manhattan. People like my parents, who spent their vital essence as clerks in the garment center, riding the subway into Times Square every weekday morning, coming back at night with the *New York Post* (then a liberal tabloid) in my father's arms, relinquished to my brother and me for the sports pages. Before the *Post* it was the *Brooklyn Eagle*, a well-written local paper but lacking, as we say, an edge.

Brooklyn spirit remains a mixture of pride and provincialism. That Brooklyn's citizens have much to be proud of is indisputable. But what's odd, for such a world-renowned place, is the rinky-dink sound of its boosterism, the narrow perspective of its free-handout newspapers, which reprint the police dockets and church bingo schedules like a small-town gazette, the defensive character of its borough president's horn tooting. Brooklyn's provincialism, be it said, is not, or not entirely, a failure to achieve cosmopolitan worldliness; it is also a painstaking, willed achievement. It's not easy to be situated next to the most au courant place on the planet and hold on to your rough edges.

*   *   *

Though Tiresias's passage between genders has always struck me as an exhausting proposition, I seem to have conducted my life so as to criss-cross another identity border only slightly less psychologically fraught: the line between Manhattanite and Brooklynite.

I grew up in Brooklyn, my family having resided just above the poverty line in the ghettoes of Williamsburg and Fort Greene, before clawing their way up the lower-middle-class ladder to Flatbush. When I went off to college in Manhattan, I vowed never to look back. Manhattan was the City, the Party, Heaven and Hell. When out-of-state friends (who didn't know any better) settled in Brooklyn, championing its civility and low-key grace, I took in the fact that they had more space and prettier apartments than I, but did not envy them. For me, the borough carried a stigma. Brooklyn was the primeval ooze out of which I had crawled in order to make something of myself, and a move back would be a defeat, a regression to childhood and family entrapment.

The rest of my family, including my parents, followed me in time to Manhattan, except for my youngest sister, Joan, who chose to live on Cheever Place, a cul-de-sac in the backwaters of Cobble Hill. Each time I took the F train to visit my sister, I pitied her for still living in Brooklyn. The wheel turns: I now live seven blocks from her old address. Just as I had expressed unconscious resistance to trekking to Brooklyn by never memorizing the directions there, asking her anew each time, so now do my Manhattan friends toy the same with me. It is as if they secretly hope to erode my patience with directional amnesia, until, in the midst of repeating these tedious instructions, I will break down and say, "Oh, all right, let's meet in the City."

On the face of it, the barrier between the two boroughs should not be so great: after all, it is quicker to hop from Wall Street across the river to Brooklyn Heights than to traverse the island all the way to northernmost Manhattan. Yet I have known many Manhattanites who never set foot in Brooklyn. I remember once asking a highly cultivated elderly couple if they might want to join me and my wife to hear a Baroque opera at the Brooklyn Academy of Music (or BAM). I was told, "My husband and I don't go to Brooklyn." These were world travelers who lived half the year in Capri. Even the more intrepid Downtown Manhattan types who, in the 1980s, started going to BAM for its avant-garde performances would often travel in packs, emerging from the subway with looks of suppressed terror, and cling to their chums like rope-climbing mountaineers until they had reached the safety of the Brooklyn Academy. As it happens, the area around BAM *is* choppy and unprepossessing, usually under construction or partly boarded up, a classic transitional zone caught between commercial, residential, and traffic conduit. I do not blame Manhattanites for being afraid to venture left or right into unknown streets. But there is more to their hesitation than fear of muggers. There is also profound confusion at the vagueness of Brooklyn's urban design. In contrast to the clear, insular certitude of the Manhattan grid, Brooklyn's vaster landmass is more like the continental United States in its potential for inspiring agoraphobia. Manhattan's grid is like a tall menu offering a hierarchical suite of neighborhoods: the merest change in signage, streetlamp, or fenestration signals, to the trained local eye, a world of information about income and class. Brooklyn is no less class-bound, but its status cues are harder to read, especially for the Manhattanite who is so used to precisely calibrated progressions of luxury and distress.

Then, too, the arrival in Brooklyn brings with it a drop in sophistication and tension (Manhattanites often equate the two) that registers immediately in the body. I have experienced it myself as a decompression: a weight lifting from my shoulders. Entering the lower-rise streetscape, compared to that of Manhattan, is like going from a tense verticality to a semiprone position. This unstiffening is one of the delights of living in Brooklyn, but for the casual day-tripper it can be alarming, like the woozy onset of a tranquilizer. The Manhattanite has learned to convert wariness into a muscle, which twitches unhappily when not stimulated; the Brooklynite has adapted to greater quantities of boredom and is less afraid of it. Everything on the Brooklyn side of the bridge is more casual; you see fewer fashion statements, passersby seem like ordinary people rather than out-of-work actors projecting a cameo-worthy intensity. Even the slackers in Brooklyn have less fiercely ideological anti-ambition than Manhattan dropouts. Brooklyn coffeehouses appear to be furnished with throwaways from the owner's aunt's living room. There is, in short, a touch of the amateur, voluntary, homemade about the place.

I remember when my wife became pregnant and we began looking for larger living space than our one-bedroom, fifth-floor walk-up in the West Village. I was determined not to leave Manhattan, but we looked uptown and down and grew fed up with the overpriced, jerry-built crawl spaces pretending to be duplexes, the apartments darker than a jail cell. I had somehow forgotten to bank $5 million to purchase a town house in the Village, so we began, reluctantly, to consider buying a house in Brooklyn. On our second day of looking in that borough, we fell in love with a Carroll Gardens brownstone and made an offer, which was accepted. That night, we had second thoughts, stealing peeks up and down the nearly deserted Court Street on a Saturday night. My stomach—the gut of a Manhattanite attuned to urban excitement—felt queasily hollow. Were the quiet streets an omen of our soon-to-be dulled existence? Were we about to make a huge mistake? Fifteen years later, we have more than adjusted, while the surrounding neighborhood has accommodated us by growing livelier and hipper. We love our house, our block, and the borough of Brooklyn. Perhaps, like the pod people in *Invasion of the Body Snatchers*, we have simply been taken over by some Gowanus legume that insidiously hypnotizes us to accept a blander life.

All I know is that, when I go into Manhattan, which I do on the average of three times a week, I enjoy the City but I do not miss living there. Yet I realize I may never be whole: I have been both Manhattanite and Brooklynite, I have identified with the imperial contempt of the former and the complacent inferiority complex of the latter, I have sampled the champagne and the Ovaltine, and will forever be split.

Not so much when world-weary as when feeling chipper, I saunter over from my house to the Union Street Bridge, to take in the restorative waters of the maligned Gowanus Canal. To do so, I first go past the modest brick, three-story homes of Union Street, with their stoops, stone angel fountains, religious decorations, and patriotic American flags and an occasional Italian tricolor, this being a long-standing Neapolitan neighborhood, where immigrant stevedores labored on Brooklyn docks to raise a roof over their families' heads, with a renter downstairs. These are not the fancy brownstones selling for several million, but awkward, cozy row houses, whose lack of cachet increases as you approach the canal. Essentially, no one of class ever wanted to live near the Gowanus, legendary for its stink and for mobsters' bodies fished out of the canal.

The old Gowanus creek had been enlarged in the 1840s to service nearby factories and move construction materials for the burgeoning habitations of Brooklyn; and this dinky little canal, one hundred feet wide and less than a mile long, no deeper than fifteen feet in high water, became one of the most trafficked watercourses of nineteenth-century America. In the twentieth century, it devolved into a one-use channel—a conveyor of heating oil, whose toxic leakage into the creek bottom and the nearby shores' sediment has complicated any future development for recreational or residential uses. The daunting, Superfund-scale cleanup costs have not prevented local community planners from fantasizing the lowly Gowanus becoming a Little Venice, with outdoor cafés hugging the narrow banks. (Inshallah, it will never happen.) The tides being too sluggish to rid the channel of pollutants, a flushing tunnel has been installed; its pumping action goes a long way toward alleviating olfactory insult.

Standing on the span, looking outward toward the north, I see what is most astonishing for this city, a good deal of sky and clouds above low-scaled structures, and a vast, sweeping view of Brooklyn that would have quickened the pulse of a Delft landscape painter. You can luxuriate in the profligate empty space ("waste," to a developer's eye) framed by the canal. On the canal's western bank, a small grassy meadow with wildflowers, bisected by oil pipes, slopes down to the greenish, petroleum-iridescent water. Along the eastern bank are lined the back ends of mostly abandoned factories, painted with graffiti and faded words like "Conklin

Brass." The thump-thump of cars passing over the bridge's metal plates competes with the contemplative mood.

Looking south, toward Red Hook, there is a parking lot filled with Verizon telephone trucks, in the distance the elevated trestle of the F train, and the Kentile Floors sign, and a factory placard which reads "Alex Figliolia Contracting: Water Mains and Sewers." All this prosaic attention to infrastructure and repair, strewn haphazardly on either side of the canal amid weeds and ailanthus trees, this strange combination of industrial, residential, and bucolic, speaks to the poignantly somnolent essence of Brooklyn. The genius of Brooklyn has always been its homey atmosphere; it does not set out to awe, like skyscraper Manhattan, which is perhaps why one hears so much local alarm at the luxury apartment towers that are starting to sprout up, every two blocks, in parts of the borough closest to Manhattan. I, being a native Brooklynite, never romanticized the place as immune from modernity, nor do I see why such an important piece of the metropolis should be protected from high-rise construction when the rest of the planet is not. But my feelings are mixed: for if the sleeping giant which is Brooklyn were to awake and truly bestir itself and turn into a go-getter, I would deeply regret the loss of sky. Perhaps it is some deep-seated, native-son confidence that Brooklyn will never quite get it together that allows me to anticipate its bruited transformation with relative sanguinity. Meanwhile, I stand on the Union Street Bridge, a fine place from which to contemplate the Brooklyn that was, that is, and that is to be.

———

Brooklyn occupies an oddly sentimental corner of the American consciousness. Recently I was in a breakfast place in Santa Fe called Bagelmania, where the walls were covered with old, blown-up photographs of the Brooklyn Bridge and other ostensibly quaint scenes from my native town. I thought of the Brooklyn Diner on West Fifty-Seventh Street in Manhattan, yet another railroad-car theme diner devoted to the bygone fifties. What is it about Brooklyn that serves as such a ready hieroglyph for nostalgia?

In the era of World War II and its aftermath, when more battleships were built in the Brooklyn Navy Yard than in all of Japan, Brooklyn became the symbol of democratic, pluralistic tolerance and earthy common decency—in short, the values for which we were fighting the Fascists. Every platoon in war movies had its GI played by William Bendix or his ilk who swore that Flatbush was "the greatest spot on oith." In the 1945 *Anchors Aweigh*, the chorine with a heart of gold is called simply Brooklyn. When soldier Robert Walker meets single girl Judy Garland at Pennsylvania Station in *The Clock* (also 1945) and they fall in love, the two, having only a weekend to commit to each other before he returns to action, and needing a glimpse of domesticity to inspire them, go to Brooklyn, where they encounter a gruff, kindly milkman (James Gleason) and his family. Another Gleason, Jackie, immortalized the frustrated hopes and dreams of working-class Brooklyn through his portrayal of Ralph Kramden in *The Honeymooners*. Just as British playwrights used to typecast Cockneys as working-class and proud, refusing to take any guff from superiors or even envy them, so American popular culture celebrated the Brooklynite as Everyman, bittersweetly contented, in the end, to stay in that grubby environment with the El train rattling the windows, because somehow it was still "the greatest spot on oith."

Nostalgia can lead to schmaltz. The late urban planner Elliot Willensky titled his book *When Brooklyn Was the World*; but Brooklyn was never the world, except for children who never left their neighborhood, so that to long for that time is to wish to stay arrested in childhood or, at the very least, parochialism. To stay in the kingdom of egg creams, stickball, and of course, Dem Bums: the Brooklyn Dodgers with their loyal fans, Hilda Chester and the cowbells. I'm sick of hearing about Jackie Robinson and Pee Wee Reese with arms around each other—how it satisfies our need to believe a simplified myth of racial harmony! And the team owner Walter O'Malley cast as a Judas selling the team to Los Angeles, with the connivance of Robert Moses. I was ten years old in 1953, and a more passionate Dodger fan did not exist. I *loved* Jackie Robinson, Pee Wee Reese, Carl Furillo, Gil Hodges, Don Newcombe, and Duke Snider.

But let's be honest: Dodgers attendance figures were already declining before Walter O'Malley moved the team to Los Angeles. The borough's breweries started closing in the 1950s, not the 1960s. So it's distorting to say that the fifties were the heyday of Brooklyn, and then blame everything bad that followed on O'Malley's desertion.

As painful as the departure of the Dodgers may have been, the real decline in Brooklyn's fortunes came about from shifting the port to New Jersey and closing the Navy Yard, and the city's loss of most of its manufacturing base. Ironically, the country was falling in love with white working-class ethnics at just that moment they were starting to be replaced by African-Americans, Hispanics, and Asians, who would find it much harder to obtain unskilled, entry-level jobs. If I am going to rue the loss of anything, it is the blue-collar world of my childhood, and the opportunity it gave to millions of people without college degrees to work with their hands and bring home a paycheck. All those egg cream–dispensing candy stores, those dairy cafeterias, delicatessens, and trolleys that Brooklyn nostalgists lament were actually cogs in a functioning working-class culture, which collapsed when several hundred thousand manufacturing jobs left Brooklyn in the 1950s and 1960s, never to return. Decades of massive disinvestment by redlining banks accompanied that deindustrialization process.

Fortunately, the tide has turned in the past fifteen years, and money has begun flowing back to Brooklyn. In retrospect, it's hard to see how Brooklyn could have ever fallen out of favor for long, given its superb housing stock and proximity to Manhattan's overheated real estate market, which makes it seem a relative bargain. Its new prosperity, as seen in gentrified bistros and boutiques, departs from the old homey, amateurish environment; it expresses a more self-conscious consumerist culture, driven by trust fund entrepreneurs and globalization's accelerated design trends.

At the same time, almost invisibly, an entirely different, labor-driven Brooklyn is taking shape: massive immigration from India, China, the Dominican Republic, Russia, Israel, and Guyana has made present-day Brooklyn a more dynamic place than the old, cozy myths allow. Parts of the borough are bursting with hidden economies. Holding on to Brooklyn's endearing-loser past obscures this new, emerging reality, its opportunities and dislocations.

———————

"Only the Dead Know Brooklyn": how often have I thought of that aptly grim title of Thomas Wolfe's. What did Thomas Wolfe know? you may ask; he grew up in Asheville, North Carolina. True, but he put in his time here; he tried to grasp the borough's true nature. In that short story, he adopts a narrative voice with a thick Brooklyn accent: "Dere's no guy livin' dat knows Brooklyn t'roo an' t'roo, because it'd take a guy a lifetime just to find his way aroun' duh f—— town." Our narrator witnesses a debate after someone asks directions to "Eighteent' Avenoo and Sixty-Sevent' Street." Some say it's in Bensonhurst, others, Flatbush. It turns out the direction seeker is an oddball trying to master Brooklyn by traveling to random places with a map. The narrator attempts to set him straight, telling him to stay out of Red Hook, but he won't listen. "Walkin' aroun' t'roo Red Hook by himself at night an' lookin' at his map! . . . Maybe he's found out by now dat he'll neveh live long enough to know duh whole of Brooklyn."

Only the dead know Brooklyn. Did Wolfe mean that we're all stiffs here, or that the place itself is a morgue? I have to admit that a good part of the borough's terrain seems taken up by cemeteries. The border between Brooklyn and Queens alone has such a concentration of cemeteries it's been called "the city of the dead." By the time you subtract all the smaller graveyards, funeral homes, mortuary headstone firms, et cetera, what are you left with? A sliver for the living.

Maybe I can't help thinking this way because the neighborhood I reside in, Carroll Gardens, has an abundance of funeral parlors: Raccuglia's, Scotto's, Russo's, Pastorelli's, Cobble Hill Chapels, Cucinella's (which specializes in foreign shipping). What saltwater taffy and casinos are to Atlantic City, burial arrangements are to Carroll Gardens. It's an old Italian neighborhood with lots of old Italians, but not enough to keep six funeral parlors thriving. I leave my house in the morning and see the functionaries in black suits running interference for limousines' parking spots, helping the florists make deliveries, or just standing on the street corner looking dignified.

On top of that mortuary concentration, four blocks away from me, just over the Gowanus Canal, is the South Brooklyn Casket Company. Many's the time I've walked by that casket manufacturer and brooded on the brevity of glory. In an effort to penetrate into the twin mysteries of Brooklyn and mortality, I once dialed the number of the South Brooklyn Casket Company that was listed in the phone book, and asked the man at the other end if I might interview him for a magazine article. My request was turned down. "We're not interested in that kind of thing," the gruff voice stonewalled. What kind of thing? I wondered. Transparency? Open disclosure? My suspicions were aroused: what were they shipping in those caskets? A recent tabloid scandal had exposed funeral parlors in the tristate area for hacking up corpses and selling body parts to be transplanted abroad.

I decided to nose around on my own.

On a warm day in March, I strode up Union Street and crossed the verdigris, irenic waters of the Gowanus and stealthily approached my target, careful first to hide notepad and pen. The South Brooklyn Casket Company occupies brick warehouses on both sides of the street. Its offices are located in a slender, aluminum-sided building topped by an American flag. I saw hard-bitten men wheeling caskets and loading them onto the backs of trucks. Trying to appear nonchalant, I wandered over, eavesdropping on two workers speaking in Spanish.

"Where are you taking them?" I asked one of the men, probingly.

"All over," he replied, enigmatically.

There was little more to glean from him, my sharp journalistic instincts told me, so I headed around the corner, knowing that sometimes more can be learned from the back of a building than the front. I peered into its windows, seeing stacks of caskets polished and shiny like new sedans, champagne-colored, taupe, all the season's popular colors. I would not like to be buried in such a metallic-looking sheath. A plain pine box, thank you. Around a truck with Canadian plates, two men were unloading product. "Are those caskets made in Canada?" I asked, shrewdly.

"Yes. We drove 'em down from there this morning," said the trucker, with what I thought was a Cajun accent.

"So . . . South Brooklyn doesn't manufacture its own caskets? It just distributes other companies'?"

"No, they make 'em too."

I had nothing more to ask. My researches had led nowhere. It was true, after all: I would probably have to wait until after I was dead to understand Brooklyn.

Robert Moses Rethought

E rich von Stroheim was billed in his acting days as "the man you love to hate." For the last thirty years, Robert Moses has been cast in that same role, as the villain responsible for everything that went wrong with New York. Even those newly arrived to the city knew enough to boo when his name came up at dinner parties. Moses (1888–1981) lived a long time, and his impact on the physical character of New York City was greater than that of any other individual in its history. This imperious master builder has seemed to many the embodiment of all of modernism's mistakes, gutting cherished working-class neighborhoods with highways, and more interested in big projects and superblocks than in preserving the past with fine-grained restorations. When, in my book *Waterfront*, taking into consideration his many parks, beaches, bridges, and other necessary transportation projects, I argued that Moses had done far more good for the city than bad, and ought to be honored as one of its greatest citizens, a friend castigated me with a note: "Who next, Stalin?"

Moses's satanic reputation with the public can be traced, in the main, to Robert A. Caro's magnificent biography, *The Power Broker: Robert Moses and the Fall of New York.* This irresistible, exhaustively researched masterwork of high journalism imposed a legible through line on its subject's complicated career and turned Moses into a dramatically divided, classically hubristic figure who went from do-gooder idealism to insatiable lust for power. Though Caro's portrait was nuanced, giving the devil his due (especially during the first half, when the "good" Moses reigned), he was still the devil, in the final analysis. And indeed, he has proven a most serviceable devil for conventional master narratives of New York over the last quarter of the twentieth century. But the stories we tell ourselves about how we got where we are need to be altered as circumstances change. Caro's book, with its ominous subtitle, appeared in 1974, when the city did appear to be going under, hit by a fiscal crisis that would verge on default, high crime and drug problems, massive loss of manufacturing jobs, a degraded infrastructure, and population contraction. Since then, the city has rebounded, reinventing itself as the capital of the world, a glamorous, exciting tourist destination, much safer, more prosperous, cosmopolitan, hospitable, and populous than it has ever been. By almost every standard—garbage pickup, Broadway box office sales, increased public transit ridership—it has improved from that low point forty-five years ago.

Maybe it is fair to ask, then, at this moment: If the city is surviving so well, to what extent should we attribute its resiliency to the changes wrought by Robert Moses? If we truly love New York, how can we hate Moses, since he did so much to reshape the city into the one we enjoy now? Such considerations may help explain the extensive revisionist reflection that is suddenly being applied to Moses's legacy. There have been exhibitions devoted to Moses at the Museum of the City of New York, the Queens Museum of Art, and the Wallach Art Gallery at Columbia University. An insightful book, *Robert Moses and the Modern City: The Transformation of New York*, edited by two Columbia professors, Hilary Ballon and Kenneth T. Jackson, has pulled together the diverse strands of current thinking by urbanist scholars, and it recasts its controversial subject in a more balanced light, without whitewashing his flaws.

The book places Moses in a broader context, showing that his decisions were in line with what was happening nationwide and worldwide. While he may have promoted the mystique of his own omnipotence to outfox opponents (which claim his critics took too credulously), he was in fact hemmed in constantly by budgetary, legislative, and special-interest constraints. His brilliance was less as an urban form-giver than as an administrator who kept finding ways to build durably and well in the face of these harsh limits. With consummate opportunism he followed the money trail, at first tapping into local budgets for the construction or improvement of recreational facilities (Jones Beach, Riverside Park, dozens of neighborhood playgrounds, and an astonishing set of public swimming pools) at Governor Al Smith's and Mayor Fiorello La Guardia's behest, then building parkways to get to the parks, then using FDR's New Deal funds for a rash of civic projects, then milking the postwar federal funds for highway construction and massive complexes of public housing. One of his gambits was to turn highway construction into a funding stream through toll collection and the establishment of public benefit corporations, like his cash cow, the Triborough Bridge and Tunnel Authority, which gave him the freedom and resources to operate more autonomously.

It would take too long to enumerate all of Moses's achievements, real and dubious. What needs to be stressed here is his vision of sustaining New York as a middle-class city. He saw that New York was losing its manufacturing base, and he tried to shore up the central city by supporting the growth of cultural institutions, universities, and hospitals. To that end, he brokered deals that brought the city the United Nations, Lincoln Center, two World's Fairs, the expansion of New York University, Fordham, and countless other academic institutions and hospitals. This is the city we live in now, for better or worse, the one in which image and Internet have replaced factories and the port, and health and hospital services have supplanted the garment industry as our number one employer. Foreseeing the increasing polarization of the city into rich and poor, Moses also tried to hold on to the middle class, by setting in motion the construction of tens of thousands of units, some with the aid of unions, such as Co-op City, Washington Square South, University Village, Kips Bay Plaza, Penn South Houses, and Stuyvesant Town.

Mentioning Stuyvesant Town reminds us that Moses did not put up a fight when its sponsor, MetLife, insisted that the project be racially restricted. A pragmatist, cavalier as too many were in his day about racial prejudice, he was more intent on getting those hundreds of units built than on protecting the civil rights of African-Americans. Kenneth Jackson summarizes this thorny subject:

> The important questions, however, are not about whether Moses was prejudiced—no doubt he was—but whether that prejudice was something upon which he acted frequently. . . . The evidence does not support Caro's claims that racism was a defining aspect of Moses's character. . . . Moses did try to place swimming pools and park facilities within the reach of black families and accessible by convenient public transportation. He did not build bridges too low to accommodate buses so that black families would stay away from Jones Beach, nor did he control the water temperature so as to discourage black patronage.

In Moses's implementation of urban renewal, which involved clearing large tracts of inner-city land for university and hospital expansion or middle-class housing, many poor and working-class families were not relocated nearby but displaced to worse neighborhoods. Let us be blunt: these were crimes against the poor. What we now need to do is look in the mirror and ask: Would we take back all those world-attracting amenities, the hospital and university buildings, the cultural complexes, if we could, even knowing that might imperil the city's future economy? The answer is not so simple.

Moses was no nostalgic sentimentalist but a realist, who did not hesitate to intervene in Olmsted and Vaux's masterpieces, Central Park and Prospect Park, by adding zoos, children's playgrounds, and ball fields, because he deemed the fashions in recreation had changed and the public interest demanded it. Some of those changes we have rolled back; others we keep and cherish. As for those highways, regardless of how much we may value today the benefits of mass transit over cars, we can see in retrospect that if Moses had not put in that interconnected highway system for the automotive age, New York City would have strangulated on traffic and stagnated economically. The problem was not that Moses built highways but that, like the Sorcerer's Apprentice, he didn't know when to stop. He had, to use Hilary Ballon's apt description, a "bird's-eye view," a regional, aerial vision when it came to transportation that tended to ignore the little people down below. Having taken care of the perimeter roadways, he began having at the inner city's innards, cutting a brutal swatch with the Cross-Bronx Expressway; and he would have done in Soho with his proposed Lower Manhattan Expressway if he had not been stopped by public outcry.

One of his most vocal opponents was Jane Jacobs, whose 1961 book, *The Death and Life of Great American Cities*, became a rallying point and primer for a new urban aesthetic. It taught us to appreciate the value of neighborhoods, street life, mixed uses, and organic, subtle changes—to redress the overscaling errors of modernist planning. Jacobs's modest, humane vision was a necessary corrective to Moses's technocratic arrogance. But the pendulum may have swung too far; we may have become too timid, too frightened of attempting any large public works. Consider Westway, or the rail freight tunnel, or various garbage-incinerating plants, or the Gehry Guggenheim design for West Houston Street, all worthy ideas shot down by neighborhood opposition. Sometimes a regional solution is called for, and when a neighborhood's NIMBY perspective clashes with the city's overall good, the former should not necessarily prevail over the latter. What New Yorkers are finally coming to understand, in this season of reevaluating their master builder, is that the choice between a Jane Jacobs and a Robert Moses, between neighborhood preservation and large-scale planning, is a false one. We need both.

City Hall and Its Park

New York City is too infinite to have a center, too hot and cold to locate its putative heart. But if one place can claim a measure of symbolism for the metropolis, it is City Hall and its adjoining park. Surrounded by Park Row, which once housed the legendary newspapers of James Gordon Bennett, Horace Greeley, Joseph Pulitzer, and William Randolph Hearst, and now plays host to more contemporary media via J&R Music and Computer World; by that majestic cathedral skyscraper, the Woolworth Building, with its beige and taupe terra-cotta cladding; by the muscular Municipal Building, a McKim, Mead & White wedding cake of Stalinist-architecture bulk; abutting the on-ramp to the Brooklyn Bridge; by the ghost of what was formerly Ellen's Coffee Shop, run by an ex–Miss Subways; and by the masses of civil servants on lunch break, shoppers frequenting bargain discount outlets, and criminals paroled from a nearby jail, the Tombs, all strolling up Chambers Street—City Hall itself is both grace note and anomaly.

An eighteenth-century *petit palais* built at the inception of the nineteenth (1802–1812), it stubbornly offers up its classical charms, looking nobly trim, without an ounce of imperial pomposity, its modest scale suggesting the perfect administrative headquarters for a city of, say, 200,000. There is something droll about this dollhouse structure, set amid skyscrapers, continuing to serve as the command post for the mayor and the city council of twenty-first-century New York.

I remember the first time I saw City Hall. I was being honored there, along with other sixth graders, for my composition on fire prevention. At twelve, what did I care about fire prevention? I was a hack, like most early achievers, turning out facile prose for my masters. The call would come down from the Board of Education for an essay competition on some benign civic topic such as Brotherhood or the Four Freedoms, and I would oblige, usually to no avail. This time I got lucky. On a sunny June day I sat on a folding chair with the other district winners, all of us goody-goodies, and listened to the fire commissioner's speech, and went up the City Hall steps to receive my Little Hot Spot silver medal. Then (I would like to imagine) I looked up at the graceful relic and my heart swelled with antiquarian pride and architectural ardor. But I know better.

You step back and think, My God, it's stood up well! But this, you discover, is not the original façade: weather, air pollution, and pigeon droppings had weakened the original soft marble surface to such an extent that, in the early 1950s, every stone, column, and capital carving had to be duplicated in sturdier materials—an amazing labor of love, testifying to the irreplaceable nature of this building in New York's mythology. The interior, though also restored, is closer to its original character. And it is the interior that is really the dazzling part, with its twin spiral staircases drawing the eye upward to the building's Corinthian rotunda. Inside, all is curved, sinuous, coquettish, in contrast to the exterior's bluff, rectangular symmetry, so that the effect is of achieving the impossible: placing a round peg in a square hole.

Paul Morand, a French writer who wrote a fine travel book about the city, *New York* (1930), penned this chauvinistic appreciation of the building:

It is not false Louis XVI, as the Woolworth is false Gothic. The City Hall was erected at the beginning of the nineteenth century by Joseph Mangin, a French architect, in association with the Scotsman John McComb, Jr. (the Frenchman was evidently the artist, and the other the contractor, for this hall is so pure a taste that it can only be of French birth). New York can laugh in turn at the false Renaissance

style of the Hôtel de Ville of Paris. The City Hall, the third building of its succession in New York, harbors great historic memories:
here it was that Lafayette was received in triumph, and here a people
filed before the corpse of the murdered Lincoln. Its style is authentic,
from the curved ceilings, the graceful pillars, the lines of the dome,
the primitive bareness of the vestibule, the classical feeling of the rotunda, to the galleries where the early magistrates of New York gaze
in effigy on the visitor with all the majesty of English lord mayors.

One tends to forget that New York is not so young; it is older than St.
Petersburg. At times, as the poet George Oppen has noted, "it seems
the oldest city in the world." But most of seventeenth- and eighteenth-
century Manhattan has been destroyed, if not by fire then by the high
cost of real estate, leaving City Hall as perhaps the oldest structure still
functioning as it was originally intended (i.e., not retired to being a museum house). A decade before it was built, around 1790, New York had
lost its status as the young nation's capital to Washington, D.C. Freed
from the stodgy atmosphere of national policy-making bureaucracy, it
could develop an identity more intensely focused on mercantile and cultural interests, a more polyglot, speedy nature. The city fathers' choice
of Mangin and McComb's sophisticated architectural contest entry for
their final City Hall shows a certain awareness of and confidence in the
destiny ahead.

City Hall was supposed to anchor the northernmost point of development, which is why the building faces south. The rear of the building
was originally clad in brownstone, not marble, to save money and, legend has it, because no one thought the city would ever extend any farther
north, though I find this hard to believe: the grid plan of 1811 already
called for rectangles to march up the length of Manhattan to Washington
Heights and beyond. Today City Hall seems to be perversely ignoring
the majority of its constituents as it eyes the narrow bunion of land, the
original Dutch colony of New Amsterdam, from which the city sprang.
But in a sense, the building's symmetry and siting marked the beginning
of a more formal approach to town planning, and foretold the abandon-

ment of the twisty New Amsterdam street layout for the geometric grid structure that New York would ultimately follow.

A century later, Henry James marveled in *The American Scene* (1907) that one can still go anywhere inside this City Hall, with an American confidence that "the public, the civic building is his very own." He compared such "penetration" to the "romantic thrill" of "some assault of the dim seraglio, with the guards bribed, the eunuchs drugged and one's life carried in one's hand." In his own exploration, he "made so free with the majority of things" that he came "into the presence of the Representative of the highest office with which City Halls are associated." Still, he worried, with characteristic Old World snobbery, whether such easy "penetralia" might rob the building of its impressiveness and prestige.

These days, your approach to City Hall, both outer steps and interior, is barred by a black wrought-iron fence and two sheds, one on either side of the building, containing metal detectors and presided over by a pair of armed policemen, who will direct you firmly away unless you are there on "official business," or have registered with an official tour. Lamentable as seems this erosion of democratic access from James's day, you would like to believe it is due to post-9/11 caution; but, in fact, the area was first closed off to the public by Mayor Rudy Giuliani before the planes ever struck the World Trade Center. In any case, it is a pity that you can no longer even dawdle on the steps of the building: something significant has been lost to the public realm and to the public's imagination.

The twelve steps in front of City Hall retain their function as the place where mayors are sworn in, ceremonial speeches are made, distinguished visitors receive the key to the city, and heroes are awarded medals. In the past, political protests, uniformed picketers, garbage strikers, school decentralization battles, all came to roost here. The rallies are still permitted, with a permit, but protesters are no longer allowed to attract a crowd, so that they seem pathetically to be addressing themselves, bent on boosting their own morale, like the small contingent I see today, chanting "They say poverty wage!—We say union wage!" Meanwhile a young male lawyer in a gray suit, ignoring the protesters and holding an attaché case, converses with a woman colleague, also in a woolen suit, chocolate brown, in the heat of summer, while their underlings, jacketless but sporting ties, carry expandable folders crammed with legal papers. Just west, where the overflow crowd used to congregate, sits a parking lot for official cars. In other words, the space in front and to the side of City Hall, once allotted for civic congregation, has been chopped up and ceded to the powers that be. The fence-protected lawn also hosts tasteful modern sculpture, part of the Public Art Fund supported enthusiastically by Mayor Michael Bloomberg, which you can enjoy from a distance beyond the palings—this curated, professionally vetted artwork now having more right to City Hall's proximity than the citizenry. It is only after you get beyond the zone directly surrounding City Hall and head south toward what remains of City Hall Park that the feeling of public space takes over again and you experience something like the originally intended "commons."

It is a pleasure to see how amicably the park is used by so many different types: office workers, vagrants, tourists, mothers with strollers. The formula seems so simple: if you want people to frequent a public space, all you need to do, as William H. Whyte sagely observed, is provide seats for them. City Hall Park has a plenitude of benches. The mature, fully grown shade trees help immensely in providing a comfortable atmosphere. For public space to function as naturally and successfully as does City Hall Park, it takes a historic walking city, a tolerable climate, and a habit of malingering. Chinese families cut through the park on their way to East Broadway and Chinatown; a troop of African-American children on a field trip pause in their march and spread over several benches; Hasidic Jews hurry to their destination. A middle-aged, chubby man in a Hawaiian shirt reads a tourist brochure on the Greek Islands. On the next bench a drunk lies sprawled, sleeping it off. Some Latino children splash ecstatically at the edge of the gorgeous, slender fountain that centers the park. Their mother yells, "Get over here! Get over here!" They run to her side and submit to inspection. "Look at the way you look, and now we have to go on the train!"

The flower beds have been artfully planted. Still, the park has a ragged, scruffy look, it is never immaculate; the grass holds its share of wrappers, tissues, cellophane, coffee cup lids. A small price to pay, it would seem, for popularity. With sirens, car alarms, Broadway and Brooklyn Bridge traffic swirling around, you can't honestly call the park an oasis of tranquillity. It's something else again: an unapologetic feast of urbanism.

I would be derelict in my duty as cicerone if I failed to mention another distinguished, albeit notorious building in City Hall Park, not far from our beloved landmark and far exceeding it in bulk. This is the Old New York County Courthouse, a handsome Victorian structure which took twenty years (1858–1878) to build, and provided the opportunity for enormous graft, kickbacks, and pocketing of public funds. Indeed, the Tweed Ring, a political machine under the control of William "Boss" Tweed, was said to have made off with $10 million out of the $14 million (in old dollars!) budgeted for construction. Despite the scandal attached to the edifice, it has inspired considerable attachment among architectural historians and New York City buffs, and was recently restored and converted into headquarters for the Board of Education. Tweed himself has been undergoing a rehabilitation of sorts by revisionist historians, who argue that the patronage system he presided over, however nepotistic and venal, at least gave many workingmen and new immigrants employment and the occasional, needed handout of food, clothing, and burial expenses, in exchange for their votes.

So "this imperfect triangle of City Hall Park" (to quote the 1939 *WPA Guide to New York City*) can be read as an allegory, embodying the metropolis's three basic types of democratic expression: a formally elected, representative democracy, as exemplified by the dignified self-containment of City Hall itself; a more corrupt (and what is more typically New York than corruption?) but approachable, direct access to power, symbolized by Tweed's courthouse; and, finally, the Whitmanesque democratic spirit, characterized by the pedestrian flow and eye contact in the public spaces of this great city, where the people exercise their sovereign prerogatives of movement and leisure.

Walking the High Line

When, in June 2009, the High Line park opened to the public, it was declared an almost unqualified success. Some architecture critics nitpicked the design, but basically they endorsed it, and ordinary folk (I include myself in that category), less fastidious, greeted it with enthusiasm. Crowds lined up for hours to have the elevated promenade experience, it became a (free) hot-ticket item in New York City, which typically overembraces a novelty for six months, then ignores it. Especially in hot weather, the challenge soon became to grab one of the reclining benches on the sundeck and tan yourself for hours, while envious masses stumbled by. The crowded, restless carnival-grounds movement of the park-goers aboveground rhymed the pedestrian conveyor-belt effect of the gridded streets below: Manhattan is a place where loitering in one place is done at your peril. Paris has boulevard cafés for cooling one's heels, Rome comes to a rest at fountains and piazzas, but in Manhattan you keep moving forward. Well and good: I approve.

The High Line kicks off at Gansevoort Street, in the meatpacking district of Greenwich Village, and continues northward to Chelsea. A second phase, from West Twenty-First Street to West Thirtieth Street, opened in time for the summer of 2011. The crowds continue to come, and the trees in the initially opened sections have already grown to an impressive, even alarming height, so that at times one has the impression of filing into a forest. The glory of the High Line as presently reconstituted lies in its variety of spatial and recreational situations: narrow and wide paths, decked and open-air routes, limited and broad views of the city, beach-like lolling areas, conceptual artworks. The northernmost, recently opened section offers a charming green lawn, a thrillingly sharp curve, and a vast, magical cityscape facing northward, over the sunken Thirtieth Street West Side Rail Yards. A final spur, from West Thirty-First to West Thirty-Fourth Street, is still in negotiation, depending on the future dispensation of the West Side Rail Yards. (These are the very same rail yards once inadvisably proposed for a Jets football stadium, a proposal blessedly defeated, though there are still plans afoot for a massive skyscraper complex to arise on platforms which would be built over the yards; should the recession ever end and this development come to pass, good-bye magnificent northern vista.) If at this stage the High Line seems a bridge to nowhere, petering out anticlimactically at around West Thirtieth Street, much enjoyment or distraction is available along the way: people watching, ambitious if palette-restrained garden plantings, the varied seating arrangements and viewing platforms, a delightful amphitheater with wooden benches that faces a pane of glass framing the traffic below.

The fact that this new amenity sprang from older industrial infrastructure says a lot about the current moment in New York's evolution. A city that had once pioneered so many technological and urban planning solutions, that had dazzled the world with its public works, its skyscrapers, bridges, subways, water-delivery system, its Central Park, palatial train stations, libraries, and museums, appears unable to undertake any innovative construction on a grand scale, and is now consigned to cannibalizing its past and retrofitting it to function as an image, a consumable spectacle. Productivity has given way to narcissism; or, to put it more charitably, work has yielded to leisure.

———

My first encounter with the High Line occurred before its present reconstruction. On a frigid winter day, a few years back, I found myself walking in air, as it were, through and yet above the familiar streets of Manhattan's West Side. I was only at second-story eye level, and yet that modest extra altitude (eighteen to thirty feet) made for a profoundly different peripatetic perspective: as in a dream where suddenly you can walk through walls, I was passing in and out of manufacturing buildings, staring into the backyards of private residences, saluting the Gothic Revival redbrick fortress of the General Theological Seminary, and hovering within sight of the waterfront like a seagull. That the route felt this magically exhilarating to a first-timer, on a day of such inhospitable weather, convinced me the High Line would make a wonderful urban prospect in any and every season.

What remains of the High Line is a 1.45-mile elevated rail structure that was built in the 1930s to move rail freight parallel to, and about a block east of, the docks along the western spine of Manhattan Island. A mere thirty years later it was deemed obsolete, due to the trucking industry's domination over rail freight and the removal of the Port of New York to nearby New Jersey. It stood for several decades as a characteristic piece of abandoned industrial infrastructure, such as has increasingly come to litter the American urban landscape. Both as a discarded engineering marvel and as a defunct railroad line that could metamorphose into a "rail trail," it offered a highly visible, symbolic opportunity for historic preservation through adaptive reuse.

Being a native New Yorker, skeptical by birth and by a lifetime's exposure to jive planning schemes, I was frankly not expecting to be enthralled by the experience of walking the High Line. I'd passed the raised, rusty brown metalwork railings for years without their registering sharply on my consciousness. (It doesn't look like much from the street; then again, you only see it at the crosswalks.) But ever since the notion of turning the viaduct into an elevated park first appeared in the media, I'd been dying to take a look. Joel Sternfeld's evocative photographs in *The New Yorker* of the High Line as a sort of junkyard meadow further whetted my appetite. Still, I knew I would have to call in several favors for permission to see it, and the prospect of thus abasing myself deterred me, until the magazine *Preservation* requested I write an article about it, providing the perfect excuse for entry.

CSX, the railroad company that at that point still owned the High Line (having inherited it, along with other properties, from a bankrupt

Conrail), assigned me a guide, Laurie, for my meander. Laurie swore me to secrecy in print about our method of gaining access to the overhead railroad line (I will say that it involved climbing from the back window of a Chelsea building onto the tracks). Until the property could be transferred over to the city government and turned into safe public space, CSX had no desire to let curiosity seekers wander there, not only because it *was* private property but because broken glass and potholes bestrewed the terrain, inviting twisted ankles and insurance suits.

We walked along the tracks, which were covered with a high meadow of weeds and wildflowers, planted willy-nilly by wind-borne seeds. It was certainly mythic, this vision of Nature surging back to reclaim the postindustrial landscape. There was also something "retro-futurist" about the High Line, reminiscent of Hugh Ferriss's fantastic 1929 *Metropolis of Tomorrow* drawings, where New York was envisioned as giddily multileveled, with elevated roads and walkways threading the skyscrapers.

One unique aspect of the High Line is that it was built in the middle of the block. At the time it went up, the public was already turning against elevated structures, such as El trains, on the grounds that their shadows gloomed the adjoining streets. It was therefore sensibly proposed that the project be erected midblock, and run through buildings of such massive industrial nature as could absorb a rail line in their midst and profit from its freight deliveries. Though the viaduct did pass by smaller residential structures, these were mostly tenements and sailors' boardinghouses; the line could never have been permitted to barrel through or by well-off apartment houses. In any event, walking the High Line that first time, I found myself looking usually at the backs of commercial buildings, a more furtive, piquant sight than offered by their street façades. Whereas the fronts of these buildings boast whatever decorative pretensions they might possess, their posteriors are barer, balder, with rear entrances, backyards, fire escapes, chimneys, parti-walls patched with tar. The effect is like spying on their private, unguarded existence.

The High Line's metal railings facing the cross streets sport handsome Art Deco details, but in an economy move, the railings not visible from the street below were constructed of blunt metal pipes. Another curiosity is that the outer railings could be manufactured only in straight angles, so that, where the train rails curved, a triangular addition had to be inserted outward for the railings to meet. These jutting nooks, which were filled with muddy, stagnant water when I encountered them on my first visit, were sure to make admirable lookouts when drained and weatherproofed.

There is a breathtakingly dramatic, unobstructed view around Twenty-Third Street, gazing west at the Chelsea Piers and the Hudson River, where the High Line suddenly widens from thirty to sixty feet. You can also see Hudson River Park, the newish bicycle-pedestrian corridor snaking its way along the river's edge. Running parallel to each other, a city block apart, the High Line and Hudson River Park seem almost to be siblings in their efforts to open the waterfront to the public. If I prefer the former, it is partly because Hudson River Park can never escape its proximity to the jangling traffic of Route 9A—a rebuilt West Side Highway in the guise of a boulevard—whereas the High Line, raised above the street, is separated from motor vehicles, and gives us an eerier, slower, quieter experience of the city. We feel lordly, seeing the metropolis we do every day, but from a more protected and contemplative viewpoint. In that respect, the High Line functions like *The Gates,* Christo and Jeanne-Claude's intervention in Central Park, whose chief virtue was that it redirected our attention to the lineaments of Olmsted and Vaux's masterpiece, or Olafur Eliasson's temporary waterfall plunging off the Brooklyn Bridge. Maybe we have grown so jaded to the modern city's beauty that we will increasingly need such reframing aids to rekindle our admiration and awe.

The High Line was originally built in the early 1930s to transport all manner of freight, but particularly New York's daily supplies of butter, milk, eggs, cheese, dressed poultry, and meat (conveniently, it passed through the Gansevoort meat market). Before it was constructed, the New York Central Railroad had operated a rail freight line at grade, or street level, along Tenth Avenue, and men on horseback ("West Side cowboys") had ridden ahead of the train with red flags or lanterns to warn pedestrians of its coming; yet even with this picturesque alarm system, so many careless, inebriated, or simply unlucky citizens had gotten run over that the street acquired the notorious name Death Avenue. For over seventy years, since the midnineteenth century, public outcry had agitated against this danger to life and limb, demanding a safer solution: thus, the High Line.

The removal of tracks from the city streets was a link in a much more ambitious master plan, the original West Side Improvement, overseen by Robert Moses. The New York Central freight line had run at grade through Riverside Park as well, and Moses, then parks commissioner, saw an opportunity to conceal the lines by building a platform over them, meanwhile greatly widening the park. The freight cars would then proceed south underground to the Thirtieth Street–West Side Rail Yards, after which they would ascend, via the High Line, all the way down to the then newly constructed St. John's Park Terminal, a huge twelve-story building that covered four city blocks, bounded by West, Washington, Spring, and Clarkson Streets, at the border of Greenwich Village and Soho. There the High Line would debouch into the terminal's vast second floor and the freight would be sorted for its final destinations.

A *New York Times* reporter waxed enthusiastic at the opening of the High Line on June 3, 1934: "High in the air, it cuts through city blocks. It passes into big buildings in its path and emerges on the other side to continue on its way, leaping any cross streets it meets. Along its new aerial course large new buildings have already been erected, and others are under construction for packing companies and similar concerns."

The vision was for a whole manufacturing and refrigerated warehouse district to spring up, spurred by proximity to the waterfront's port cargo. The president of New York Central, F. E. Williamson, predicted at a dedication ceremony for the West Side Viaduct:

With the completion of the West Side Improvement, of which this viaduct is one of the more important features, West Side manufacturers, distributors and merchants in general will have transportation facilities unsurpassed anywhere. I think it is a safe prediction to say that in time this viaduct and other portions of the route will be covered with air-right buildings whose tenants can bring in their raw materials and ship out their finished products swiftly, safely and efficiently over rails at their very doors. This simple event today may well mark a transformation of the West Side that will affect its development for the better for decades to come.

Some of that transformation did occur: the National Biscuit Company, the Morgan Parcel Post building, the Merchants' Refrigerating Company, and other factories and packing houses congregated around and benefited from the line. The preexisting Bell Telephone Laboratories provided a particular engineering challenge: special design precautions had to be taken, including laying new foundations, to insulate the laboratory's delicate equipment from excessive noise and vibrations during the railroad line's construction and subsequent operation, straight through the building itself.

The double-line viaduct, built of steel with concrete floor construction, was strong enough to supply two fully loaded freight trains—overbuilt, in fact, since the thought had been that trains would keep getting bigger and heavier, which didn't happen. What did happen was that trucks and airplanes cut so significantly into the rail freight business that by the 1960s the railroad line was operating deeply in the red. The southern part of the structure, which ran from Greenwich Village's Gansevoort Street to St. John's Park Terminal at Houston Street (some fifteen city blocks away), was dismantled. A great shame and missed opportunity, in retrospect, though it seemed to bother no one at the time. The last freight delivery on the remaining northern part of the line took place in 1980. There that northern section sat, awaiting the wrecking ball, its complete demise deferred only by the interminable litigation that accompanies any property matter in New York City.

Then, in 1999, the Friends of the High Line, started by Joshua David and Robert Hammond, campaigned for the structure to be turned into an elevated public promenade. This idea, at first improbably romantic, began to gain momentum, thanks to its organizers' political acumen and ability to attract A-list supporters, but also to the lack of valid reasons why it shouldn't be done. The structure was sound; it would require a sophisticated new design for pedestrian access and repaving, but not that much overhauling. With a newly elected mayor, Michael Bloomberg, enthusiastically behind it (New York's previous mayor, Rudy Giuliani, had been all for tearing the line down), and the High Line's owner, CSX, amenable to turning over the facility to public use, it only awaited approval by a Washington railroad oversight bureau (and the settling of a legal challenge by one recalcitrant property owner) to become a reality.

Key to advancing the promenade idea was the Federal Railbanking legislation, which had been drawn up to protect defunct railroad lines from seizure by adjoining property owners, by putting them in a "railbank." This provision ensured that, even if the rails were physically removed, the route itself would not be lost as a national resource, and could be returned to rail use at some later date for national security or other reasons. In the meantime, some routes could be converted into "rail trails," allowing walkers to promenade picturesquely past rivers or suburban neighborhoods. Obviously, when the abandoned rail line ran through a busy city neighborhood, the permit process would become much more complex and the perambulation a different experience.

As it happened, there already existed an extraordinarily successful model for the conversion of an abandoned railroad into an elevated urban walk: the Promenade Plantée in Paris. I visited that facility one summer, when it was so lushly abloom it looked like a levitating botanical garden. My first thought was, the French really know how to pull off this sort of show; we could never manage to do it so elegantly in New York. The Parisian promenade is also much wider than the one in Manhattan, and the total walking distance is longer, so its landscaping opportunities are consequently more lavish. Added to which, their original line was built for passenger service, not freight, and the adjoining 12th Arrondissement is a residential neighborhood rather than a manufacturing zone, which makes for a cozier surround of private flats, skylights, mansards, and Art Nouveau apartment houses. Finally, the Paris viaduct is a freestanding edifice, built on top of large vaulted spaces, which have been converted into fancy boutiques that sell furniture, computers, or wine, and which draw shoppers to the elevated park. There is no way the underside of New York's High Line could ever be turned over to similar retail uses, particularly since much of it already passes through buildings and is not even visible from the street. In short, the High Line could never be anything as *grand* as its Parisian counterpart. But it could be more peculiar, fugitively spying on the workaday, like a coal tram passing into and out of mountain seams.

The High Line passes through West Chelsea, a "neighborhood in transition"—usually the euphemism for blight but, in this case, the opposite. What began as a ragtag assemblage of warehouses, factory buildings, and four-story tenements has been transformed, in the last decade, through Manhattan real estate mania, into a high-end art district: the large floors of unbroken space, formerly given over to industry, have proven perfect for chic, austere galleries displaying large sculpture or multimedia installations. Meanwhile, restaurants, watering holes, Japanese tearooms, and ancillary cultural offices have taken root near the galleries. The new Chelsea, which has supplanted Soho as New York's premiere art district, flaunts a spacious interior aesthetic that makes the most of its industrial origins (exposed timbers, tin ceilings, concrete columns), embracing plain, functional warehouse architecture as the new purity. In a densely crammed city where space-envy trumps all other deadly sins, several thousand unobstructed square feet in a Chelsea art gallery translate visually into the quintessence of good taste.

Looking east from the High Line, along Tenth Avenue, you also see an atypical (for Manhattan) number of parking lots, taxi garages, gas stations. They bring their own raffish film noir atmosphere to the area. But these underused lots also read ominously, to the New Yorker's trained, nervous eye, as markers held in place for future speculative high-rise development. Here we face a paradox: the Friends of the High Line have defended the expense of constructing and maintaining a free elevated promenade by saying that there is no need for this public space to pay for itself; its costs will be more than offset by the increased real estate values of properties abutting the new amenity. True enough: but raised real estate taxes will only spur owners of the land to compensate by developing their own properties. The many unobstructed views the High Line presently offers, thanks to the generally low height of buildings and parking lots alongside its route, could dramatically change, should a wall of luxury high-rise spring up on either or both sides. This is already starting to happen.

Much of the High Line's present magic stems from its passing through a historic industrial cityscape roughly the same age as the viaduct, supplemented by private tenement backyards and the poetic grunge of taxi garages. It would make a huge difference if High Line walkers were to feel trapped in a canyon of spanking new high-rise condos, providing ant-like visual entertainment for one's financial betters lolling on balconies. The High Line exemplifies a preservation conundrum: how do you not only protect the older structure itself, through intelligent adaptive reuse, but also retain the flavor of its original surrounding context? A certain amount of luxury high-rise will inevitably occur along this route: the question is how much. Only strict zoning regulations might prevent a forest of new apartment buildings from flanking the High Line, but the city seems to be encouraging more, rather than less, high-rise residential development in the Far West Side. We can only pray that the current recession, which has temporarily brought a halt to some of the new construction, will last as long as possible.

While wringing our hands, we should also remember that, when the High Line was built, one of its initial purposes was to spur "air rights" development over the site. Living cities change and grow; they cannot remain picturesquely frozen in time. Whatever happens, the High Line will still afford spectacular unobstructed views eastward, at street corners, and westward, at a good many spots, to the river.

———

It seems another paradox that fragments of the industrial past can be preserved only if they are willing to relinquish their uses. In their postindustrial phase, cities are undergoing a complex revaluation: factory buildings, once regarded as soul-destroying blights on neighborhoods, "dark, satanic mills," have come to be cherished as honest, noble architecture, and then converted into festival marketplaces. The infrastructure of viaducts, overpasses, elevated highways has evolved, in a hundred years, from engineering marvel through hideous eyesore to charming troglodyte Erector set. The industrial archaeology movement, which began in Europe, has done much to enlighten city dwellers about the historic and aesthetic values of these remnants. Other, more pragmatic motives are at work, of course: space-hungry metropolises, looking to turn over their last available undeveloped land to a mix of recreation, office, housing, and retail, find such parcels mainly in their emptied-out manufacturing zones. So brownfields are tamed, power plants converted to museums, and chimney stacks treated like venerable memento mori, as castle ruins were regarded in the Romantic period.

I've sometimes thought the best, most radical use of the High Line would have been to restore it to its original function. New York, alone among major American cities, has no freight rail delivery system, making it overly dependent on trucks, which pollute the environment and raise local asthma rates alarmingly. A rail freight tunnel under New York Harbor has been sensibly proposed, and never built, for close to a century. So the High Line was hardly redundant. CSX, shortly after it took over the line, did a study to see if it made financial sense to employ the elevated structure again for moving freight, and decided in the negative. Here we may pause to ask whether a wise national policy might have yielded another outcome: since the triumph of the airline and automotive industries over shipping and rail freight did not come about merely through impersonal "laws of the marketplace" but was aided by countless governmental subsidies, direct and indirect, could we not have developed a more sanely balanced transportation policy? And should we not fight for one still? Pragmatically speaking, it was probably too late to return the High Line ever to rail freight service—it would have cost too much to rebuild the southern, dismantled section, and the present upscale Chelsea community would never stand for a noisy reactivated railroad line in its midst—so we may as well just guiltlessly enjoy the new promenade.

Anyone who had the good fortune, as I did, to walk the High Line in its "natural" state cannot help wishing that more of its self-seeded, primeval meadow look had been retained. But to make it safe for the public to walk on, the entire surface—uneven, potholed concrete, gravel, debris, rails, soil, and meadow—had to be stripped, and the lead paint removed: there was no getting around that fact. A competition was held for the redesign of the High Line, and the winning design team, James Corner Field Operations (landscape architects) and Diller Scofidio + Renfro (architects), devised clever, cutting-edge solutions for retaining some of the unruly charm of the city-pasture wilderness into which it had fortuitously evolved. The new surface consists of planking composed of precast concrete, which meanders in a winding path along the High Line's length. The planks (sometimes diverging into two smaller paths, sometimes rising up or dipping down) taper and blend into the plantings, and vice versa, so that the effect is of grass coming up through cracks in the pavement. The planned mix of native grasses, flowering meadow, and woodland thicket suggests a conscious effort to retain some of the scruffy, weed-like feeling (as opposed to a formal French garden), with emphasis on wildflowers and self-sustaining, low-maintenance plants that can coexist. Of course the landscaping is still in its earliest stages, and we won't get the full effect for at least another twenty years. The plantings will vary seasonally, attuned to patterns of visual interest, much as with the city's green roof gardens, and with the same sort of soil and drainage considerations, or headaches.

The aesthetic effect of the High Line as a whole may be more busily contrived than beautiful, more self-consciously theoretical than inevitable, in a way that sums up the dilemma of making new public spaces or monuments during a period when late modernist minimalism and fussy postmodernism have fought to a standstill. Still, the resulting design is as good as these things get nowadays. So I am happy with it—as I would be with any new public space that worked, in this era of relentless privatization.

Since the promenade needed to be made easy to get up to and off of, access has been provided in the form of regularly placed stairways, and a few elevator-stairway combinations. Some of the entrances are designed to deliver the public from the street to midpromenade in a rather gradual manner, through stairs and ramps which offer a chance to inspect the undersides of the elevated structure, its steel girders and hand-hammered rivets, and appreciate its engineering sophistication, while preparing visitors for the amble aboveground. In its proposal, the design team promised to "refer to" the freight rail line by reinstalling a few rail fragments, which they have done, as well as letting the planking system "evoke" the rails themselves. (*Refer to* and *evoke* are architectural jargon that usually means the eradication of history, followed by reinsertion of obscure design metaphors meant to be read as palimpsests.) It would be a tall order indeed to get tourists or, for that matter, native New Yorkers to perceive the High Line's historical place as an essential link in the ambitious West Side Improvement, that is, in a massively integrated regional transportation system that included the then-ubiquitous piers, the Holland and Lincoln Tunnels, the George Washington Bridge, the lighter system that floated railroad cars on barges from New Jersey rail terminals across the Hudson River, where they were brought into the Starrett-Lehigh Building's enormous elevators, loaded onto trains of the High Line, and sent a few miles south to St. John's Park Terminal. Nor, even with the best efforts to illustrate this past through design cues or interpretative signage, would it be easy to convey what a daring engineering feat once was necessary to hack through existing buildings without unsettling them.

So let us not exaggerate the educational effectiveness of High Line Park as a history lesson. Some strollers may experience it more as a dinky curiosity than an archival thrill, a sort of tame, horizontal roller coaster that has ground to a halt. Still, what matters is that a piece of the freight rail line has been rescued from extinction, and that the city will have gained a well-used, effective public space, which offers an escape from the street at the same time as an intriguingly fresh angle on it. If this mysterious structure vexes the visitor with unanswered questions, that is all to the good. May it also stir the imaginations of future urbanists, and send them back to the library to understand what such an improbably elevated promenade was once all about.

Getting the South Wrong

What do I know about the South? Practically nothing. But ever since Montaigne, lack of knowledge has often served as the starting point for personal essays. Perhaps if I can fruitfully interrogate my misconceptions, my ignorance, my flat-earth notions, it will throw into sharper relief the experts' deeper insights.

I first became conscious of the South when I was growing up in Brooklyn, in a largely black neighborhood. Surrounded as I was by a Southern black ambience transplanted to Brooklyn—all the great touring gospel choirs sang at the church on our block, and we could hear their lusty voices and the congregation's clapping and shouting—I became infatuated with black culture. I fell in love with the blues, but my deepest respect was reserved for the so-called pure country blues of 78 rpm recordings: Blind Lemon Jefferson, Robert Johnson. Even the urban blues musicians I listened to, such as John Lee Hooker and Muddy Waters, had to have a Southern pedigree.

The South seemed the cradle of all the music I loved, and I dreamed of going there. True, it was frightening, with Governor Faubus ranting racist nonsense and dignified Autherine Lucy having to walk a gauntlet through spitting crowds on her way to school; but I instinctively rejected the North's smugness that we were more tolerant, since I knew the North to be equally segregated residentially. I was at least halfway prepared to accept the Southern apologists' argument that more intimacy and warmth existed between the races down South because of the way blacks and whites were raised together, although it did seem fishy to me that all this interracial closeness among Southern children should suddenly transform itself into venom at age fifteen. In sum, I was attracted to the *idea* of the South, not least because it was a little scary.

During the 1950s and 1960s, there was another element in the attraction that Northerners with some cultural pretension felt toward the South, or what we took to be the South. I am speaking of the infatuation filmmakers and actors trained in the Actors Studio had for that region. A partial list of relevant titles would include *Cat on a Hot Tin Roof, Pinky, The Chase, The Fugitive Kind, Panic in the Streets, Sweet Bird of Youth, The Long, Hot Summer*, and *The Sound and the Fury*, but would not alone capture the flavor of that collision. One has only to watch Eli Wallach, the quintessential New York Jewish actor, trying to warp his Brooklyn accent into a plantation drawl while drooling over the sex kitten Carroll Baker, in Elia Kazan's overwrought *Baby Doll*, to appreciate that, for these ethnic Northerners, first- or second-generation European immigrants, the South was both the exotic Other, home to a jungle of deliciously primitive id emotions, and an analogous ghetto, with its somehow familiar emotional mother tongue.

How or why these practitioners of the Method, rooted in Stanislavsky, Yiddish theater, and the thirties political Left, made such a smooth transference to the South is fascinating to consider. The Actors Studio constellation wanted to be in what we would now call independent movies, and were naturally drawn to adaptations of culturally prestigious properties. If the greatest living novelist, William Faulkner, and the greatest living playwright, Tennessee Williams, were Southerners, opportunism alone dictated it might be a good idea to stake out a Southern franchise. The legitimate theater was the crucial third corner of the triangle between movies of that period and the South. Elia Kazan, the driving force between the postwar marriage of Broadway and Hollywood, had made his reputation directing Williams's plays onstage, and he went on to specialize in Southern locale movies (*Pinky, Panic in the Streets, A Streetcar Named Desire, Baby Doll, A Face in the Crowd, Wild River*). It was convenient for him to cast the character actors he trusted from past stage

collaborations, like Zero Mostel, Rip Torn, and Eli Wallach. Other directors, such as Martin Ritt, Richard Brooks, and Sidney Lumet, readily cast
as Southerners stage veterans such as Geraldine Page, Ed Begley, E. G.
Marshall, Barbara Bel Geddes, and Maureen Stapleton. Nebraska-born
Marlon Brando made a habit of playing Southerners, as did Cleveland-
born Paul Newman. So it was that movies based in the South became a
kind of summer stock for New York Method actors.

Another attraction was what might be called the Freudian connection. Thanks partly to the themes developed by Williams, Faulkner,
Flannery O'Connor, and Carson McCullers, the South came to be seen
as a swamp of incest, homoeroticism, cretinism, gigolos kept by older
women and child-women kept by older men, castration, impotence, a
fulminating passel of Big Daddys (Lee J. Cobb, Burl Ives, and Luther
Adler bellowing their gored-ox versions of Southern patriarchs), hysterical spinsters . . . The South seemed a place where women acted
superficially like neurasthenics but were sluts underneath; where men,
when not delivering flowery speeches about the moon, often brayed like
animals in heat; and where youngsters lay their heads on their big black
Mammy's breast, like the famous Ruth Orkin photograph of Julie Harris
and Ethel Waters at the cast party for *Member of the Wedding*. In other
words, all bubbling subconscious drives were brought to the surface,
which was catnip to the Actors Studio crowd, for whom psychoanaly-
sis had immense cachet. The South became a code, liberating the filmmaker to explore taboo subjects. It was as though anthropologists had
found a tribe where the unrepressed continued to thrive, where they still
yelled at the dinner table. (Later on, when the New South had undercut
that fantasy, the role of the unrepressed would pass to the ethnic Italians,
blacks, and Latinos.)

In all this ferment, one constant remained: the family's primary role
as the nexus of conflict, neurosis formation, and consolation. If these
Northern directors and actors found it relatively easy to tap into the emotional dynamics of Southern stories, it was partly because they revolved
around explosive family tensions. Particularly for those with Jewish
backgrounds, the material had a biblical resonance: the Old Testament

is filled with narratives about sibling rivalry, incest, betrayed patriarchs, secret conniving, and family guilt. Southern culture was steeped in the same Bible stories: not for nothing did Faulkner concoct titles like *Absalom, Absalom!* and *Go Down, Moses.*

The moral smugness that Northern or Hollywood liberals felt toward the South during that region's desegregation struggle also contributed to the vogue for Southern stories. With the South perceived as a bastion of racism, it was easier to construct narratives of good and evil, tolerance and bigotry. It goes without saying that these films presented a distorted, caricatured view of the region. There was little recognition of Southern intellectual life, or of the more nuanced, worldly attitudes of Southern moderates, such as might be found in the stories of Peter Taylor. On the other hand, the Method group's filmed version of the South paid it an inverted compliment as an outpost of vitality in an overcivilized world. Russian Jewish performers projected nostalgic memories of their peasant culture onto the South.

I should say a few words in general about the instant simpatico that Northern Jews sometimes feel for the South, and vice versa, though this topic is bound to take us into suspect generalities. Briefly: these sympathetic connections seem based on each group's perception of itself as an outsider or underdog (the South, defeated in the Civil War; the Jews, historically persecuted); on the shared preference for comfort foods, hospitality, family gatherings (what Southerners call "down-home," Jews call *haimische*); on an appreciation for language, storytelling, chatter, grisly humor, wit; and, finally, on their substantial differences, which act as an erotic magnet: dark Talmudic Jewish men, blond, flirtatious Southern women.

By the way, one should not forget there is a long, complex history of Jewish communities in the South, but the Northern Jewish artists who come visiting these parts are generally not that interested in their Southern Jewish brethren. The experience they seek from the South is that of being able to confront Christian America and embrace the enemy on terms that suddenly seem more empathically possible. Whatever misunderstandings and disenchantments subsequently occur, as each group uses the other for spurious healing purposes, could not be otherwise, their not having delved deeply enough into the other's specific histories and mores.

I discovered some of these things by going out with a woman from Mississippi named Kay, a poet and graduate student. We were together off and on for seven years and almost got married. Kay was in fact the marrying kind, having been hitched and divorced twice by the time she was thirty; she wanted to know quite seriously from the first night we slept together if my intentions were "honorable." This seemed a quaint, charming Southern locution to me, and I respected in principle the code of honor she seemed to be alluding to, though I had no intention of being rushed into so important a decision—especially once I came to realize that Kay was fairly neurotic. She was alluring, brainy, moody, and explosive as all get-out. In those years I often went out with loony, affected women. Kay was certainly the looniest of the bunch. She would bat her eyelashes and parody the Southern belle ("Why, Mr. Lopate, I do believe you are paying me a compliment") or play the reproving schoolmarm, lecturing me on how a "ma-toor" gentleman was expected to behave where she came from.

This relationship took place not on the porch of an old plantation manse but on the Upper West Side, Manhattan. I made a few trips back to Kay's home in Mississippi, but for all her enthusiasm about Southern flora and fauna, she was essentially a runaway, with little intention of moving back home. Kay introduced me to a circle of expatriate Mississippians living in New York—bankers, bohemians, modern dancers, artists. In fact, I attended the first two annual Mississippi Day picnics in Central Park. These were warm-weather affairs with plentiful food, gossip, lolling on the grass, the occasional microphone remarks from a visiting politician (former governor Winter spoke one year), and a gracious display of regional chauvinism, which conveyed the message that though we Mississippians deign to live among you uncouth Yankees, we are infinitely above you and you will never understand us.

I was not offended, because by then I had been told often enough by Kay that I would never get it. What "it" was, exactly, I could never be sure, but in my mind "it" took on the character of an Arthurian myth, with courtly rules about appropriate behavior. "It" seemed to be partly a system of social class knowledge, like the English distinction between "U" and "non-U." Or perhaps "it" was none of these things, but only the code name for the distance couples feel when they are not getting along. Easier to label me "New York Jew" and her "Southern Belle" than get to the bottom of that mistrust.

I remember on our first trip down South, Kay was continually worried that I might offend someone by my New York abruptness. It's true I can be abrupt. When I put in my order at the Atlanta airport food stand where we changed planes, she told me afterward I had spoken in a manner that was too brusque, and might have upset the counterwoman. So far as I could tell, this waitress was used to receiving requests from travelers in a hurry and seemed not in the least offended, but Kay would not speak to me again until we landed.

Kay's old friends in Mississippi seemed to accept me warmly, with no evidence of language or custom barrier. I suspect Kay needed to believe I didn't understand her background so that she could maintain a constant anger toward me in the absence of marriage proposals. On my end, I had become more and more loath to entertain the idea of spending a life with her when half the time she acted as though she hated me. And when she was unfaithful—to get back at me, she said, for my lack of commitment—I stiffened my resolve to break off with her someday. Meanwhile, I'd received an education about Millsaps College, Eudora Welty, and kudzu; I had managed to visit John Lee Hooker's Tupelo and William Faulkner's Oxford; I had met some very friendly, cultivated Mississippians; and I had internalized the beauty of crepe myrtle trees and shotgun houses and Delta river towns.

So, in 1980, when I was offered a teaching post in Houston, Texas, I leapt at the chance, already prepared to be at home in that steamy, semitropical environment. By virtue of its climate, pace, manners, and proximity to New Orleans, Houston is much more a Southern city than a Western one. Dallas is Western, Houston Southern. Especially if you scraped away the boom that had catapulted its population from 500,000 in 1950 to several million in 1980, you would still find a poky Southern city where all the prominent families knew each other and major business and political decisions could be made in a downtown hotel room over poker.

This time I was not just visiting but living in the South; careful not to offend by speaking abruptly or making disparaging comparisons to the North, I imagined by now I had a sixth sense about the sensitivities of Southerners. I deliberately sought out Houstonites who knew the city's past. It was a pleasure to unravel its layers of history: to learn, say, the story of the building of the Ship Channel, or the efforts of blacks and liberal whites to integrate the downtown area, or the Army Corps of Engineers' role in taming the bayous, or Mrs. de Menil's initial impact on the art scene. Because there were so few literary lights, I could befriend all the painters, architects, composers, and wealthy patrons in town, as I never would have been invited to do in New York City.

During the eight years I spent teaching at the University of Houston, I came to appreciate a calmer, courtlier, more indirect style of communication. I would talk to some businessman or scholar, and he would politely and attentively cock his ear while looking mostly away from me, maybe at his shoe, and I would come away having learned one surprising fact, and knowing that the next time I met him I would come away with a little further understanding of the big picture, there was no hurry; or I would run into a woman I vaguely knew at a museum opening, and suddenly she would exude the most flirtatious promise and feminine enchantment, and most of the time it meant nothing except that Southern women knew exquisitely how to flirt. They always gave the impression of being several steps ahead of me, though occasionally I caught up with one long enough for something romantic to ensue.

So it came to pass that again I went out with a Southern woman whom I almost married. This woman, Helen, was as sane as her predecessor had been nutty, as true as the other had been faithless. She was, in fact, the nicest woman I had ever been with, and I kept trying to talk myself into falling in love with her so that I could avail myself forever of her kindness and tact. But it was not to be: I had already schooled myself too well in loving women who were angry, depressed, hysterical, and mean to me; I apparently needed that friction to feel erotically engaged. At least I had come to learn that there are many types of Southern women, including the generous and forbearing.

When I think about the South, I find myself almost instinctively equating it with femaleness. I suppose this is another cliché: the notion of the North as steely, industrial, masculine, and the South as pliant, botanical, uterine. My cultural misinterpretations abound: often when I met a refined, educated Southern man, my first assumption, based on the way he talked, dressed, and carried his body, would be that he was gay. At least half the time I was completely off-base. It occurs to me that one reason I link the South with feminine associations is that, by traveling in its art world, I stayed far away from the intimidating redneck, testosterone types—the football-playing, hard-drinking trucker with gun rack, imagery that attaches to the Southern macho. For better or worse, almost everything I know by experience about the South comes from contacts with women, gay males, and cultivated, soft-voiced men with a bisexual style, if not practice. This, as the sociologists say, constitutes a skewed sample.

IV

LITERARY MATTERS

"Howl" and Me

I have to say that "Howl" struck me from the first as a little ludicrous and overblown. I must have been fourteen and still in junior high school, around 1957, when I first encountered Allen Ginsberg's groundbreaking poem. How it crossed my path I'm not sure; probably my brother, Leonard, who was seventeen and mad about García Lorca and Blake, tossed it my way, as he did all of his poetic discoveries. We went around for weeks intoning favorite passages—the first two lines, of course, "I saw the best minds of my generation . . ." down to "looking for an angry fix," and "fucked in the ass by saintly motorcyclists, and screamed with joy" and "boxcars boxcars boxcars," which for some reason always cracked us up. We loved the poem for its phonic fireworks and flaming images, but we also mocked its solemn oracular quality, applying an adolescent penchant for parody to any target within easy reach.

Much as we embraced Kerouac and Ginsberg as a retort to the "tranquilized fifties," we were not immune to the ubiquitous parodies of the Beats in popular culture. Who could not giggle at Bob Hope's beatnik routine, wearing a beret and a fake goatee, banging bongos, snapping his fingers, and crying "Yeah, man!" Still, we were much more pro- than anti-Beat; and "Howl," by virtue of giving America the finger, fit neatly into our bag of anarchic provocations, along with *Mad* magazine, the raunchier lyrics of rhythm and blues, Mort Sahl and Lenny Bruce.

Some shards of Ginsberg's dangerous shrapnel lodged more deeply in my subconscious than I realized, because, soon after reading it, I wrote a poem called "I Hate It All" and turned it in to my English teacher for creative writing extra credit. This lurid rant enlisted every cliché about "gnawing rats," "crying men," and "the dirt of the slums," disguising my personal resentment, no doubt, at my parents for making us live in a ghetto, before coming to the noble realization, "But I am of it, of this thing I hate." It was, if you will, a precociously James Baldwinish moment of identification with all I was trying to flee. My English teacher, Miss Loftus, responded with sour surprise, "Phillip, I thought you were one of our most well-adjusted students!" and sent me down to the guidance counselor.

You must understand that, for all my extracurricular dabbling in anarchic culture, I was pretty much a *good* boy, and had gotten myself elected student president, no mean feat in a mostly black school, so that, when I began poetically denouncing the squalor of my immediate environment, the adults grew alarmed. Getting sent to the guidance counselor was not the pat-on-the-head, extra-credit response I had anticipated. I found myself in a jam, needing to explain my ode to hate as somehow not really reflective of my true feelings, and I began saying it was a creative put-on, spouting show-off references to the Dadaists and Surrealists. My dodge, I could tell, did not convince the guidance counselor; but she had no choice, given my refusal to admit what was really bothering me, except to send me back to class.

The odd thing, I see now, is that I kept doing this, modeling the role of the perfectly calm, responsible, civic-minded A student, while sending out flares that something was not right inside. In high school, I again got myself elected to office, this time chief justice of the student court, meanwhile writing a provoking piece about my feelings of alienation for a citywide essay contest. When my high school English teacher, Mrs. Gold, accused me of trying to shock the middle class (she used, for the first time in my hearing, the French expression *épater le bourgeoisie*), I mocked her behind her back as a provincial spoilsport. I wanted to express honestly a little part of my adolescent confusion, darkness, and dread, while protecting my privacy by pretending I was merely being literary and experimental.

All this self-divided behavior culminated in my getting accepted to Columbia on a full scholarship, and trying to kill myself sophomore year. The combination of virginal frustration, too much Dostoevsky and Nietzsche, poverty, poor diet, finding myself adrift living away from home for the first time in the maddeningly impersonal and competitive atmosphere of Columbia of those years combusted with my own neurotic impatience to yield the conclusion that life was not worth living. The point is that I knew more than I cared to admit about the screaming rage and shock expressed by "Howl"; I had my own personal howl going on inside my head, and I was trying to keep a tight lid on it.

Having survived this adolescent crisis of yearning and negation, I would spend the rest of my life striving for skepticism and stoicism. You might say I turned away from "Howl," with its suicidal grandiosity, gutter ecstasies, and apocalyptic nightmares, trading them in for the smaller promise of humor, equilibrium, and the everyday (i.e., don't take yourself so seriously). Allen Ginsberg, fellow Jewish writer and a Columbia dropout, was like an older brother (exactly seventeen years older) who had pioneered a path not to be taken. I would stay in college and guard my scholarship, graduate in four years, and get married at twenty, eager to show everyone what a mature, responsible fellow I was for my age.

The strongest pull that "Howl" exerted on me thus was cautionary. If it seemed an advertisement for madness, drug addiction, vagrancy, homosexuality, and rhetoric as the road to enlightenment, I knew that those were not for me. Ginsberg might romanticize madness, saying: "I'm with you in Rockland / where you scream in a straightjacket" or "bang on the catatonic piano the soul is innocent" while awaiting "fifty more shocks." I had come close—too close—to ending up like Carl Solomon in Rockland State Hospital: having landed in the St. Luke's psych ward after my suicide attempt, I'd suddenly needed to convince the staff that I was perfectly all right, I did not require any shock treatment, thank you. Needles had always terrified me, so becoming a junkie held no appeal. I was dead set on clawing my way out of ghetto Brooklyn and into the middle class, too close to the poverty line to entertain romantic notions about bums and clochards. Limited as my sexual repertoire was, I did not want to get fucked in the ass by anyone, much less "saintly motorcyclists." And why "saintly"? I'd seen Marlon Brando in *The Wild One* and the motorcycle gangs in *Scorpio Rising*, and real live Hells Angels menacing the Lower East Side, and not a scintilla of sanctity did they radiate. If Allen Ginsberg wanted to have an orgasm with a guy, fine with me, but why insist that it was saintly, or that the sailors who blew him were "human seraphim"; that part struck me as sentimental. Besides, why was a good Jewish boy like Allen bothering with all that Christian-saint imagery? Perhaps the "saintly" bothered me more than the "motorcyclists." (I'm not sure I thought that then, but I do now.)

"Howl" proffered one more temptation which I resisted mightily, and which was contained in the words "my generation." This may not be the proper occasion to explore what lies behind my distrust of that (to my mind) smug, self-mythologizing notion. Oh, what the hell. To quote Ben Hecht: "It is, as I have long suspected, very difficult for a writer to write about anybody but himself." Certainly true for me. In any case, I find the words "my generation" presumptuous; I don't feel it's my right to generalize for all those who happened to be born during the same decade as myself. Or perhaps it isn't humility but vanity that won't allow me to speak of myself in any but idiosyncratic terms, resisting sociological categories that would place me in a collective epoch. Or am I merely envious that I never belonged to a glittering artistic set, like the Parisians around Picasso in Roger Shattuck's *Banquet Years*, or the Harvard crowd who went on to constitute the New York School of Poetry? Here was Ginsberg, lovingly canonizing his particular set of friends ("Holy Peter holy Allen holy Solomon holy Lucien holy Kerouac holy Huncke holy Burroughs holy Cassady") as not only a generation but "the best minds of" his generation. And what entitled them to this accolade? That they ran naked through "the negro streets," smoked dope on rooftops, dropped out of the academy—in other words, that they made a mess of their lives. Am I being too literal here? Are we supposed to think that they started off as the best minds of their generation, and then the evil capitalist Moloch society ruined them, or was it their own exquisite sensitivity that brought them to collapse?

Throughout the poem, Ginsberg seems torn between portraying his buddies as the divinely chosen accursed ones, *maudits*, and extending a more democratic laurel of beatitude to all the downtrodden and losers, as when he says "holy Cassady holy the unknown buggered and suffering beggars holy the hideous human angels!" What about all those working stiffs who would not end up raving lunatics, who could not afford to drop out—were we automatically judged mediocre, and condemned to a lower status than "the best minds," by dint of neglecting or refusing to fall apart? Of course "Howl" is a young man's poem, and maybe I ought not to be subjecting it to this querulous, middle-aged class analysis when what it has most to recommend it is its jazzy, generative enthusiasm, and its wholesome desire for redemptive embrace. The poem ends with these lines:

Holy forgiveness! mercy! charity! faith! Holy! Ours! bodies! suffering! magnanimity!
Holy the supernatural extra brilliant intelligent kindness of the soul!

Okay, I can buy that. Not sure what it means, but I'm all for kindness and forgiveness. Where I have trouble is when the poet says: "the soul is innocent." He invokes the word *innocence* several times in "Howl," like a son pleading before a stern father-judge, demanding amnesty for all self-destructive acts, and shifting the blame disingenuously onto Society, Moloch. Why not accept that we are not innocent?

Well, that is one reading of the poem, and probably the most conventional one. A contrary reading would be that Ginsberg himself was something of a detached observer, more stable than the others, portraying clearly though with sympathy the screwups of those around him, even envying them their loss of control, yet in his own way being cautionary, undeceived by their pitiable attempts to rationalize all that insane behavior—and cautious himself, getting on with the business of a literary career. For instance, is there not some irony when he speaks of those "who threw potato salad at CCNY lecturers on Dadaism and subsequently presented themselves on the granite steps of the madhouse with shaven heads and harlequin speech of suicide, demanding instantaneous lobotomy"? Or when he refers to "Dreams! adorations! illuminations! religions! the whole boatload of sensitive bullshit!" Yes, the whole boatload of sensitive bullshit. That is what "Howl" throws at us, and also what the poem attempts to surmount—and it manages, at times, to have it both ways.

I will always be grateful to "Howl" for preparing me for the beauties of Walt Whitman, whose cornucopic inventories and one-line portraits seem both gorgeous and inevitable. These two American masters share a love of cities and public spaces, the undersides of bridges, the streets, rooftops, alleys—the whole consoling urbanistic shebang—as when Ginsberg conjures up those

> who faded out in vast sordid movies, were shifted in dreams, woke on a sudden Manhattan, and picked themselves up out of basements hung-over with heartless Tokay and horrors of Third Avenue iron dreams & stumbled to unemployment offices."

These days when I read "Howl," I forgive the Blakean seraphic bluster and attend to the superb atmospherics of place, which mean more to me the older I grow.

The poem of Ginsberg's that really floored me was "Kaddish." I could be indifferent, finally, to "Howl"'s Carl Solomon rotting in Rockland's mental wards, indifferent to Neal Cassady's priapic triumphs ("secret hero of these poems, cocksman and Adonis of Denver—"), but I could not be indifferent to Naomi, given my own embarrassed love for a difficult mother.

Years later, when I was a fellow traveler of the New York School of Poetry, I would run into Ginsberg at parties and readings. We gave each other a wide berth; he seemed much more interested in cute young boys than in my own person, and I, for my part, did not go out of my way to cultivate him, the more so as I drifted away from a bohemian mind-set. Instead I added him to that list of famous writers I knew casually but was unable to bring myself to cultivate, which I now only partly regret.

Once, after the Stonewall riots in 1969, I volunteered my services to a benefit poetry reading for gay rights, thinking it important for straight writers such as myself to show solidarity publicly with the gay community. I read a long, comic, mother-son poem that night called "The Blue Pants," and Ginsberg closed the reading with some new poems. Afterward, he came up and told me I should have read a little faster. What a *putz*! I thought. Here I was "magnanimously" going out of my heterosexual way to participate in a gay rights reading, and he was criticizing my delivery. Years later, I wonder if he may have been paying me a compliment: recognizing a fellow entertainer, though one much less experienced than he, and giving me a bit of professional advice. I probably *should* have read the poem a touch faster.

In 1984, I was on a committee to select the Pulitzer Prize in poetry. The Pulitzer is decided in two stages: first the writers' committee goes through all the nominated books in its designated area and sends up three recommendations, then a group of newspaper and magazine editors makes the final selection. Since the editors are usually not as well-versed in poetry as one might wish, they often pick the most conventional, user-friendly collection. In any event, I pushed hard for Allen Ginsberg's *Collected Poems: 1947–1980* to be named one of the three finalists. It was a huge volume, eight-hundred-plus pages, and of course inconsistent in quality, but the high points were amazing: that Ginsberg was a major American poet of towering achievement seemed self-evident. I did not, however, succeed in convincing the other two literary judges to include him (there was still that curious fussiness about Ginsberg's coloring outside the lines of the well-made poem), so I took the unusual step of filing a minority recommendation, obliging the editors who would have final decision to consider his *Collected*, along with books by the other three finalists (Carolyn Kizer, Charles Wright, and Robert Duncan). As it turned out, the editors also rejected Ginsberg for the Pulitzer, choosing Kizer. By this time Ginsberg and I had developed a friendly nodding acquaintance, and had spoken a few times on the phone. I phoned Allen at his home to tell him he had at least been one of the finalists. He was philosophical about it, saying, "They don't want to give the big prizes to me. They still hold against me all that stuff from the sixties."

I suppose you can be either King of the May or Poet Laureate, but not both in the same lifetime. By now he was elderly and infirm, and we chatted for fifteen minutes, mostly about his ailments, but also about teaching creative writing. (He knew I had been active in the writer-in-the-schools movement.) I don't remember anything specifically that he said—nothing except for the tone, which was extremely amiable. He struck me as a nice guy, a sweet, elderly, realistic Jew of a sort I was familiar with from my youth, and I chastised myself for having misjudged him before as a *putz*.

The truth is that he was probably both, a *mensch* and a *putz*.

I may have misjudged "Howl," and am probably misjudging it still. How to evaluate such a torrent with objectivity? That poem is lodged in my psyche, at the crossroads of my adolescent confusions, and I can't be too hard on myself for failing to see it clearly or extract it from that tumult.

The Poetry Years

For about fifteen years I wrote poetry. I published poems in countless little magazines, gave readings all over, earned a living of sorts as a poet in the schools, teaching the art to children, and put out two collections: the first in 1972, the second in 1976. When I look back at those years during which being a poet formed such an important part of my identity, I am tempted to rub my eyes, as though recalling a time when I ran off and joined the circus.

How had I started writing poetry in the first place? I can honestly say I had no early ambitions along those lines. True, in elementary school I was by default the class poet, just as there was a boy who drew horses well and another boy who ran fleetly at Field Day. When Thanksgiving approached, I would be expected to craft a few stanzas about the Pilgrims' feast. In junior high I wrote several tortured poems under the Beats' influence. But by high school I had forsaken poetry for prose: I was going to be a novelist.

In college, joining the literary circle around *Columbia Review*, I befriended the poet Ron Padgett. The Oklahoma-born Padgett and I had heard of each other by freshman rumor, circling each other like two gunfighters; he had even put the word out through mutual friends that he was going to break my butt. I, having hailed from the streets of Brooklyn, let it be known he was welcome to try. Of course when we finally met, no fisticuffs occurred: he showed me a superb paper he had written for English about Pound and the medieval troubadours, I showed him a paper on Yeats, and we were off to the races.

Padgett had precociously started a poetry magazine back in high school, writing to poets he admired for contributions; and he came to New York to attend Columbia in 1960 as part of a Tulsa émigré gang that also included Ted Berrigan, Joe Brainard, and Dick Gallup, and that affixed themselves to the New York School of Poetry. The charismatic Kenneth Koch, who taught in the English Department, had lured Padgett and friends to Columbia. I attended the lunchtime readings Koch gave of his own poetry, and a memorable one of Bad Poetry, which he delivered with chortling oratory. Koch embodied what struck me as a refreshing, zany poetics that drew equally on comic strips, mock-epic parodies of Ariosto, and Dada game structures. I would later come to revere him as one of the most farsighted poets of our era, and in the last decade of his life we became friends; but as an undergraduate I was too intimidated to take a course from him. So I settled for becoming a prose-writing hanger-on of the New York School of Poetry, with entrée to the scene provided by Ron Padgett, all of us worshiping at the shrine of Koch, Frank O'Hara, and John Ashbery.

The one whose poetry appealed to me most at that time was Frank O'Hara, partly because of his unapologetically urban, movie-mad sensibility, partly because of his doctrine of Personalism:

You just go on nerve. If someone's chasing you down the street with a knife you just run, you don't turn around and shout, "Give it up! I was a track star for Mineola Prep." . . . How can you really care if anybody gets it, or gets what it means, or if it improves them? Improves them for what? For death? Why hurry them along? Too many poets act like a middle-aged mother trying to get her kids to eat too much cooked meat, and potatoes with drippings (tears). I don't give a damn whether they eat or not. Forced feeding leads to excessive thinness (effete). Nobody should experience anything they don't need to, if they don't need poetry bully for them. I like the movies too. And after all, only Whitman and Crane and Williams, of the American poets, are better than the movies. As for measure and other technical apparatus, that's just common sense: if you're going to buy a pair of pants you want them to be tight enough so everyone will want to go to bed with you.

His example gave casual permission to construct a poem out of anything at hand, from a friend's remark to a movie star's collapse to a headline or honking car or sudden mood change.

Just as there was a *politique des auteurs* among film buffs, so a sort of *politique des poètes* existed, with battle lines drawn between the more Establishment, prize-winning poets of the day, such as Robert Lowell, Richard Wilbur, John Berryman, Elizabeth Bishop, Richard Eberhart, Anthony Hecht, and Anne Sexton, and the New York School, who drew their inspiration from the French modernist poets and the painting of Willem de Kooning, Larry Rivers, and Jane Freilicher. Koch's poem "Fresh Air" was a manifesto that thumbed its nose at everything solemn, high-minded, ethically worrying— "academic," in a word—and called for a poetics of sensuous, playful experimentation. In it, he ridiculed poetry "Written by the men with their eyes on the myth / And the Missus and the midterms, in the *Hudson Review*."

Of course these divisions grew fuzzier the closer you examined the matter: Koch himself taught at Columbia, and who could be wittier or more linguistically playful than Richard Wilbur? But there still seemed this antagonism as between opposing teams, the one (the so-called Established writers) using poetry as a tragic criticism of life, the other (the New York School) as a giddy celebration of art. I remember visiting Ted Berrigan in his East Village pad, and being told by him that he never mixed life with art. Art came from art, he said, not life. Anyone reading Ted's heartbreaking, autobiographical *Sonnets* (or O'Hara's personal poems, for that matter) would be hard-pressed to concur with his assertion, but that was at least the party line.

When I first read the poetry of Berryman, Lowell, Bishop, Sexton, and Sylvia Plath, I felt guilty, like a Catholic reading books on the Index, and even guiltier for liking them so much. Lowell's *Life Studies* was a revelation to me, with its acerbic honesty ("Tamed by *Miltown*, we lie on Mother's bed"); Berryman's *Dream Songs* a grim delight ("Life, friends, is boring. We must not say so."). Surely it was possible to like both anguished confessional and breezy diaristic poetry? But I kept my taste for the former under wraps around the New York School crowd.

I remember attending a reading by Ashbery at NYU around 1967, when he premiered some of the brilliant poems from *Rivers and Moun-*

tains. Perhaps to distance himself from the prophetic, baton style of Robert Duncan or the shamanistic intoning of Allen Ginsberg, Ashbery read his poems with an ironic disdain, as if he had just bent down and picked up a piece of trash that had some improbable gibberish written on it:

> *These decibels*
> *Are a kind of flagellation, an entity of sound*
> *Into which being enters, and is apart.*
> *Their colors on a warm February day*
> *Make for masses of inertia, and hips*
> *Prod out of the violet-seeming into a new kind*
> *Of demand that stumps the absolute because not new*
> *In the sense of the next one in an absolute series*
> *But, as it were, pre-existing or pre-seeming in*
> *Such a way as to contrast funnily with the unexpectedness*
> *And somehow push us all into perdition.*

I had no idea what any of it meant, but I liked listening to its tantalizing flashes of music and meaning. Afterward, I hung around long enough to get invited to the cocktail party. At parties after New York School poetry readings, you would receive your literary marching orders. Reading tips were offered within an acceptably avant-garde framework that included such writers as Gertrude Stein, William S. Burroughs, Ronald Firbank. When I spoke to Ashbery after the reading, he recommended to me de Chirico's *Hebdomeros* and Raymond Roussel's *Impressions of Africa*, both hieratic texts in a Surrealist vein, and the relatively obscure poets F. T. Prince and John Wheelwright. I later came to suspect he was throwing acolytes off the scent, and that he himself had perhaps been more deeply influenced by Wordsworth, Bishop, and Auden.

Myself, I could not get enough of *Rivers and Mountains*, and read it until the spine cracked. Later, in 1968, when I began writing poetry, I spent a fruitless summer trying to imitate Ashbery's elegant opacity. No one could have shown less aptitude for writing in the Ashbery mode than I, given my penchant for the straightforward; but he was *the* most influential poet of the period, and so I had at least to give it a try.

What I took from my days as a New York Poetry School fellow traveler was less aesthetic than social. I had the privilege to watch the way a lively poetry scene mushroomed at St. Mark's Church in-the-Bowery, in the East Village, under the nurturance of the Poetry Project's director, the glamorous Anne Waldman (she had even acted in television's *The Mod Squad*). This was the closest I would ever come to being part of a literary circle, a generation, a movement, a bohemia, and though I have always considered myself a loner, it gave me a clear glimpse of how such a network functioned. I accepted the poets' generous invitations to parties, to passed joints, to publications in mimeo magazines, to friendships and acquaintanceships. What they made of me I have no idea. My first wife, Carol, and I lived way uptown, at the northern end of Manhattan above the Cloisters: one time we threw a party and invited the St. Mark's crowd to it, though they seemed wary ever of venturing above Fourteenth Street. They arrived late, having brought with them on the A train enough reading matter for an ocean crossing. Immediately they headed for the bedroom to get stoned, ignoring my other friends. But if the St. Mark's poets were insular, they were also warmly loyal. I was fascinated by the way they supported each other. I once asked Ron Padgett how he and Ted Berrigan critiqued one another's poems. "I just say, 'That's totally terrific, Ted,' and when I show him mine he says, 'That's totally terrific, Ron' to me," he answered. Whether this was strictly true I have my doubts, but the lesson seemed to be that critical fussiness was passé. Another time I was visiting the poet/ future art critic Peter Schjeldahl in his apartment, and I commented with surprise that he kept WABC, a Top 40 rock station, on all the time. What did he do when bad songs played on the air? Schjeldahl said obstinately, "There are no bad rock songs today." Was he pulling my leg, or did he really believe that? I felt like a visitor from the nineteenth century.

I also watched with surprise and maybe some envy how the poets and their mates swapped partners. Ted Berrigan read a poem at St. Mark's Church that went something like: "When you sleep with your best friend's wife / She gets fucked / He gets fucked / And you get fucked."

Loud titters were heard from the cognoscenti, who knew the poem's other referents, both of whom were in the audience that night.

As eye-opening as all this was, it did not necessarily make me want to be a poet. That came about another way.

Living on the brink of poverty, I was looking for some freelance editorial work (often a euphemism for ghostwriting, which I did extensively during this period), when I came upon a notice requesting readers to help edit a new poetry anthology. Reading was one thing I felt sure I could do; I did very little else. So I answered the ad and was summoned to an interview at the home of one Hyman Sobiloff.

Mr. Sobiloff, often referred to in those days as "the businessman-poet," was a wealthy venture capitalist who lived in a very tony town house on East Seventy-Seventh Street in the Upper East Side. He had several servants, and his town house had its own elevator, which impressed the hell out of me. A Chinese servant answered the door, brought me into the parlor, and told me to wait, as Mr. Sobiloff was just getting up. (This was noon.) I had time to examine the antiques and indifferent paintings before the great man himself appeared, in a silk striped robe: his fleshy, curt, bald-headed, imperial manner put me instantly in mind of Louis Calhern in *The Asphalt Jungle*, some sort of mobster kingpin or political boss (Calhern also played the title role in *Julius Caesar*). Sobiloff explained the nature of the project, which was to revise the immensely popular poetry anthologies that had been edited by his late friend Oscar Williams. I was happy to tell him my own mother had read aloud from them to us, when we were children, such favorites as Alfred Noyes's "The Highwayman." Poetically, you might say, Oscar Williams's anthologies were mother's milk to me. Sobiloff gruffly cut me off, saying the point was that they needed to be updated. He had undertaken the chore as an act of devotion to a friend who'd passed away. He pointed to several precipitously tall stacks of poetry books on French Empire chairs and said, "I know all this stuff cold, but I can't be bothered to go through 'em, I'm too busy. I need an assistant." Somehow I doubted he was as familiar with the contents of these volumes as he pretended, but I played along, familiar as I was with my ghostwriting clients' need to pretend omni-science. On my end, I bluffed like crazy about my knowledge of poetry. The interview lasted fifteen minutes. He seemed satisfied; we agreed on a salary, and I took away a few shopping bags full of books.

I had now to educate myself as quickly as possible in the English and American poetic canon. I was overwhelmed by the vast amounts of poetry I would have to absorb, but I began by plowing through the original Oscar Williams anthologies. I quickly saw that Oscar had put his friend Hy in the books, as he had his own wife, Gene Derwood, and himself, though their verse hardly seemed in the same league as that of Keats and Whitman. Sobiloff, I learned, was philanthropically active, and a heavy supporter of poetry societies and magazines. I was too shy to ask Sobiloff how he had made his millions, but someone in the know told me that he had started in the furniture business, and had perfected a scheme of buying a second, failing business and transferring all the assets from the first failing business to the second, then shutting that down and transferring all the assets of the second to a third . . . in any case, some kind of fiscal legerdemain.

Shortly after beginning the job, I learned I was not the only poetry reader; Sobiloff had hired two others, like a gambler placing bets across the board. At first he kept us strictly separate; but in time I was able to contact them, and consolidate my position as First Reader, *primus inter pares*, by offering to coordinate the project for a higher fee. He appreciated my ruth-lessness, I think. It was Sobiloff who said once in passing that he was flying off to vacation in Barbados, leaving the city because "I'm tired of all those ghetto faces," a statement so appalling to me that I was almost charmed by its brazenness. I myself came from the ghetto and wondered when he would ferret out that fact. On another visit to the boss, I met a lady friend of his whom I took to be his mistress, a woman in her fifties with the body of an ex-showgirl and a face that looked like it had seen everything. When Sobiloff left the room for a minute she warned me not to take advantage of her Hy, if I knew what was good for me.

Believe me, I had no intention of cutting corners. My work schedule con-sisted of reading four poetry books a day minimum. Most of them came from the library, some from used book stores—our boss had given us permission

228 / PORTRAIT INSIDE MY HEAD

to augment his limited stock, and I saved the receipts for him. I would wake up and eat breakfast while starting on the first, get dressed, finish reading the book, take some notes about possible selections, and go off for a walk with a bag lunch around noontime, often ending on a bench in Riverside Park (my wife and I had by this time moved down from Inwood to West 104th Street, near Columbia), where I would read a second book, and then begin paging through a third . . . By now I was starting to feel headachy from eye strain and nauseous from a surfeit of poetic expressiveness, so I would give it a rest, then turn to book four in the late afternoon, and maybe book five that evening, if I had anything left in me. I recommend this brutal pedagogic method of saturation reading to anyone with literary ambition. Overstuffed like a goose for the manufacture of foie gras, I had no choice but to secrete my own poems. Out of sheer survival I needed to have my say.

Two other factors, besides the anthology reader gig, sparked my entry into poetry in the years I am describing, 1967–69: the political upheaval of the antiwar movement and the breakdown of my marriage. They were not un-related. Living as we did fairly close to Columbia University, I got swept up in the 1968 student revolt and reentered my old alma mater as a trouble-making alumnus. Just as I had been a hanger-on at the New York School of Poetry scene, so now I became a fellow traveler of the New Left, par-ticipating in demonstrations, political meetings, and study groups, read-ing Marxist texts alongside all that poetry. I never felt entirely comfortable with my posture of radicalism, nor could I embrace deep down the hope of making revolution, being an ex-scholarship kid from the ghetto still trying to crawl into the middle class. But the heady sixties talk of sexual liberation and down-with-the-bourgeoisie and smashing monogamy had a destabi-lizing effect on my domestic arrangements. Not that I can blame the failure of that first marriage on the revolutionary Left. I had married too young, at twenty, and hadn't a clue; we both made our mistakes.

Meanwhile, my first novel had not found a publisher; it was intensely embarrassing to have a sympathetic witness to my failure living in the same apartment with me. I was unable to take defeat in stride and start on a second one. Writing novels requires a calm, settled, bourgeois existence, and the payoff is deferred for years. The fragmentation I felt so painfully in those days would not permit me to submerge myself again in a prolonged alternate dream-narrative: I was too antsy, too much at the mercy of jittery day-to-day reality. I needed a form I could turn to with quicker results, snatching a few hours here and there from a patched-together freelance existence and the emotional confusion of whether to leave or stay. Hence, poetry.

My first poems seemed to emerge from conjugal dilemma. I still hoped we could salvage the marriage, if we both behaved responsibly and maturely. (Yeah, right.) These poems now strike me as tentative and hypocritical, the way a couple in their last stage bullshit during marriage counseling while secretly eyeing the exit. Formally, I was feeling my way into poetry at the same time I was feeling my way out of the marriage. By the time our marriage had definitively collapsed, I was on much firmer ground. Incidentally, I have always derived poetic inspiration from breakups. The rejection of love produces an emotional clarity in me, while the return to solitude arouses a need to solace myself, with either lyrical resignation or revenge.

I had decided to leave Carol and New York for California, the promised land of youth culture. Before I decamped, I turned in my lists of recommendations for the updated anthologies. It's funny to recall what I thought then would make for such substantial improvements. I had wanted the collections to seem less stuffy, so I added Bessie Smith and Bob Dylan lyrics, and Native American chants, and a slew of black poets, and of course increased the selections of the New York School poets, and F. T. Prince, John Wheelwright, Robert Creeley, George Oppen, Ed Dorn, and Allen Ginsberg, among others. Sobiloff looked them over without saying a word. Years later, when the revised anthologies appeared, I had a hard time finding any evidence of my labors. But the job had served its purpose: it had given me a condensed poetic education.

The poets who influenced me the most at the beginning of my poetic career were William Carlos Williams, Frank O'Hara, Pablo Neruda, Vladimir Mayakovsky, and Randall Jarrell. I was happy to purloin Williams's three-line stanzas, or O'Hara's splattering of words across the page; to imitate Mayakovsky's mock-megalomaniac outbursts, Neruda's surreal inventories, or the loquacity of late Jarrell. Later on I would fall in love with the dramatic monologues at the back of Pasternak's novel *Doctor Zhivago*, and Cavafy's deceptively simple lyrics and history poems, and Pavese's *Hard Labor*, with its dense materialist details of working-class life.

I was searching for something that made me happy whenever I found it, but I still didn't know how to characterize it. Though I had been a fan of Neruda's, when I attended a reading of his at the Ninety-Second Street Y, he put me off with his hammy, amphitheater delivery. It was another Chilean poet, Nicanor Parra, who crystallized for me what I was looking for, with the title of his collection *Poems and Antipoems*. This taste for "antipoetry," for grubby reality, was addressed by Wallace Stevens in his preface to the 1934 *Collected Poems* by William Carlos Williams, when he described Williams as someone for whom "the anti-poetic is that truth, that reality to which all of us are forever fleeing." I was drawn to the antipoetic for a number of reasons. First, my training had been in fiction, and I was still charmed by the sound of conversational prose. Though literary critics might disparage a poem as being "chopped-up prose," that was insufficient to condemn it in my eyes. Quite the contrary: it interested me, perversely, to see how far one could go in that direction and still get away with it. A storyteller at heart, I also continued to like narrative. Some of Parra's and Cavafy's poems were like little short stories: a room, a memory, a pickup.

Second, I was much more intrigued by poetic statement than by metaphor, simile, and image. When I heard it said that great poets were characterized by their gift for metaphor, it bugged me. I did not go out of my way to find metaphors; if an apt one swam into my brain while I was writing a poem, I put it in; if not, not. A profusion of metaphor and simile seemed to me, at this point in my poetry writing, forced. I even developed a theory that the late manner of certain poets, such as Pasternak and Montale, favored unadorned poetic statement, because they no longer felt the need to show off with metaphors in order to prove their poetic bona fides.

Third, I was rebelling against the lingering idea that poems should contain language or ideas that were suitably "poetic"—the beauties of nature, flowers, finches, rapture, elevated sentiment; I was drawn to a more sardonic poetry that would traffic in mundane commercial objects, business terms, legalese. It pleased me beyond measure to be able to use a word like *bicameral* in a poem on Allende. A city rat, I had no command of the names of flora and fauna, and needed to stake my claim with vocabulary that would verge on the prosaic and antiromantic.

Finally, being poetically self-taught and, despite having read many books on prosody, finding that very little of it stuck to me, never able to master my quantities, meters, and values, never having gone to graduate school to study poetry, I still composed poems largely intuitively, on the basis of what rhythms or combinations "sounded right" to my ear. This awkward situation made me feel at a disadvantage among trained poets. But it also drove me to embrace the antipoetic tradition that ran like a heretical streak through poetic history. Essentially I was trying to turn a limitation (my ignorance) into a strength (my preference for the antipoetic).

To some degree, I was taking permission from the era's looser standards. The 1960s allowed for a wide open, pluralistic (some would say amateurish) poetics. The ascendance of the oral, from the Beats' first-word-best-word through the black activist rappers such as Gil Scott-Heron and the Last Poets, the cultural enthronement of rock troubadours, the proliferation of open readings and mimeo magazines, the promotion of children's poetry and ethnopoetics, all contributed to the idea that anyone could write poetry, or had the right to call himself a poet; one didn't need a graduate credential. It may have been an invitation to charlatanism and self-delusion, but it also made for a no-holds-barred, anything-goes freedom; and I suppose I sneaked in under that umbrella.

A key determinant for me during these years was becoming friends with the poet Bill Zavatsky, a friendship I am happy to say has lasted over forty years. Zavatsky is a largehearted, open, funny man and a very fine poet, as well as a capable jazz pianist. When I first met him around 1968, he was writing ebullient verse that ran arpeggios in all directions. His verbal fireworks showed the influence of the French Surrealists, particularly André Breton, whom he later translated. At the same time, he was trying to master a leaner lyric with more sincerity and humanity, to put more honest emotions, situations, and characters into his poems. Robert Lowell once commented that he found it hard to "people" his poems. I, with my fiction background and interest in psychological cul-de-sacs, found that part relatively easy; my poetic struggles occurred on another plane. In any case, Zavatsky was drawn to what I was doing, and he encouraged me to keep writing situational, reality-based poems.

Zavatsky had recently gotten an MFA in poetry writing at Columbia, where he'd studied with Stanley Kunitz and Harvey Shapiro, and he introduced me to a circle of young Kunitz-Shapiro-trained poets, which included Hugh Seidman, Mark Rudman, and Louise Glück, who hung out at the West End Bar and other venues in Morningside Heights. Soon I was participating in their open readings. Through them I became familiar with another poetic model, the Objectivists (Oppen, Zukofsky, and Rakosi), and their younger allies, Shapiro, Armand Schwerner, and David Ignatow. I was particularly taken with the hard-bitten, wry, tight urban lyrics of Shapiro and Ignatow. Some of my poems seem to have come directly out of an attempt to write like them.

But the poet in the Objectivist orbit who came to affect me most was Charles Reznikoff. He was still alive then, though elderly, and had been rediscovered, championed by younger poets, who were as moved by his example of humility and noncareerism as by his spare, tender poems. Reznikoff had for years published his own verse, gone his own solitary way. He had fashioned a poetics of daily observation and reflection, taking long walks and then drafting his urban encounters into concise accounts in verse. His poems eschewed all verbal razzle-dazzle, yet they shimmered with a sympathy and humanity which never sentimentalized, including as they did the recognition of human cruelty. In person—I met him a number of times—and on the page, he had a quality of resignation or acceptance (which was it? both, perhaps) that suggested spiritual wisdom. And no one was more exposed to the charge of being prosaic or "antipoetic." His long-lined autobiographical sequence, "Early History of a Writer," reads stubbornly close to chopped-up prose—an engrossing personal essay with a ragged right-hand margin.

What made him, in the end, truly poetic was his economical use of language and his limpid vision of reality, which might be compared to Bashō and Li Po:

In the street, nine stories below, the horn of an automobile out of order
began sounding its loudest
steadily—without having to stop for breath.
We tried to keep on talking
in spite of that unceasing scream;
raised our voices somewhat, no longer calm and serene.
Our civilization was somewhat out of order, it seemed.

But, just as we began to knit our brows,
tighten our jaws, twist our lips,
the noise stopped;
and we dipped our heads,
like ducks on a stream, into the cool silence,
and talked again quietly, smiling at each other.

Reznikoff provided a solution to my guilt about not being able to achieve the proper (MFA-approved) poetic surface: I had only to write down what I saw, heard, and thought, as honestly as possible, and the poetry would take care of itself. The problem was that I could never be as pure a being as Reznikoff, and some of my attempts to write like him misfired from disingenuous oversimplicity. I also had an incurable taste for the ironic, rationalizing, or mischievously analytical narrator, which led me in distinctly non-Reznikoffian directions. But Reznikoff was never far off, once I had admitted him into my pantheon as a benign conscience, a figure of enduring through failure.

Two other, nonliterary influences on my poetry during that time deserve mention. The first was psychotherapy. I was seeing a Jungian psychologist named George Romney, a Cuban émigré who smoked cigarillos and had wavy black hair and an infectious laugh; it became my secret goal to provoke that laugh of his as often as possible in sessions. I would tell him about my experiences, and sometimes in the midst of my relating them they would cohere into a kind of improvised poem, which would make him chuckle and which I would then go home and try to write down. In this way my long poem "The Blue Pants" came about. George also frequently asked me, as therapists are wont to do, what I was feeling in the moment, directing my attention to the emotion physiologically manifesting and gurgling in my body. Out of this practice of attempting to pin down emotional states came poems such as "Numbness," "Not Sadness Which Is Always There," and "Clearing a Space." The very ambition to write poems anchored in the present moment—to open myself to the here-and-now, as it were—derived from techniques I'd been learning in psychotherapy.

The second crucial nonliterary influence on my poetry was teaching inner-city youth. I worked as a Poet in the Schools for over a dozen years, first helping high school dropouts in East Harlem get their equivalency degree, then directing a program for Teachers & Writers Collaborative at P.S. 75 in the Upper West Side of Manhattan. Along with my first published prose book, *Being with Children*, a number of poems resulted directly from that work experience, which also brought me closer to my own memories of childhood and early adolescence.

Teaching kids grew partly out of a desire to be socially useful: to put my political ideals into practice. At the same time I was looking for ways to incorporate my politics into my poetry. In one case, I had been leafing through a picture book of Cuban revolutionary art, and I came upon a propaganda poster with the title "Solidarity with Mozambique," and wondered how on earth I could ever feel my way into bonding with a struggle that seemed so far away and so abstract. I began writing about daily occurrences in New York City, then tried to reach, by concentric circles leading farther and farther away from myself, the rebels in Mozambique. (Not that I ever convincingly made it.) My poem "Allende" required no such elaborate device: I was simply shaken by the overthrow of the Chilean leftist's government and wanted to register my dismay without resorting to the usual consoling *venceremos* clichés.

Finally, I took scraps from everything around me and built a poetic nest with them: movie references, which were hard to resist, given my lifelong cinephilia; musical refrains (I kept playing Lotte Lenya's album, and her crack-voiced rendition of "Lost in the Stars" seeped into my bones); the economic recession and New York City default scare of 1975; the exploding gentrification that followed in my Upper West Side neighborhood; phone conversations with exes; the parade of failed romances and breakup scenes, always good for a poem.

Around 1977 I started writing personal essays and also went back to longer fiction. I see in retrospect that I was handling the same material, the same themes, in poetry and prose. The single person learning to be alone is a theme sounded in many of the poems of this period no less than in the prose that makes up my first essay collection, *Bachelorhood.*

Regardless of the genre I happened to be working in, I found myself resisting the transcendent. I was skeptical of all triumphalism, both positive (redemption) and negative (apocalypse). I threw in my lot with ordinary life, "the daily round." This mistrust of transcendence was another way in which I felt myself out of step with the ideological presuppositions of much contemporary poetry. But again, I was trying to turn weakness into strength: the inability to reach the stars, to achieve anything like spiritual sublimity, became a stubborn claim that the earth is all we have—a brief for groundedness.

To go back to 1972: I had been amassing sufficient poems for a first collection when a printer based in Northampton approached me and offered to put them out in a chapbook. The plan was for me to spend the month of August at his print shop, learning to operate a letter press and assisting in the production of the book, to be entitled *The Eyes Don't Always Want to Stay Open.* When I arrived in Northampton, however, I discovered that the printer and his wife were about to divorce, and he was temporarily closing the business while they sorted out the division of conjugal assets. I was welcome, he said, to stay in their house for the month of August, now that it had been vacated by both husband and wife, each of whom had moved in with a new lover. As I had no other plans for summer vacation, I decided to stick it out and explore the town and the surrounding Massachusetts countryside. I was at first miserably lonely, and felt foolish and hollow. But as it happened, an elderly, poetry-loving woman neighbor befriended me. She knew how to operate the letter press. So we set in type exactly one of my poems, the paranoid epistle "We Who Are Your Closest Friends," as a broadside. (Anne Lamott, to my surprise, included this poem in her popular writing manual, *Bird by Bird*, thus bringing it to thousands of readers it would otherwise not have reached.)

Returning to the city, discouraged that there would be no chapbook after all, I visited Bill Zavatsky and his wife, Phyllis, the first night back, hoping they might cheer me up. Zavatsky, who edited the poetry magazines *SUN* and *Roy Rogers*, had been mulling over the idea of starting his own line of poetry books. Seeing me so disappointed, he told me not to worry; he would put out my collection himself. To my astonished gratitude he began retyping the manuscript immediately, and stayed up half the night finishing the job, while I slept (more or less) on his couch. Thus was born SUN Press, which would publish Padgett, Harvey Shapiro, Jaimy Gordon, Paul Violi, Raymond Roussel, Paul Auster, and Zavatsky himself, but whose maiden publication was *The Eyes Don't Always Want to Stay Open*. My second collection, *The Daily Round*, would follow in 1976.

What remains to be told is how or why I gave up writing poetry. There is a simple answer and a complicated one. First the simple one:

In 1980 I moved to Houston, Texas, to teach at the University of Houston. I had been recruited as the creative writing program's first prose writer, on the basis of my memoir about teaching, *Being with Children*, my novel *Confessions of Summer*, and my soon-to-be-released personal essay collection, *Bachelorhood*. If in New York City I had been accepted as a poet, such was not the case in Houston. I was not permitted to teach poetry courses. I need not have taken it personally: my colleagues Rosellen Brown and Ntozake Shange, both of whom had published two poetry books as well but were hired as prose writers, faced the same prohibition in that university writing program.

A higher, "purer" standard of what it took to be a poet seemed to reign over that corner of academia, based partly on the possession of an MFA credential, and partly on the networking of the professional poetry world. I got a real taste of the way the poetry guild mentality operated: the mentoring and bestowal of the blessing on a chosen few acolytes, whose books would then be lobbied for publication. The nonexclusionary ethos of the sixties and early seventies had ended in the face of the writing program–generated mystique of technique. The impression was conveyed that the poet was someone like a prophet, of rare vatic powers, and there could only be at most two dozen poets in an era who'd received the vision. I knew I'd never gotten a message from on high: I did not fit that bill. My sense of myself as a poet began to shrivel up.

But that simple explanation is false. It would be wrong to blame my colleagues for killing the urge, since anyone who can be discouraged so easily from writing poetry is not cut out to be a poet. The truth is that I had already begun moving away from poetry before I came down to Houston, having fallen in love with the personal essay and its possibilities. I found in the personal essay a wonderful plasticity, which combined the storytelling aspects of fiction with the lyrical, associative qualities of poetry. If, as Robert Bly recommended, American poets should learn to "leap" freely from line to line, thought to thought, and subject to subject, I realized I could do that as easily in the personal essay as in a poem. Moreover, I could never have been deterred from writing poetry if my Houston colleagues' judgment had not jibed with something already inside me, some insecure spot that made me feel that, on some level, I was an impostor. It had been a good long run, but it was time to stop pretending I was a poet.

The Stubborn Art of Charles Reznikoff:
The Style of "No Style"

Among those who cherish his tender, translucent, humane poetry, Charles Reznikoff is a venerated figure, a role model of integrity and sustained excellence. During most of his lifetime (1894–1976) he had been so underrated and neglected that he developed a kind of stoical, resigned shell, going his own way. In person (I saw him on numerous occasions before he died), Reznikoff gave off an obliging, almost meekly humble impression, but there was a stubborn will underneath; his dedication to his art was unshakable. You can see it from his correspondence, that remarkable, moving record in *Selected Letters of Charles Reznikoff (1917–1976)*. If publishers would not accept his poetry manuscripts, he would print them himself. He also had that grain of selfishness that all writers need, however annoying to their loved ones. Though his wife, Marie, yearned for years to quit her high school teaching job, Charles, the most devoted, uxorious of husbands, nevertheless was not much of a provider. He refused to practice law, though he had a degree. Instead, he held down jobs that would afford him the mental freedom to pursue poetry and fiction: he wrote tedious legal definitions for textbooks, sold hats, and, ill-suited as he was temperamentally to service the Hollywood dream factory, polished screenplays for his boyhood friend, the producer Albert Lewin.

Toward the end of his life, he was taken up by the younger members of the New York School of Poetry and the descendants of the Objectivists, and treated by them reverently as a fragile, priceless grandparent, a last link to the pioneers of the twenties and thirties. Reznikoff, glad for the appreciation, did not know quite what to make of it, just as he had been puzzled decades earlier when championed by Louis Zukofsky (whose abstruse criticism he could barely decipher) as a sort of instinctual Objectivist poet. The problem with that annexation was that Reznikoff was no primitive: he was extremely intelligent, rigorous, and, in his unshow-off way, committed to an ambitiously austere aesthetic program of his own.

Thematically, his work showed a lively, unsentimental sympathy for those underdogs in the urban sweepstakes: the laborer, the beggar, the immigrant, the store owner trying to eke out a living. Stylistically, he hewed to the diction of ordinary American speech, carving his material into tight, haiku-like images and wry vignettes that could best convey the often comical sufferings, struggles, contradictions, and consolations of the everyday human beings he observed, including himself. He also went to sources such as legal documents (*Testimony*), historical records (*Holocaust*), and biblical stories ("King David") for his often unsparing, sometimes gruesomely realistic, verses.

His poetry, immensely appealing as it is, lacks only one quality that has so far kept it from being fully embraced by the academic literary Establishment: "difficulty." There is nothing remotely arcane about it that would require professional interpretation; it speaks for itself . . . or so it would at first appear. I would argue that Reznikoff's work is very sophisticated and requires a good deal of unpacking, precisely because it seems so simple and straightforward. If true for the poetry, how much more so for the fiction.

Reznikoff wrote two novels: the first, *By the Waters of Manhattan*, was published in 1930, just as the Great Depression was getting under way. One associates this writer with the Depression, partly because of the gray air of diminished expectations and pinched circumstances that seems to unify his characters, though their chronic money troubles had predated the 1929 stock market crash and would outlive the postwar boom years. Actually, 1930 was a high point for Reznikoff: he had won the hand of the lovely Marie Syrkin and convinced her to divorce her second husband, and he had finished his first novel, which the respected firm of Charles Boni agreed to publish.

(His second novel, *The Manner Music*, was found in his desk after he died and published posthumously, in 1977. It is very bleak, set in the Depression years as well, and full of fine cutaway descriptions of the city, as two old friends engage in marathon walks, conversing about their dashed dreams and the bitterness of married life, stopping only for the occasional coffee and Danish in a cafeteria. It has many grace notes, but does not hold together nearly as well as his first.)

By the Waters of Manhattan is a diptych. Part One tells the story of Sarah Yetta, who emigrated on her own from Russia to the United States and at great personal sacrifice established a family in New York City. In his letters Reznikoff referred to this narrative as his mother's autobiography. It seems that Sarah Reznikoff wrote an account of her life called "Early History of a Seamstress," and her son reworked this material into the first part of *By the Waters of Manhattan*, just as he would later rework the harsh documentary summaries of nineteenth-century American legal cases into the poems that would constitute *Testimony*. And, as if it were a dry run for *Testimony*, oftentimes horrific events such as serious illness, death, betrayals, pogroms, hostility between family members, swindles by trusted partners, are told with a deadpan terseness, as vignettes offered up in the no-nonsense manner of oral storytelling: the shocks of fortune laid out and the aftershocks allowed to register in the reader's mind, with no attempt to milk emotion.

The language of this first part has a slightly foreign inflection. The *New York Times* reviewer who panned the book complained: "Too often one feels as if one were reading a jerky and not particularly felicitous translation." The anonymous reviewer was correct to sniff out a "translated" quality in the prose—Reznikoff was channeling his mother's immigrant voice—but wrong to think it was an accident or mistake. Nowadays we are much more aware of the contributions that Jewish-American writers such as Saul Bellow, Bernard Malamud, and Philip Roth have made to our literature by twisting and torquing the language and giving it a playful Yiddish tinge. We have also become, I suspect, more grateful to immigrant literature as a whole, whether its source be European, Latin American, African, or Asian, for these priceless accounts of the newcomers' struggles to adapt to the

United States. The impatience of the *Times* reviewer in 1930, however, suggests that there was still embarrassment about sounding like a greenhorn. Reznikoff's deliberate cultivation of this alienation effect in the novel's first part can be read as a stubborn provocation or an entrancing coloration.

The peculiar spin on diction begins with the very title of the novel, *By the Waters of Manhattan*. This title was a favorite of Reznikoff's: he used it repeatedly, almost like a good-luck charm, for a 1929 annual that contained stories, poems, and the first part of the novel; for the 1930 novel; and for his 1962 selected verse. It is hard to say why this phrase held such appeal for him, but I hear in it an echo of Longfellow's *Song of Hiawatha*: "By the shores of Gitche Gumee." The locution "By the . . ." also sounds biblical (the Old Testament was never far from Reznikoff's mind, and he named two poetry collections *By the Well of Living and Seeing*). New Yorkers are notorious for disregarding the fact that their city is on the water, so the emphasis on *waters* (plural) suggests an ironic, archaic undertone: in any case, a learned idiom.

Part One ends with a telling line of dialogue, spoken by Sarah Yetta, which operates as a hinge between the halves: "We are a lost generation," she says. "It is for our children to do what they can." The paradox, for us, is that these first-generation immigrants, who braved dangers so resourcefully and sacrificed so much for their offspring, seem to possess a wholeness of self and spirit, while their relatively more privileged children seem the lost, fragmented ones.

The second part focuses on Sarah's son, Ezekiel, who (we learn from Reznikoff's letters) was modeled not on himself but on his friend Joel. It is significant that this Ezekiel bears the same first name as his grandfather, a *luftmensch* who secretly wrote poetry. When Grandfather Ezekiel died, his wife, Hannah, burned all his verses, thinking they might contain some reference to Nihilists and get the family in trouble with the Russian police. "As she put the first into the fire she said, 'Here's a man's life.' " With characteristic understatement Reznikoff the novelist leaves it at that; but Reznikoff the man was deeply affected all his life by the burning of his grandfather's poetic output, which actually happened, and his own persistence not only in writing but in seeing the work published at all costs, even setting the type and printing it himself, was clearly in part a defiant response to that earlier erasure. This point is eloquently made by Stephen Fredman in his fine study of Reznikoff, *A Menorah for Athena*:

> Here is the primal scene of poetry for Charles Reznikoff. His grandfather's lifework, his secret self, written in Hebrew, language of the Torah—not Yiddish, language of the Diaspora, or Russian, the cosmopolitan language—is destroyed out of fear and ignorance. . . . This "sad story" was related by Reznikoff obsessively in interviews and in the family histories he wrote in prose and verse. . . . Making manifest his inheritance, Reznikoff's poems are the great-grandchildren—as though the dead, cremated manuscript had produced, through the intermediary of Charles's mother, this new breed of American Jewish poems.

In the novel, Reznikoff's character, Ezekiel the younger, is not a writer, however, but a touchy malcontent, a would-be artist without an art. "If he had studied music, if he could draw and paint . . . ," he broods.

The two parts of the novel are radically different from each other: the first flows with the folkloric sound of a family chronicle and spans decades, while the second slows down, covers a chronological period of months, and is much more introspective, taking us into Ezekiel's thoughts and stream of consciousness. The language in the second part is also different, having lost its foreign tinge and become American-educated, sprinkled with poetic quotations and references to Wordsworth and the Buddha in the Metropolitan Museum. Most crucially, the psychology is vastly different: the first part has an extroverted, indirect psychology, similar to that of Gertrude Stein's *Three Lives*, where the working-class protagonists are barely aware that they have an unconscious, much less that they are expressing it in every statement they make. Sarah Yetta acts forthrightly and maturely, even as a young girl, with consistent rectitude. She may sorrow at the changeable nature of people's emotions, a neighbor who goes from friendliness to frosty hostility, but she herself is solid and dependable. Ezekiel, her son, is more unstable in his emotional response, as we see so dramatically and frankly in his sudden satiety with the previously unattainable Jane once she submits erotically to him. Prone to defensive rationalizations, Ezekiel suspects his own motives and is already tired to death of his narcissistic air of superiority, knowing full well he has accomplished so little. (Such neurotic self-suspicion would have been a luxury for his mother, who needed to hold on to any shred of self-respect in the face of a community that denounced her as prideful when she struck out on her own.)

Thematically, the two parts connect to each other with an organic rightness, telling the whole painful story of immigration in America as it has tended to play out on the family front. Still, the halves are in many ways radically unlike: so it is puzzling that both the novel's defenders and its detractors paid so little attention, in 1930, to the differences between the two parts, thereby scanting the book's haunting strangeness.

When first published by Boni, it contained an introduction by the then-prominent literary figure Louis Kronenberger. He began by saying: "It is a long time since I have read a story so obviously sincere—and so tellingly simple. The simplicity, from the first paragraph to the last, is not an incidental virtue or a trick of technique; it is essential. It bears no relation to the over-cultivated monosyllables which have come as a reaction to our over-cultivated (and belated) Eighteen Nineties. Here is nothing falsely *naïf* in story or in style. There is, in fact, no 'style.' " Though Kronenberger goes on to praise the novel for its severe refusal of romantic theatricality, and for the realism of its inconclusive ending, I am struck by the application of this backhanded-compliment critical vocabulary ("simple," "sincere," "no 'style' ") to Reznikoff.

The great critic Lionel Trilling, who also praised the novel in a glowing review that appeared in *The Menorah Journal*, was similarly taken with Reznikoff's sincerity and purity:

> Certainly it is not great prose in the sense that it is exciting or compelling. It makes no pretension to this. Perhaps it is merely such prose as we should expect at the least from every writer—each word understood and in its right place; each word saying exactly what it should say and not forced beyond its meaning. . . . In short, style becomes

its writer's morality. . . . The charm of Mr. Reznikoff's book lies in its avoidance of . . . falsification. His book has true words, hence truth—solid, raw, sociological truth.

This is a splendid tribute, but I wonder if such points of view have not done Reznikoff's literary reputation more harm than good. To make of Reznikoff an angel of sincerity and raw sociological truth-telling seems to me to slight the selectivity of his artistry and the lyrical beauty of his language. Let us consider some examples:

He was glad to find himself on the bridge, the tenements and office buildings behind him, his face towards the sky. Soon the roadway changed to slats of wood, springy under his feet after so many miles of asphalt. Ezekiel was pleased, too, after the even curves of gutters and the straight lines of pavements and houses to see the free glitter of the water. He was now in the rhythm of walking, that sober dance which despite all the dances man knows, he dances most.

No "style"? Reznikoff speaks enthusiastically of "a new science, city-craft," and his novel is replete with urban tableaux that offer up the verbal equivalent of John Sloan's or Edward Hopper's New York paintings, like the marvelous descriptions of the Automat or the barber shop or the Italian procession. There are astute little aphorisms dropped into the text: "Somewhere there must be a woman—so a girl, he thought, dreams of the man she hopes to marry and at last puts up with her husband." Or: "He decided not to drink. After a while his thirst would pass, as it often did, just like hunger and cold. The body, he had found, makes its needs known and after awhile, unanswered, concludes its master cannot satisfy it, though he would, or is busy, and courteously becomes silent." This is lucid, spare writing, yes, but styleless? I find it elegant in its concise shifts from the man's to his body's perspective, and from the needy particular to the philosophically general.

There is also a richness of sensory description, the way a character tries to shake off "his familiar despondency" and adhere to the available charms of the present. "In the bright morning he looked eagerly at the houses, at each horse and milkwagon." "The silver of the thin dime was an unexpected pleasure." "How good to rest." "He ate slowly, to taste each morsel to the utmost, and praised God." This elemental side of Reznikoff most resembles his contemporary William Carlos Williams, who ended the poem "To a Poor Old Woman" about the solace of eating plums in the street with the simple repeated "They taste good to her."

If the novel ends inconclusively, it is because Ezekiel's hopefulness and discouragement have fought to a legitimate standstill. He has managed to start his own business, a bookstore in Greenwich Village, with virtually no capital, though now he has little time for an inner life, and feels imprisoned, tied down to work; he has shaken off virginity and has a robust sex life, though now he is growing tired of his mistress; he decides one moment to drink "the bitter night of his life" and the next moment is diverted by a girl passing by; he looks at himself and sees both an ordinary young man and a swindler. He is, in Reznikoff's words, "Janus-faced," turning one visage to the world and another away from it. He lives on a knife edge between optimism and despondency. Just when everything seems depleted inside, there is an upturn. This bobbing-up reflex in the midst of potentially drowning is a deeply moving trope in Reznikoff's prose and verse; he reverts to it again and again, as his way of bearing witness to the human spirit's resiliency within a punishing world. "It seemed to Ezekiel that his thoughts at last brought out the sun, whose brightness they had been touching and leaving and returning to, as a bird pecks at a golden fruit." The power of one man's thought to bring out the sun—that is true magic, an indication of why *By the Waters of Manhattan* is finally a poet's novel.

The Improbable Moralist

Leonard Michaels (1933–2003) was an original; everything he wrote, like it or not, came alive. His prose kept moving at a fast clip, and paid readers the compliment of assuming they could match his mental velocity, with a concise, pungent, and pyrotechnic style that tolerated no flab. It won him admirers as diverse as Susan Sontag, William Styron, Larry McMurtry, and Charles Baxter—Michaels's reputation always stood higher with fellow writers than with the general public. One reason may have been his avoidance of make-nice redemptions and his insistence on hard truths (like the waiter in his delicatessen story who blurts out to customers: "There is no such thing as lean pastrami"). But it's also fair to say that his preoccupation with betrayals, sexual randiness, and aggression could strike some readers as nasty, hard to take. There was another side of Michaels, tender, appreciative, and compassionate, which gained strength as he grew older. The publication of his collected stories should win him many new fans, offering as it does ample proof that he was among the few essential American short story writers of the past half century. His short roman à clef, *Sylvia*, also reissued, about a hideous start-up bohemian marriage in Greenwich Village, is one of the most powerful pieces of autobiographical prose to have resulted from this age of the memoir.

Michaels burst on the scene in the sixties with the incendiary stories that were collected in his first book, self-deprecatingly entitled *Going Places* (1969). Many of these stories followed the adventures of Philip Liebowitz, a young man on the make, driven by envy and id, set loose in the mean streets and salons of Manhattan. Down below were "the street fighters, the city's most deeply kicked, stabbed and slashed"; up above, in fancy Central Park West apartments, another kind of violence. In "The Captain," Liebowitz, desperate for employment, goes to a party and tries to butter up the hostess:

> "Do you really want the job, Mr. Liebowitz?"
> I said, "Let's fuck."
> She blinked and shook her head. She sighed.
> I had been too quick, too smart. I shrugged like a man with nothing more to say, and looked across the room at them, sitting close on a couch, talking. To express life's failure, I lifted a cigarette.

These stories satirize the bourgeois swingers who rationalize bad behavior with pronouncements like "I'll kill you. To me the connection between love and death is very close" or "I will say one thing, Cosmo, you meet people in an orgy." Again and again, Liebowitz finds himself having sex almost inadvertently with the hostess while her husband (sometimes his best friend) is banging on the door. The sex is usually compulsive and sprinkled with literary references: "I caught her hand, dragged her down like a subaqueous evil scaly. We kissed. She bit me. I bit her ear. We kissed and there was no outside except for the phone ringing again. I let it. We had D. H. Lawrence, Norman Mailer, *triste*." The clipped sentences mock a hard-boiled persona: Philip Marlowe by way of that other Philip, perennial English-lit doctoral candidate Liebowitz.

These early stories merge recognizable Gotham settings with Oedipal nightmare surrealism. A father bursts in on his daughter in bed with the naked Liebowitz, who scurries out onto the street without his clothes; there he is admonished by the elderly doorman for not being nice; he slips back to his girlfriend, only to discover that her father has had a massive heart attack and is in the hospital; she whispers, "Fuck me." The characters seem helpless, dread-filled, driven by blind appetite and impulse.

If these early stories resist garden-variety realism, the ones in Michaels's second book, *I Would Have Saved Them If I Could* (1975) go further in the direction of the postmodern: list stories, parables, fragments, pastiches. The title story, for instance, is a brilliant collage of reflections about the author's immigrant family, Lord Byron, Karl Marx, Borges, and the concentration camps. Right in the middle is a section entitled "Black Bread, Butter, Onion," a sort of urban pastoral prose-poem, which conveys Michaels's talent for capturing the everyday, while measuring the guilt-ridden distance his character has come from the Old World sufferings and sacrifices of his relatives:

> The black bread should be Pechter's, but the firm went out of business, so substitute bialys from the bakery on Grand Street, between Essex and Clinton, on the right heading toward the river, not Soho. With your thumb, gauge and tear bialys open along the circumference. Butter bialys. Insert onion slices. Do this about 3:00 a.m., at the glass-topped table in my parents' dining room, after a heavy date in Greenwich Village. My parents should be asleep in their bedroom, twenty feet away. Since my father is dead, imagine him. He snores. He cries out against murderous assailants. I could never catch his exact words. Think what scares you most, then eat, eat. *The New York Times*, purchased minutes ago at the kiosk in Sheridan Square, is fresh; it lies beside the plate of bialys. As you eat, you read. Light a cigarette. Coffee, in the gray pot, waits on the stove. Don't let it boil. Occasional street noises—sirens, cats—should penetrate the Venetian blinds and thick, pleated drapes of the living-room windows. The tender, powdery surface of the bialys is dented by your fingertips, which bear odors of sex; also butter, onion, dough, tobacco, newsprint, and coffee. The whole city is in your nose, but go outside and eat the last bialy while strolling on Cherry Street. The neighborhood is Mafia-controlled, completely safe. You will be seen from tenement windows and recognized. Smoke another cigarette. Take your time. Your father cries out in his sleep, but he was born in Europe. For a native American kid, there is nothing to worry about. Even if you eat half a dozen bialys, with an onion and coffee, you will sleep like a baby.

In subsequent collections, such as *Shuffle* (1990) and *A Girl with a Monkey* (2000), Michaels would continue to juggle the roles of good son and bad boy. His superb list story "In the Fifties" records: "I knew card sharks and con men. I liked marginal types because they seemed original and aristocratic, living for an ideal or obliged to live it. Ordinary types seemed fundamentally unserious. These distinctions belong to a romantic fop." Meanwhile, "I was a teaching assistant in two English departments. I graded thousands of freshman themes. . . . I wrote edifying comments in the margins. Later I began to scribble 'Awkward' beside everything, even spelling errors."

"Are you experienced?" Jimi Hendrix demanded. Michaels came of age at a time when being experienced seemed to require forcing yourself to violate prudence and common sense: like Norman Mailer's "White Negro" or Philip Roth at his raunchiest, or the filmmaker James Toback in *Fingers* and *The Gambler*, Michaels had a naïve craving to be "cool." But he always acknowledged self-mockingly the potential shallowness of such adventures. Is the nature of experience to sleep with as many women as possible, to gamble, to hang out with gangsters, kill a man, sell drugs? Or is it to learn to sit in one's room, calmly and contemplatively, as Pascal recommended.

Michaels took a teaching job in Berkeley, where he lived for the last decades of his life, save for a period near the end in Italy. As James Baldwin fled America for Paris to save himself from being eaten by rage, so Michaels abandoned New York, which he saw as a ruthless killer-city, for the milder climes of the Pacific. Reading *Sylvia*, that excruciating, harrowing account of his first, mutually punishing marriage to an emotionally disturbed woman who, when he finally decided to leave her, took revenge by committing suicide in his presence, you understand why he had to get away.

In middle age, Michaels's stories deepened and mellowed; he grew fonder of ordinary people, more stoically realistic. There was less evidence of a player's need to show off. Oh, occasionally he would still relapse into razzle-dazzle sensationalism, as with the silly "Viva la Tropicana," where Jewish gangsters spray bullets and take Cuban mistresses. But overall, a solacing sadness replaced frantic hysteria. He began to look back at his youthful competitive angst with detachment, as in the story "Honeymoon":

> I felt envy, a primitive feeling. Also a sin. But go not feel it. According to Melanie Klein, envy is among the foundation stones of Brain House. Nobody is free of it. I believed envy is the chief principle of

life: what one man has, another lacks. Sam is smart; hence, you are stupid. Joey is tall; hence, you are a midget. Kill Sam and Joey, you are smart and tall.

Ultimately, this Social Darwinist outlook, bred in the Lower East Side ghetto of Michaels's youth, where bright Jewish boys vied like rival gang members for college scholarships and dates, had to give way. But not before it had propelled Michaels through a careening, womanizing existence; he married four times. He could be, as they say, "difficult." This may be the moment to admit that I knew Lenny, and considered him a friend, though we rarely saw each other, living as we did on opposite coasts. He was a handsome, moody, casually erudite man who strutted (he loved Latin music, the sensual art of its dance movements) and brooded (he had a touch of the obsessive about him, and seemed to go around sniffing hostility in the air). On the other hand, he was one of the kindest, shrewdest men I've ever known. Wendy Lesser, who often published him in her *Threepenny Review*, has written a wonderful portrait of Lenny, loving yet clear-eyed, in her 2007 memoir, *Room for Doubt.* She admits his temperamental, touchy side; also, that he was enormously generous, especially toward younger writers, a rare trait in the literary world. I find it interesting that Lesser says she prefers Michaels's essays to his stories. I would not go that far, though he was a marvelous essayist (Montaigne was his god). I will say he increasingly tried to complicate the frontier between fiction and nonfiction. He published diary extracts as short stories, fascinated with how the minimalist journal entry could bear the heart of a tale. As the guest editor of a special fiction issue of *Ploughshares*, he published my "Against Joie de Vivre," though I kept insisting it was a personal essay. Michaels had a broader, more inclusive idea of genre. He insisted on calling *Sylvia* first "a fictional memoir," then "a novel," though it was, from what I gather, entirely factual. In any case, I read it as a memoir.

One of the ways in which his own fiction writing evolved in an essayistic direction was that he became increasingly receptive to aphorism and digressive reflection, what may be called the "wisdom aside." Nowhere was this shift to wisdom more pronounced than in his final, impressive suite, the Nachman Stories. These seven beautiful short stories, brought together for the first time in his posthumous *Collected*, feature a protagonist-mathematician who lives a quiet life in California. We are explicitly told that Nachman "wasn't especially sensual," that his "need for ecstasy was abundantly satisfied" by working out mathematics problems and playing the violin, that he was "a strict observer of limits. He didn't fool around." In other words, he is not ruled by appetites—in some ways the opposite of Michaels's earlier alter ego, Philip Liebowitz.

The tension in these last stories thus shifts from the consequences of acting out to those of restraint and right action. In one story, Nachman goes so far as to place his hand momentarily on the thigh of a Vietnamese haircutter on whom he has a mad crush, and agonizes afterward about possibly having disrespected her, though she is clearly interested in having an affair with him. In another story, he wonders whether it is proper to burst the balloon of a mathematician who has claimed to solve a celebrated problem, by showing him where he has gone wrong in his demonstration. In yet another story, he broods about whether to tell his best friend, Norbert, that his wife, Adele, has been cheating on him. "People who told unbearable news to friends, as if it were their duty, then felt very good about themselves while their friends felt miserable— Nachman was not like those people. Besides, to feel good about oneself was important only to narcissists." He does tell the wife, with whom he is also friends, that she is talking nonsense when she says she was "helpless" to resist the affair:

> "I don't believe that experience, for its own sake, is the highest value. . . . There are limits."
> "I think you mean morals."
> "O.K., morals. Yes, morals. You have something against morals?"

In the Nachman Stories, Michaels openly acknowledged that he was a moralist. Of course, he had been one from the start; but now he was willing to identify with a good man who insisted that we take responsibility for our actions, that experience is not the end-all. I am not saying that Michaels *became* Nachman, any more than he had earlier been Philip Liebowitz; but I am saying that he'd reached a stage in his life where he was interested in exploring a surrogate self who believed in boundaries, in acting like a *mensch,* and whose sense of value would derive in large part from work. Nachman's friend Norbert mocks him: "You live a small life. Somebody gives you a pencil and a piece of paper and you are a happy Nachman. Like a kid on a beach." Nachman calmly explains: "When I solve a problem, I collect a piece of the real." Here, I think Michaels was directly speaking about his life as a writer.

This is how Leonard Michaels put it in a journal entry: "Writers die twice, first their bodies, then their works, but they produce book after book, like peacocks spreading their tails, a gorgeous flare of color soon schlepped through the dust."

That *schlepped,* placed where it is, testifies to his capacity to goose a sentence. If prose makers can be divided into sentence writers and paragraph writers, then Michaels was more a sentence writer, in the manner of Isaac Babel, who famously declared a period should come with the piercing effect of a bullet. But *schlepped* also signifies Michaels's debt to Yiddish. Many of his vivid sentences exist in a kind of syntactical exchange between English and Yiddish inflections: "Perhaps a girl with so much needed someone like him—a misery." Just before he died, he wrote a fine essay in *Threepenny Review* about the Yiddish language. And it was surely no accident that he gave his last protagonist the same name as that great Hasidic storyteller, Rabbi Nachman of Bratslav. Michaels never stopped reflecting on the condition of being Jewish. Now that he is gone, it is easier to place him in a broader context, as part of that astonishing flowering of American Jewish writing that included Bellow, Malamud, Mailer, and Roth, toward which he can be seen as both filial heir and mischievous critic.

James Agee:
Nobility Overload

In 1958, three years after James Agee suffered a terminal heart attack in a taxicab at forty-five, his self-described friend and fellow film critic Manny Farber wrote an essay called "Nearer My Agee to Thee." The title captures Farber's characteristically mischievous attempt to wrest the real writer from his pious followers: "Even when he modified and showboated until the reader got the Jim-jams, Agee's style was exciting in its pea-soup density." In retrospect, Farber's effort to forestall sanctimony by objective assessment seems doomed, because Agee was such a prime candidate for literary sainthood: handsome, tortured good looks, a cross between Montgomery Clift and Robert Ryan; body-punishing habits (alcohol, cigarettes, work jags, insomnia), a rebellious streak, many loves, obsession with integrity, and an early death. He belonged to that bruised, vulnerable, too-good-for-this-world poster club of actors, writers, and rock stars whose authenticity was vouchsafed by premature passing.

The canonization of James Agee appears to be complete with Library of America's two-volume set, bringing together all his fiction and film criticism, plus some high journalism and *The Night of the Hunter* screenplay. In a way, Agee is a perfect fit for the LoA, which, having published the obvious national classics by Hawthorne, Melville, Twain, James, et cetera, has since branched out to include "major minor" writers such as Dawn Powell, H. P. Lovecraft, and Carson McCullers, whose careers can be polished off in a volume or two. If these forays have exposed the LoA to criticism for diluting the house's founding standards, they have also provoked fruitful reassessments of marginal literary figures by calling the question in this way, while putting into readers' hands impeccably edited and elegantly printed texts that might otherwise be scattered or out of print.

Beyond his thanatoptic mystique, Agee's reputation rests on three claims: a hugely peculiar nonfiction tome, *Let Us Now Praise Famous Men*; an impressive body of movie criticism; and a beautiful, heartbreaking novel, *A Death in the Family*. Having now bolted down almost sixteen hundred pages in the two volumes, I find it easier to agree that Agee's overall achievement merits inclusion in the LoA's list than to know what to make of my lingering ambivalence toward this literary charmer.

Agee was born in 1909 and grew up in Knoxville, Tennessee. When he was seven his much-loved father, Jay, died in an automobile accident. This tragedy, and the grief and longing that ensued, helped shape his consciousness for life. His mother placed him in the St. Andrew's School, where his Anglo-Catholicism deepened, under the influence of a teacher, Father James Flye, who became a surrogate father, mentor, and friend. Agee, an excellent student, enrolled in the Phillips Exeter Academy and later was admitted to Harvard. At some point early on he developed that high-minded, solemn, strutting rhetorical style which would be his calling card and his nemesis. His literary gods were Joyce and Faulkner, and, as with Faulkner, his first love was poetry.

While still a senior at Harvard, Agee wrote a parody of *Time*, which landed him, after graduation, a job at *Fortune*, the business magazine recently started by Henry Luce. It is significant that Agee's entry into the Luce empire should have been by way of parody, because it epitomized his own conflicted relationship to the journalistic teat. Sometimes he was Luce's fair-haired boy, sometimes the independent Joycean who refused to compromise with the media's expectations of clear copy. His journalistic bona fides gave him access to the larger world, but also required him to pretend an interest in business affairs. Sent to cover the Tennessee Valley Authority, he came back with crème de la crème descriptive prose that delighted his bosses. Agee, a fan of Pare Lorentz's documentary *The River*, with its orotund naming ("Down the Monongahela. . . ."), commenced his own piece with "The Tennessee River system begins on the worn magnificent crests of the southern Appalachians, among the earth's oldest mountains, and the Tennessee River shapes its valley into the form of a boomerang, bowing it to its sweep through seven states." *Fortune* sent him out again, with the great photographer Walker Evans, to report on cotton tenant farmers in Alabama, and he returned with hunks of the impenetrable rock or uncut diamond that would become *Let Us Now Praise Famous Men*. They rejected it.

Let Us Now Praise Famous Men (the title comes from Ecclesiastes) is often glibly spoken of as a classic, but if it is, it must be one of the most unread and unreadable classics, which educated people would rather compliment than endure. I tried twice in the past to get through it, and only managed a third time by taking on this reviewing assignment. What makes it so difficult to read is its thick fog of lyrical rhetoric, and its total lack of forward momentum. It essentially breaks down into a series of prologues: for four hundred pages Agee keeps starting the book, promising and backing away, introducing us to the ostensible subjects and then refusing to describe them. Originally called *Three Tenant Families*, it purports to be about three interrelated, hardscrabble clans, the Gudgers, the Ricketts, and the Woods. However, Agee had such scruples about any traditional approach that might conceivably exploit, betray, or simplify these poor folk—the journalistic, the psychological, the aesthetic, the anthropological—that he was left with his hands tied, reduced to meditative mini-essays about roosters, mules, and bedbugs, whose feelings would presumably not be hurt by his speculations. Some of these passages are marvelous, but all leave us frustratingly outside the main drama because he disdains to develop his subjects as characters. "There will be no time in this volume to tell much of their personalities," he says about the farm children, in a volume that seemingly has time for everything else. The book turns out to be more about Agee's shy, reverential feelings toward these salt-of-the-earth farmers, and his hunger to be liked by them, than about the people themselves. (How little he actually knew them becomes clear in *And Their Children After Them*, a valuable book written fifty years later by Dale Maharidge and Michael Williamson, who studied the Agee families' survivors and progeny, and uncovered their incest, abuse, and other goings-on.)

Despite Agee's reluctance to aestheticize his subjects, he ends up doing exactly that, as though he had come upon a set of intact Doric statues in an Alabama field. Of course he was competing with the daunting success of Walker Evans's photographs, which Agee adored. Even more than treating the tenant farmers as visually uncanny, his response was to imbue them with "sacramental" wonderment. Again and again, Agee has an epiphanic response to the tenant farmers, their "helpless innocence" and "beatitude." (At such moments, he sounds like an early Beat.) "The least I could have done was to throw myself flat on my face and embrace and kiss their feet," he wrote about encountering a young Negro couple on the road, not without a trace of self-parody. When he is taken in by the Gudgers for the night, after his car runs aground, he makes it into a biblical parable, as though he is an angel and they are hospitable patriarchs.

In a way, Agee remained primarily a religious writer. His faith in Anglo-Catholic practice may have wavered, but his attraction to the spiritual, his attempt to convey the "predicaments of human divinity," as he put it, never faltered. His first book, a collection of poems called *Permit Me Voyage*, and his first extended fiction, a labored novella called *The Morning Watch*, about an adolescent altar boy having a crisis of faith, both attest to this preoccupation. In *Let Us Now Praise Famous Men*, he really let loose.

The book is a catchall, with reveries, documents, inventories, surveys (Agee throws in his testy response to a *Partisan Review* questionnaire about the state of American literature). Though he began writing it when he was twenty-seven, there are times when he still comes across as a brilliant undergraduate, who cannot stop compiling lists of his favorite enthusiasms, like the list of "unpaid agitators" that includes Blake, Céline, Ring Lardner, Jesus Christ, Freud, and the blues singer Lonnie Johnson. Alongside his celebration of tenderness, there are sudden, outrageously adolescent outbreaks of hostility against everyone who doesn't understand, especially those intellectuals back up North, who dare to fling around words like *sharecropper* and who have "absorbed every corruptive odor of inverted snobbery, marxian, journalistic, jewish, and liberal logomachia, emotional blackmail, negrophilia, belated transference, penis envy." Agee himself was of course a progressive, a self-described lapsed communist, but he mistrusted armchair radicals who did not go out into the *field*, as he did. He expresses frustration that he is unable "to blow out the brains with it of you who take what it is talking of lightly, or not seriously enough." Then he catches himself and admits: "Oh, I am very well aware how adolescent this is."

You have to admire the freedom and wild stubbornness of the enterprise, but the *Times* reviewer who called it a "distinguished failure" may have gotten it right after all. *Let Us Now Praise Famous Men* is a failure, as Agee keeps telling us, but in the end, like Walter Benjamin's Arcades Project, a fascinating ruin.

Assigned by *Fortune* to write a little piece about Brooklyn, Agee moved into the borough and responded with "Brooklyn Is," a dizzying if random Whitmanesque catalog, which was again rejected by the magazine's editors and has only recently resurfaced in a little book put out by Fordham University Press, which optimistically labels it "a New York classic." You would think Luce had had his fill of Agee; but no, the two were made for each other, commerce and culture; St. Jim was his class act, and soon he was back at *Time*, not only writing reviews but obliging whenever Luce needed a valedictorian on staff to strike a lofty tone. The death of FDR? The atom bomb? Get Agee. In an August 20, 1945, piece called "Victory: The Peace," he concludes: "Man's fate has forever been shaped between the hands of reason and spirit, now in collaboration, again in conflict. Now reason and spirit meet on final ground. If either or anything is to survive, they must find a way to create an indissoluble partnership." This sort of immensely talented blather (*you* try it sometime) belongs to the history of oratory and hack writing, in the highest sense.

Between 1942 and 1948, Agee juggled regular film critic chairs for *Time* and *The Nation*, sometimes filing conflicting reviews of the same film. His reviews in *The Nation* tended to be lengthier and more essayistic; those for *Time* shorter, breezier, and more pinned to celebrities. Before he quit to write screenplays in Hollywood, he left a substantial record of moviegoing that has inspired many reviewers since, while irritating the hell out of others.

I consider Agee one of the five major American film critics, the others being Otis Ferguson, Manny Farber, Andrew Sarris, and Pauline Kael. He is always stimulating to read on the movies, but of the five, I disagree with him the most. It may well be a mistake to evaluate a critic on the basis of whether we share his judgments today, since we tend to forgive, in the name of period charm, certain melodramatic or sentimental false notes that would have rubbed a discerning contemporaneous viewer the wrong way. Still, again and again, he seems to get it wrong (by our current cinema studies standards): "Welles has little if any artistry," Billy Wilder makes pictures that are like "a good Ph.D. thesis," Ida Lupino's great performance in *The Hard Way* has an "expression of strained intensity [which] would be less quickly relieved by a merciful death than by Ex Lax." He has little of Farber's visual/formal acuity. Compare Farber's and W. S. Poster's complex appreciation of Preston Sturges with Agee's schoolmaster grading of Sturges as "a never-quite-artist of not-quite genius."

Agee was always on-the-one-handing, on-the-other-handing in his movie reviews. His torturous judgments, particularly on the typical Hollywood product, became almost comic in their whirling-dervish pivots. Frequently he would settle the matter with a series of fuzzy, decorous moral encomia such as "noble," "healthful," "pure." For instance, take this assessment: "I very much like Olivia de Havilland's performance [in *The Dark Mirror*]. She has for a long time been one of the prettiest women in movies; lately she has not only become prettier than ever but has started to act as well. I don't see evidence of any remarkable talent, but her playing is thoughtful, quiet, detailed, and well sustained, and since it is founded, as some more talented playing is not, in an unusually healthful-seeming and likable temperament, it is an undivided pleasure to see."

Agee could never quit bemoaning the sorry state of filmmaking in the forties, which now looks like a pretty good era in retrospect. He lacked Otis Ferguson's savvy enthusiasm for the collective craft of the well-made studio picture. More and more, Agee seemed dead set against commercial filmmaking, period. "Quite a few Hollywood people amused themselves as best they could in their captivity by making such nostalgic and amusing, if far from original melodramas as *The Killers*, *The Big Sleep*, and *The Dark Corner*. Such harmless little slumming parties were treated by a number of critics, reviewers, and editorial writers as if they were a sinister mirror of American morals, psychology, society and art." So much for film noir.

While reviewing the film at hand, Agee always seemed to be *willing* another kind of movie into existence. He wanted, he said, to see pictures "made on relatively little money, as much at least by gifted amateurs as by professionals," shot on location, using nonprofessional actors, eschewing music scores, not "hindered by commercial work in studios." Impatient with set-building artifice, he became the prophet and avatar for a shoe-string, independent cinema of social themes, which he found at the time in war documentaries and Italian neorealism. (He also lent his energies to this type of filmmaking, participating in Helen Levitt's *In the Street* and Sidney Meyers's *The Quiet One*.) Not surprisingly, Agee championed *Open City* and *Shoeshine* when they first debuted, mounting a very high horse indeed for the latter: "The elementary beginning of true reason, that is, of reason which involves not merely the forebrain but the entire being, resides, I should think, in the ability to recognize oneself, and others, pri-marily as human beings, and to recognize the ultimate absoluteness of re-sponsibility of each human being. (I can most briefly suggest what I mean by a genuine recognition of human beings as such by recommending that you see the Italian movie *Shoeshine* and that you compare it in this respect with almost any other movie you care to name.) I am none too sure of my vocabulary, but would suppose this can be called the humanistic attitude."

It's astonishing that he could get away with this arch, Elizabethan style in a movie review. W. H. Auden famously applauded Agee's "column as the most remarkable regular event in American journalism today" while acknowledg-ing that "I do not care for movies very much and I rarely see them." No doubt Auden liked it that Agee was sticking it to Hollywood, while sustaining a for-midably literate tone that the great poet placed "in that very select class—the music critiques of Berlioz and Shaw are the only other members I know—of newspaper work which has permanent literary value."

Agee thus became the darling of an educated middle-class reader-ship which was suspicious of popular culture and cinephilia. He had little feeling for genre, and little willingness to make excuses in its name. Nowadays, we might judge Minnelli's *The Clock* to be as fine a humanistic statement in its own way as *Shoeshine*, but Agee, while pulling for it, could only see its virtues as hopelessly compromised and "softened" because of an intrusive music score and a romance plot he judged safe and saccharine.

Agee's distaste for Hollywood smoothness caused him at times to overrate the awkward and unpolished, as in his hype job for an intriguing, clumsy curiosity like Malraux's semidocumentary *Man's Hope*, about the Spanish Civil War:

> The heartsick peasant in the disastrous plane is great movie poetry. The descent of the broken heroes from the desperate stone crown of Spain, as from a Cross, to the maternal valley, a movement so conceived that a whole people and a whole terrain become one sorrowing and triumphal Pietà for twentieth century man, falls possibly short of its full imaginable magnificence, considered syllable by syllable; but in its mass it is poetry even greater. Homer might know it, I think, for the one work of our time which was wholly sympathetic to him.

Whenever Agee mentions movie poetry, you can bet some crucifixion imagery will follow. Praising William Wellman's fine (now neglected) war film, *The Story of G.I. Joe*, he says about the Robert Mitchum role: "And the development of the character of the Captain is so imperceptible and so beautifully done that, without ability to wonder why, you accept him as a great man in his one open attempt to talk about himself and the war, and as a virtual divinity in the magnificent scene which focuses on his dead body. This closing scene seems to me a war poem as great and as beautiful as any of Whitman's." It is not much of a stretch to see that Agee is conflating here the body of his dead father with those of Mitchum and Christ.

In his superbly accomplished autobiographical novel, *A Death in the Family*, Agee got the chance to dilate lovingly over the dead father's body, laid out after a car accident. *A Death in the Family* is modest in scale but rides a deep current of feeling. Agee had brooded over and tried to write this novel all his life; he knew the setting (the Knoxville of his childhood) and the characters (drawn from his immediate family and relatives) inside out. That is to say, he knew them far better than he ever did the tenant farmers in Appalachia, and could tap their flaws and humors with far more honesty and noncondescension. These are people who read Thomas Hardy, *The Nation,* and *The New Republic,* agnostics who worry, but try not to show their horror, because one of them has gotten "religion." The shrewd aunt who takes the young boy Rufus shopping; the boy's gullibility in letting himself be teased by bigger kids on the way to school; the unthinkable and all-too-real, irrevocable loss of the father, whom we have already come to love; the young mother's vacillation between stoicism and hysteria; the alcoholic, self-pitying uncle—all these and more are perfectly achieved. Though Agee left the manuscript unfinished at his death, it doesn't need anything else; the emotional arc has more or less been completed. The novel was published posthumously two years after he died, and won the Pulitzer Prize in 1958. The book testified to Agee's successful digging out of his narcissistic gulch and gaining an objective, shifting perspective on a half dozen protagonists. Perhaps the experience he had had writing Hollywood screenplays (*The Night of the Hunter* and *The African Queen*) had strengthened his sense of structure, even as it made him less resistant to satisfying a bourgeois audience with accessible, vivid storytelling and fully developed characters.

Michael Sragow, the series editor, has done an excellent job selecting the texts and, in his biographical notes, keeping straight all of Agee's similar-named wives, Via, Alma, and Mia. He has omitted Agee's poems (no great loss) and his other screenplays (then again, Agee was a much better novelist than a screenwriter). I may have wanted to see some correspondence, especially a few letters to Father Flye and Robert Fitzgerald, but I think we have enough to go by here. The totality suggests a hardworking, self-destructive writer with flashes of greatness and equal expressions of bluff artist, whose poignant legacy deserves our continued and sympathetic, if unillusioned, regard.

On Not Reading Thomas Bernhard

S ome years ago I received a request from a friend, the deeply and
widely cultivated Katharine Washburn, that I send her something
for a literary journal she was coediting about Thomas Bernhard. Always
eager to satisfy Katharine, in spite of my reservations on the subject, I
eventually wrote the following in the form of a letter to her.

Dear K.:

   When you asked me to contribute to your special number on Thomas
Bernhard, I told you that I'd read only one book of his and had no plans to
read more, and you replied with your irresistible voice of throaty mischief
that that too could be the subject of an essay: *Why* did I not read Bernhard?
At the time it seemed an amusing but far-fetched proposal, which I had no
intention of accepting, since an honest answer to that question would have
only exposed my intellectual limitations and unsupportable taste prejudices before an audience of unsympathetic Bernhardites. However, having
just read Robert Craft's longish appreciation of Bernhard in *The New York
Review of Books*, I was struck by the realization that, based on Craft's summaries of the plays, novels, and memoirs in the Bernhard corpus, I was still
not in the least tempted to read further. You ask me why this should be so.
Well, for starters, the approving portrait Craft drew was of someone fero-
cious, solipsistic, bracingly intransigent, despising mediocrity and mother-
land—in other words, a self-important pain in the ass. Of course dedicated

Bernhardites (one imagines them meeting in cellars around the Upper West Side) might well feel that the Craft article did not really do justice to their man, was shallow or typically *NYRB*-magisterial, missing the point, and that I ought not to be swayed by it. The point is that I wanted to be swayed by it, so as to steel myself for a lifelong neglect of this apparently important writer. If Craft is right that Bernhard will one day be studied in every American university, then I had better get some momentum going in refusing to read him further, before my courage collapses.

It wasn't always this way. I remember the first time I came across a fresh copy of Bernhard's novel *Correction*, around 1983, in the Rizzoli Bookstore (was it the original Rizzoli on Fifth Avenue, which I loved, with its Brazilian mahogany staircase and upstairs gallery and sexy monastic ambience, those premises since taken over by Henri Bendel's department store, or the second, present version on West Fifty-Seventh Street, which is more impersonal?—I think it was the old Rizzoli), on a table next to several other paperbacks from a new line, Aventura, the Vintage Library of Contemporary World Literature. This display was almost pornographically tempting to me: first, because I am a sucker for book packaging that creates a snobbish, happy-few aura, and these trade paperbacks, featuring four-color painterly illustrations surrounded by lots of white, on thick white-card cover stock, and the bold calligraphic slash of an *A* for Aventura (the name itself conjuring one of my favorite movies) suggested the realized literary wet dream of a hotshot editor capriciously neglecting the bottom line; second, because my preferred reading consists of neglected foreign writers—I suppose I feel too competitive with my American contemporaries, but I am a comparative literature buff down to the toes, just give me an obscure book by a foreigner with worldly irony, something by Svevo, Pavese, Machado de Assis, Narayan, Pérez Galdós, Milosz, Bassani, Tanizaki, Soseki, Kundera (before he went popular), Eça de Queiroz, Canetti, Zoshchenko, and I'm in paradise. So I had every hope of adding Bernhard to my list of witty melancholics. The paperback carried a quote on the front from George Steiner, [*London*] *Times Literary Supplement*: "The feeling grows that Thomas Bernhard is now the most original, concentrated novelist writing in German." "The feeling grows": that gave me pause. Not Steiner's feeling but *the* feeling, the sentiment of educated readers everywhere. And where were you, Lopate, while this feeling was growing? Were you not, admit it, paying too much attention to the Mets, or going to movies, or reading only *dead* authors, okay, even dead German authors like Walter Benjamin and Robert Musil, but shamefully ignoring the living German writers, so that you were unable to offer a single rival of equally "original, concentrated" merit to refute Steiner's claim? You thought you knew which way the wind was blowing, and yet all along a Bernhard monsoon was collecting offshore. Well, you had better get with it, my friend! On the other hand, George Steiner—do I really respect this man, or is he just some sort of pompous know-it-all? He writes serious, solemn book reviews in *The New Yorker*, which some people say are brilliant, but which always seemed to me no more than respectable—oh, respectable to the highest degree, mind you, it is probably only my stupidity that fails to grasp Steiner's unique contribution to modern thought. He did write that highly regarded essay on Russian literature, *The Hedgehog and the Fox*—no, wait a minute, that was by Isaiah Berlin, and Berlin really *is* brilliant . . . although, come to think of it, I've often finished one of Berlin's essays in *The New York Review of Books* and not understood what was so wonderful about it either. No, Steiner is the one who wrote that other little book about Russian literature, *Tolstoy or Dostoevsky*, which I read as an undergraduate and which left no impression on me. (Years after this Rizzoli episode, I went to a lecture by Steiner in the hope of settling the question once and for all, was he brilliant or not? His public manner seemed to me very impressive, erudite, definitely brilliant, though a day later I couldn't remember anything he'd said, except it was about a passage in Homer. Several feminist women friends of mine who were at that lecture told me later that Steiner was an old-fashioned male chauvinist who was trying to hide the fact in his public presentation, but I suppose it says something about my own untrustworthiness along these lines that I failed to pick up a hint of this tendency in him, just as earlier, when I read Bernhard's *Correction*, I didn't even notice that it was "deeply marred by misogyny," as Craft puts it—or anyway, that wasn't what bothered me about the book.) I then turned the paperback over and saw "Astonishingly original, a composition of strange new beauty" (Richard Gilman, *The Nation*). Wasn't Richard Gilman basically a theater critic who had married the powerful literary agent Lynn Nesbit? Was he trying to establish himself as more of a cultural heavyweight by trumpeting this dense, feverish (I had already peeked at the prose) Austrian writer, the way some movie critic will write a paean to an unassailable literary figure like Primo Levi, just to keep his intellectual stock up? On the other hand, maybe Gilman was already *there*, at the center of our intellectual life, and I had simply failed to realize this fact while spending too much time watching Mets games. Caught in a pincers movement between the combined authority of Steiner and Gilman, finding myself in a quandary of indecisiveness, I thought: oh, what the hell, it's not that expensive, and bought the book and left Rizzoli's. For a while it sat on my coffee table, impressing, I hoped, those visitors who might chance to examine the current pile. Then one afternoon, feeling rigorous and strangely clearheaded, I began reading *Correction*. Initially the fact that there were no paragraph breaks annoyed me, it meant that every time my eyes blinked I would lose my place, there were no chinks to provide footing on those solid cliffs of prose, I worried about eyestrain, plus the absence of visual caesurae made it harder for me to pace myself, to decide that a certain number of pages would constitute the day's quota, there were no chapter endings to aim for, so I kept reading, feeling vaguely migrainous, which I realized may have been the point, since the writing itself was so feverish, claustrophobic, resistant to characters or plot in the traditional sense, it was a sort of meditation, all well and good, I understood what he was doing, I wasn't born yesterday, it's not for nothing I read all those difficult books in my youth, Henry James's *The Golden Bowl*, all those hyperventilating narrators and tortured philosophers, Dostoevsky, Céline, Kierkegaard, Nietzsche, Handke, it was to prepare me for just such an experience as Bernhard, with his obsessively brooding tone, going around and around, bouncing like a metal bead in a pinball machine, wasn't this analytical stuff just the kind of thing I liked? Just my cup of tea? And yet, as I patiently plowed through the novel, twenty pages an hour at one clip, a little voice inside me was saying: This is hard going and is it really worth it? I pushed this thought aside, because I was eager to have a Bernhard under my belt, to have *done* Bernhard, enough to be able to brag that I'd gotten to him sooner than my friends. And indeed, when I finished the book I went around town telling everyone how brilliant it was, how they really ought to read it, *had* to read it, I was overstating my enthusiasm because after all I wanted some reward, some intellectual street credit for the effort I'd put in. I wanted to be part of that growing *feeling*, marching shoulder to shoulder with George Steiner and Richard Gilman and Susan Sontag and the rest, and even if none of them recognized me or acknowledged my greeting as we marched along, I knew, *I* knew that I had done my homework, I wasn't just a layabout watching the Mets game, I was someone who both watched the Mets *and* read Thomas Bernhard. I was a well-rounded individual, sound mind in sound body, *mens sana in corpore sano*, as we used to say back in Columbia College.

It so happens that whenever I discover a writer I like, I start acquiring all of his or her books, stockpiling them for that first summer day when I'm free from student papers and can read purely for pleasure. But I noticed that something seemed to be holding me back from acquiring other Bernhard titles. There was something a little too fanatical about him for my taste— too hothouse, too punitive, what have you. I wondered if he had a true sense of humor. What I missed in him that I enjoyed in my favorite ironists, from Montaigne to Machado de Assis, was that gyroscopic balance and self-skepticism, or modesty, which would rescue the analytical work from megalomania, so that even when the narrator seems self-delusional we can still catch the smiling sanity of the author underneath. I wasn't sure whether I could trust that Bernhard was truly detached from his ranting narrator. Maybe he was trying to show that detachment and objectivity were a myth, by bringing us into a claustrophobic space in which no distance, no per-spective would be allowed—to rub our noses, so to speak, in the myopia and unhealthiness of self-absorption that he took to be the universal condi-tion. If so, he had made his point, boy had he made it, like a dentist's drill, he deserved all sorts of credit for daring, experimentation, practicing on the cutting edge, a writer's writer, but it still seemed pretty much a trick, a tour de force, and I wanted—a novel. Better to praise him than to undergo the experiment again. If, as Craft informed us, "*Correction* is Bernhard's most profound work," I had all the more reason to keep away, since I had found his best not exactly to my taste.

My resistance to further burrowing in Bernhard was of a piece with a conscious effort to distance myself from what might be called "the blackmail of the avant-garde." Ever since I was a teenager, I'd swallowed the argument that I should experience a certain difficult artwork because it kept faith with the logic of modernism, so for decades I had paid my dues, digesting works whose stimulations barely compensated for their longueurs: I had waited patiently for the next theatrical image in a Robert Wilson opera to change onstage, listened to hours of Philip Glass's musical repeats, watched Michael Snow's mechanically programmed movie camera scan a barren landscape in 360-degree arcs, dutifully read Hans Haacke's polemical conceptual artworks about Manhattan real estate in art galleries, perused William S. Burroughs's cutup poems in columns scissored from larger texts, all in the hope that I could convince myself that tedium was a necessary prelude to ecstasy. Now all at once it occurred to me that I had never signed a paper committing myself to the army corps of modernism. Nor did I regard myself as an antimodernist. It was simply that I could no longer be coerced into endorsing something because it claimed to be the next aesthetic step. If Bernhard extended Beckett, did that alone make him worth reading? Bernhard was a Jeremiah, the last angry, conscience-torn Austrian. Okay, let him have his fun, but I can't go along with a man who, for instance, makes such a big deal out of hating his country—not that one should necessarily love one's country, but why act so personally injured, so outraged, so *surprised* when it is run by mediocrities? Certainly Austria had much to answer for, having condoned anti-Semitism and Kurt Waldheim, but if indeed it is a ghost living on past grandeurs of the Austro-Hungarian empire, that should inspire pity, not odium. The narrator in Walker Percy's *The Moviegoer* may think "Only the haters are alive," but Percy went on to disprove that by writing a lively novel about gentle human beings incapable of hate.

I'm not saying hate can't produce good literature. Céline, one of my favorite writers, makes an interesting comparison to Bernhard. Céline and Bernhard are both incessant chatterers, fanatics of a sort, unfair witnesses. So why do I tolerate fanaticism in the French writer, whose politics after all were completely reprehensible, unlike Bernhard, who was, if not a democrat, at least an anti-Fascist? It could just be that I stumbled on Céline in my adolescence, when his rage spoke to mine, but I rather think it's because he created vivid scenes and unforgettable characters in the great novelistic tradition, because he possessed a perverse comic genius filled with self-mockery and compassion that gave the lie to his self-proclaimed misanthropy, and because he engineered a cathartic release—that release that Bernhard for the most part puritanically refuses us. Of course I could be all wrong about Bernhard, having read only one of his books. But this letter is not meant to be a serious critique of Bernhard, only an analysis of my resistance to Bernhard. As such, it is also an analysis of my ignorance, for what else could you call the refusal to learn more about a subject? If it has any value, it is only to suggest how we retain calculated prejudices against this or that artist, so as not to be eaten up by the monstrous demands of high culture.

Another reason I have for neglecting Bernhard, which is also not the man's fault, has to do with the way that literary reputations are orchestrated in America—particularly the reputation of an estimable, difficult, supposedly underappreciated foreign writer. American readers are always being scolded by our cultural arbiters about how stupid and lazy we are, how we have no intellectual life compared to Europe, and how we can at least make a start in the right direction by consuming the intellectual flavor of the month. I feel conflicted in this regard, because I would give a lot to be one of those arbiters of cultural fashion, and I suspect that our intellectual life may indeed be small potatoes compared to Europe's (though how can I be sure, having never been a part of European intellectual life?), and I also agree that Habermas, Rulfo, Chiaromonte, et al. are worthwhile authors. On the other hand, I still freeze up at the thought that *they* may be trying to put one over on us, by exaggerating the merits of some of these foreign writers and soft-pedaling their flaws. For instance, I happen to be fond of the Swiss author Robert Walser, but I still can't accept his being packaged as a major writer when he is really an intriguing minor figure, on the order of Lautréamont, who may have inspired the Surrealists but was no Balzac or Baudelaire. Sometimes scholars become so hypnotized by the Lautréamonts and Walsers precisely because of their marginality, or because of their lopsided incompleteness, which allows for all sorts of speculation. Recently I was asked by an even more obscure journal than yours to contribute to their special issue on Robert Walser, for an equally invisible fee, and, being obliging, I turned in an enthusiastic commentary on *The Walk*. It *is* a beautiful story, but I didn't have the guts to state my deeper reservation, which is that, for all of Walser's eccentric charm, and he certainly deserves to be read—a barrel of laughs compared to Bernhard—I still can only take him in small doses before his precious, doll-like, arrested-development sensibility, whether faux-naïf or genuinely childish, gets on my nerves. He is, to put it bluntly, *cracked*, just as Bernhard seems to me, on some level, deranged. When I read either one, the obsessive language has a visionary intensity that can give exquisite insights into the limitations of normalcy. But it's also exhausting, the same way it is exhausting to listen to a paranoid schizophrenic for more than ten minutes. I have had some experience along these lines, a friend of mine had a mental breakdown that took the form of incessant panicked verbalization, logorrhea, the clinical term for which, I believe, is logomania. It was very distressing; it lasted for years; he would phone around eleven o'clock at night and talk in a rush for an hour until I had to hang up. In the end, he killed himself. Perhaps in saying this I have stumbled upon the key to my allergic reaction to Bernhard: I am made too nervous, too threatened by being put in proximity to that aggressive, suicidal, circular discourse, logic's noose, produced on the borders of sanity. That may be as close as I can get to an answer.

Sincerely,

P.

The above was written some time ago. My wonderful, husky-voiced friend Katharine died of lung cancer, after a lifelong smoking habit; Richard Gilman passed away as well, and any day I expect to read an obituary notice for George Steiner. In the meantime, I have read a second novel by Thomas Bernhard, *The Loser*, which struck me as magnificent, satisfying in every way, including character and plot, and an entertainingly haranguing, hilarious collection of essays, called *My Prizes*. I expect to go on reading this author with pleasure. Having expressed all my reservations about Bernhard, I am now free to like him. Go figure.

Worldliness and Regret:
The Charterhouse of Parma

S tendhal first came into my life through the impassioned offices of Dr. Floyd Zulli. Improbable as it may sound to a younger generation, this professor with dark-rimmed glasses, a crew cut, and a zeal for world literature had mesmerized our household and thousands like it into getting up at 6:30 a.m. and turning on the television set to catch his lectures on the novel, in a program called *Sunrise Semester.* Many took the TV course for college credit, but my folks did it for enlightenment. When I think about my parents, lowly textile clerks with no more than high school diplomas, setting the alarm early to hear a lecture on Balzac or Dickens and trying to keep up with the reading, I could weep. Weep, too, for the quaint assumption that the cream of culture should be offered to everyone, and that the people were hungry for it.

In any case, Floyd Zulli (what a name! suggestive of a Hungarian charlatan) kicked off his course with an interesting choice, Stendhal's *The Red and the Black.* We had never heard of this classic; its writer was not a "given," like Dostoevsky or Kafka, in our Brooklyn working-class autodidact ghetto. I was immediately drawn to the mystical sound of "Stendhal," an author with one name, like a magician (or a charlatan, likewise). Of course Zulli made it clear that his real moniker was the more prosaic Henri Beyle, but Beyle's invention of a new identity for himself appealed to me. I, slogging through the indignities of high school, had some self-invention in mind as well.

At college, we read a few chapters of *Le Rouge et le Noir* in French for our language requirement class; while it seemed witty and absorbing, I decided to defer the pleasure of reading the whole novel on my own as long as possible, maybe keeping it for a kind of dessert. Also, by this time I had picked up the snobbish prejudice that the very popularity of *The Red and the Black* made it a little common, whereas *The Charterhouse of Parma* seemed to exude the aroma of a delicacy, literary caviar. So I took up my education in Stendhal with his last great novel. It was assigned for our senior colloquium seminar, come to think of it; I had no choice in the matter.

Colloquium was a semi-big deal at Columbia; you had to get in, and supposedly only the most brilliant students, with the highest grades and best academic minds, made the cut. In practice this meant that I was thrown in with a bunch of dull, overachieving premedical students seeking to become well-rounded, and only a few of my humanities soul mates. To this disappointment was added my unspoken shame, because most of the seniors were entering their second year in the seminar, while I had been rejected the year previous for junior colloquium. I didn't help my cause in that first interview by dismissing the playwright Jean Giraudoux as a lightweight, only to discover later while idly going through the Butler Library card catalog that one of the professors interviewing me had done his doctoral dissertation on Giraudoux! In those days I was perennially provoking Columbia's (to my insecure eyes) genteel faculty with my working-class defensiveness, sometimes intentionally, sometimes not. An intentional provocation, surely, occurred in the first semester of senior colloquium, when instead of writing an analysis of *Rameau's Nephew*, I did a cheeky dialogue in imitation of Diderot about the colloquium itself, satirizing everyone in class, including the two professors, F. W. Dupee, a lion in the English Department, and Richard Kuhns, a younger, tweedier man from Philosophy, who cotaught the class. They were not amused, and demanded a substitute paper, which I never handed in. Dupee forgave me: he was a dear man, sympathetic to revolt, and a fine critic with a subtle prose style; how I could have twitted him so maliciously I'll never know. My next paper would be on *The Charterhouse of Parma*, and this time I resolved to play by the rules.

The Charterhouse of Parma has been characterized as "a miracle of gusto, brio, élan, verve, panache" by its most recent translator, Richard

Howard—all of which is true, but it remains a rarefied pleasure. I took to the book immediately and avidly. Why this rather recherché novel should have so delighted me at twenty requires some background. I'd already been in thrall to a group of writers who specialized in paradox and analysis— Nietzsche, who loved Stendhal, saying, "The man was a human question-mark. . . . Objection, evasion, joyous distrust, and love of irony are signs of health, everything absolute belongs to pathology"; Gide, who declared *The Charterhouse of Parma* his favorite French novel; and Dostoevsky, my mentor, with his penchant for acerbic insight—and they had prepared me for Stendhal, who fit right into this lineage. I also loved the tradition of the comic novel: Fielding's tongue-in-cheek addresses to the reader in *Tom Jones*, Sterne's digressions within digressions in *Tristram Shandy*, Diderot's sabotage of normal plot flow in *Jacques the Fatalist*, Svevo's rationalizing narrator in *Confessions of Zeno*, Machado de Assis's sardonic, pithy style in *Epitaph of a Small Winner*. What tickled me most, I think, was voice—the sound of outrageous candor cutting to the point, combined with a touch of irony insinuating that it could never be that simple.

In Stendhal, I found the exemplar of a spasmodic, abrupt voice whose very impatience signaled vitality. Where another writer might take para-graphs to prepare an insight, Stendhal would polish the business off with a terse epigram, such as "Courtiers, who have nothing to examine in their souls, notice everything." His mind was so generously well-stocked he could afford to throw away one-liners. His paragraphs lacked topic sentences: rather, they were all topic sentence, one atop another. He dispensed with transition sentences whenever it suited him—a prose predecessor of the jump cut I so loved in French New Wave directors like Godard and Truf-faut. "Let us skip ten years of happiness . . ." was a typical brazen shortcut by Stendhal. To leave out the plodding intermediate steps, you need to possess sophistication about the deep structures of narrative, supreme confidence in your own experience of life, and an almost unimaginable faith in the in-telligence of your readers. Stendhal wrote with freedom unconstrained by popular criticism; he wrote, he said, for "the happy few" (the oft-quoted final words of *Charterhouse*) and for an audience a hundred years hence who would truly appreciate him. I was that audience, I liked to think.

I was especially smitten with the early battle scenes, wherein Fabrizio, our Italian hero, voluntarily enlists in the French army. Barely seventeen years old at this point in the story, he runs away from home with a head full of romantic notions and an allegiance to his idol Napoleon. It soon becomes clear that he has no idea what either war or life is about. As he darts from one place to another, following dubious escorts, dodging bullets, getting his horse stolen from him, trying to discover whether he has actually participated in a battle, and encountering all the cowardly behavior of an army in hasty retreat (this is Waterloo, remember), Stendhal observes with comic detachment that Fabrizio did not grasp in the least what was happening. Ah, to understand what is happening to you—the pattern underneath ephemeral events!

If I had to summarize in one word what I cherished about *The Charterhouse of Parma*, that word would be *worldliness*. At twenty I had a romance, almost a mystique about worldliness. Not for me the adolescent pulings of *A Catcher in the Rye*: if the price of entering adulthood was the forfeiture of innocence and whatever residues of childhood wonderment I still possessed, I could not pay that price quickly enough. Disenchantment was my goal. So when *Charterhouse*'s Count Mosca, that worldly diplomat, advises his adored, Gina, the Duchess of Sanseverina, to marry an elderly man who can give her wealth in return for her title, we may be bothered that this nobleman appears to be pimping his heart's desire, but we appreciate his overall grasp of circumstances. In the same pragmatic manner, Mosca advises his handsome young rival Fabrizio, whom he rather likes, to enter the priesthood with an eye to becoming bishop: a strange choice for a libidinous young man, we might think, one requiring years of patient execution, but which makes sense in the context of nineteenth-century ambition (either the red of military life or the black of the clergy). He also advises Fabrizio to take a mistress from a conservative family, and to read in public cafés only the stupidest Ultra newspapers. We are none of us romantic heroes living in isolation; we are social animals, being watched by our potential friends and enemies. Mosca is a realist: what bothers him is not that he has been cuckolded by his wife but that she has embarrassed him by sleeping with a political enemy.

To be worldly is to accept the consequences of knowing that men and women are not angels, that they have appetites they will seek to satisfy as well as justify, and that vice and self-destructiveness play their inevitable parts. Choderlos de Laclos, the author of *Les Liaisons Dangereuses*, another favorite worldly novel of mine at the time (and still), certainly went further in depicting depravity as the common rule: the strategies of seduction that Valmont and the Marquise de Merteuil suggest to each other in that novel turn sex into a chess game to ward off boredom. Stendhal was more interested in demonstrating the political machinations of court life, the techniques of winning by appealing to the courted party's vanity or petty spite. But in both cases it was reason aligned with recognition of appetite that intrigued me. I found the same combination in the Marquis de Sade, whom I also gobbled up at twenty. Youth, largely powerless, is often fascinated with satanic forces, and I now see what a cliché I was. But the Gothic never appealed to me, because as much as I sought evidence of evil, I was listening for, indeed craving, the sound of reasoned analysis, of calm French logic, even when it took a grotesquely hypertrophied form, as in de Sade.

The Charterhouse of Parma and *Les Liaisons Dangereuses* were both books that swept through my family, much discussed by me, my brother, Lenny, and my sister Betty Ann (the youngest, Joan, was still playing with dolls). Betty Ann, who was a year younger than I, dark, attractive, and moody, was particularly drawn to portraits of strong-minded, independent, active women; she modeled herself in adolescence on Duchess Sanseverina, Mme de Merteuil, and Billie Holiday. For Lenny and me, the duchess, Gina, was a sort of fantasy ideal, an older, worldly woman of passion, beauty, and intelligence by whom we dreamed of being taken in hand. I found myself identifying (as did, I think, Stendhal himself) with Count Mosca, a man of icy intelligence and affectionate warmth, whose impressive overview of life is not enough to win him first place in the heart of his beloved Gina. She remains much more taken with her nephew Fabrizio, that gilded youth and heedless naïf.

Wherever he goes, women fall all over themselves to please him. (" 'Speak more respectfully,' said the Countess, smiling through tears, 'of the sex which will make your fortune, for you will always displease the men—you have too much spirit for prosaic souls.' ") Yet even older men, like the bishop, are fond of him, inviting him to take over their stations at some later point. Placing himself forever in danger, he is continually being rescued by the interventions of guardian angels, most notably his adoring aunt.

I did not begrudge Fabrizio his triumphs, but in no way did I identify with him. Already at twenty, I was seeing myself as the witty secondary, who would not get the girl.* A few months later, when we read *Sentimental Education* for colloquium, I again identified not with the dreamy, aristocratic Frédéric but with his resentful lower-middle-class pal, Deslauriers. Possibly so did Flaubert. I wonder if this is a professional deformation: the writer, stuck at his desk, avenges himself against his dreamboat protagonist by making him seem a little vapid, condescending to or undercutting him.

At Columbia, I watched with fascination two of my classmates, Mitch and Jon, who seemed to me golden boys by virtue of their looks and breeding. I befriended both; you might even say I had crushes on them, or at least envied them. They seemed always to be in the midst of complicated troubles, torn between several girls vying for their attention, undecided between different spiritual paths and aesthetic directions. They would come to me for suggestions, and I would, despite my envy, manage to feel superior to their quandaries and dispense advice from my perch of ironic detachment. Why I should have been certain so early that I did not have it in me to be a ladies' man is a question that nags at me. Cowardice, probably, or lack of sustained interest. I don't think it's ever entirely a matter of looks (nor was I ugly) but, rather, of a certain persistence, or receptivity to the chase, which may bubble up from an incompleteness of self that requires amorous adventure to fill—that hazy incompleteness that is often more enticing to women, who see a chance to fill in the blanks, to mold improvements, than the man who projects himself as a "finished portrait" (such as I was already attempting to do). Gina cannot love Count Mosca with all her heart because he is too cautious and too aware of each consequence, while Fabrizio has the reckless, impetuous, disregarding spirit of

---

* Technically, Count Mosca does get Gina, making her his mistress and later his wife, but it is her nephew she loves: the proof is that she lives only for a short time after the death of Fabrizio, "whom she adored."

a sleepwalker, which she associates with capacity for passion. (She's right, it turns out, though his passion will be for Clélia, not for her).

What did I make of Fabrizio when I first read the book? I could never retrieve those responses, were it not for the fact that I happened to keep my colloquium paper. Here it sits before me—typewritten on onion-skin, with Professor Dupee's penciled comments—a shipwrecked sailor rescued from the ark of time. "Fabrizio, the Unconscious Hero" was the title. At the risk of being laughed at for exposing my undergraduate prose, I will quote the beginning:

> The unconscious hero was a favorite character of novelists in the eighteenth and nineteenth centuries. He seemed particularly adapted to a form which was reaching fruition at the time, and which grew from the picaresque novel in many respects: the comic novel of adventure. Fielding is without question the main exponent of his form, just as *Tom Jones* and *Joseph Andrews* are the works which give it definition. However, the formula he perfected—the unconscious hero's ejection from the secure surroundings of his childhood into the larger world, his naïve attitudes when confronted with obvious examples of evil, his near-passive participation in a string of marvel-ous incidents which thrust him into the path of danger and grotesque characters, and finally, his arrival at a stable position—was employed in works as diverse as *Candide, Roderick Random, Gulliver's Travels, Justine,* and *The Charterhouse of Parma.*

After more literary contextualizing, I went on to say:

> The lack of great consciousness in a novel's protagonist seems to in-crease his susceptibility to coincidence. The rational, active, tragic hero in literature constructs his own destiny, and if he is defeated by fate the implication remains that he himself laid the groundwork for his failure. The unconscious hero, however, becomes much more controlled by the laws of chance. As such he is usually more fortu-nate, for he can always be saved by the accidental discovery of a faith-

ful servant like Ludovico, who will nurse him back to health, or by
the coincidence of a passport inspector who happens to know Giletti,
and who lets Fabrizio through in order to protect his friend. . . . A
hero like Joseph Andrews, Tom Jones, or Fabrizio possesses other
characteristics which become closely associated with his unconsciousness: he is incredibly handsome, so much so that most people
are immediately won over to him by his physical appearance; he is
graceful, strong, courageous, and sufficiently proud of his honor to
fight against personal attacks; he is naïve, gallant, and susceptible to
romantic notions; he is frequently passive. A character with these at-
tributes is quite useful to the writer of an adventure novel, because
the writer must be able to create a perpetual stream of incidents and
plot twists. If the hero is handsome, then at any moment a woman
may fall passionately in love with him, arouse her lover's jealousy, and
incite a duel, which will probably end in our hero wounding or killing his adversary and fleeing the police.

In retrospect, it seems to me I was taking a little mocking revenge against
the popular, handsome boys who were my friends. Though Mitch and Jon
were exceedingly intelligent, I took as my consolation prize the prejudiced
view that they were unconscious Fabrizios and I, the ever-alert Count
Mosca. My dream was to become Stendhal, never his romantic hero.

The rest of the paper supported my thesis by showing the many ways
the novelist employed to demonstrate and analyze Fabrizio's unconsciousness. For example, the anticlerical Stendhal blamed Catholicism,
"the instruction given him by the Jesuits of Milan. That religion *deprives
one of the courage to think of unfamiliar things,* and especially forbids *personal examination,* as the most enormous of sins, a step towards Protes-
tantism." Or he blamed his character's youth: "Fabrizio's reasoning could
never succeed in penetrating farther; he went a hundred ways around
the difficult without managing to surmount it. He was too young still; in
his moments of leisure, his mind devoted itself with rapture to enjoying
the sensations produced by the romantic circumstances with which his
imagination was always ready to supply him. He was far from employing

his time in studying with patience the actual details of things in order to discover their causes."

I cited Fabrizio's unconscious cruelty toward his aunt, after she had rescued him from prison: "He tortures his benefactress and savior by ignoring her completely and doting on the memory of her rival, Clélia." I went on to indict him: "His passion for Clélia ultimately leads to the death of his love, their child, the Duchess, and Fabrizio himself. Yet none of this tragedy would have occurred had Clélia and Fabrizio taken a rational course of action." (This is definitely a twenty-year-old talking!) I quoted Stendhal's seeming preference for reason over imagination, which delighted me: "The presence of danger gives a touch of genius to the reasoning man, places him, so to speak, above his level: in the imaginative man it inspires romances, bold, it is true, but frequently absurd."

In the end, I gave Fabrizio his due by noting that his instincts had elevated him above the common run of man, and won him the adoration of his priceless aunt. To show that this heroism was of a peculiarly unconscious nature, I quoted Gina herself, letting her have the last word: "I love in him his courage, so simple and so perfect that, one might say, he is not aware of it himself."

In the next twenty years, I stockpiled Stendhal's books: going on vacation, when I wanted something I knew would amuse me, I would pluck a title of his from the shelf. *The Red and the Black* proved to be, like *Vanity Fair*, one of those marvelous books whose vivacity and charm far exceed anything you might expect from a classic. I now regard it as Stendhal's best. Some of his lesser novels, like the refined novella *Armance*, the rather slight *Lamiel*, and the multivolume *Lucien Leuwen*, are interesting on every page but never come to any point (in fact, *Lucien Leuwen* was probably left unfinished because Stendhal realized he was spinning his wheels). I have come to the conclusion that Stendhal may not have been a natural novelist; like Kafka, he would get deeper and deeper into a story and not know how to plot an exit. I've also read his Italian tales, such as "Vanina Vanini," which have the economy of Kleist, if not the same payoff. In these short stories he seems to be forcing himself to complete a narrative arc. Their plots did not stay with me, but the storyteller remained good company throughout.

Finally, I turned to Stendhal's literary nonfiction, and was deeply enchanted. *On Love*, his book-length meditation, is such as astonishing fountain of wisdom, observation, philosophy, reverie, and paradox. It excited me enough to try to imitate the master with a chapter called "Journal of Decrystallization" in my novel *Confessions of Summer*. Later, after I had gravitated to the personal essay, I gobbled down his two autobiographical texts: *The Life of Henri Brulard* and *Memoirs of an Egotist*. The "I" in these unfinished memoirs is one of Stendhal's greatest characters: irascible, enthusiastic, pedantic, defiantly Oedipal, despising his father and adoring his mother. I also read his *Roman Journal* and some of the *Life of Rossini*. By this time, he had become for me one of those writers, like Montaigne, whose sentences are incurably interesting, regardless of whether the piece they are embedded in comes together.

Recently I returned to where I started and reread, for the third time, *The Charterhouse of Parma*.

I am getting old. This fact, which troubles me immensely, cannot help but inspire indifference in you, the reader. I completely understand your refusal to be moved by my aging. I even applaud it. And in part I feel it myself: Who cares? But I ask myself: What has all this aging accomplished? It has made me lose the ability to appreciate as keenly as I once did a literary masterpiece.

This has happened to almost all the literary enthusiasms of my youth. Kerouac and his hitchhiking epics I can no longer take seriously or read for pleasure; Dostoevsky's hysteria seems bullying, its shrillness repels me. The Stendhal who ruminates on love, travel, and other experience continues to replenish me; but I find *The Charterhouse* a bit tiresome. Not all of it, of course. I still love the battle scenes, and the great interior monologues of Count Mosca and Fabrizio in Chapter 7, and Gina flinging herself into her nephew's arms. I still love many of the analytical aphorisms. But as a whole, it feels a little precious, artificial, forced. *The Charterhouse of Parma* was dashed off, we know, in fifty-two days, at the end of 1838, and the swiftness of its composition shows, in its excessive penchant for summary, its likeness to a single whoosh of sustained exhalation, its bravura, tour-de-force qualities, and its repetitions and hasty windup.

Stendhal's recurrent brickbats, such as using the warmhearted Italians to reproach the French nation's calculation and materialism, have grown stale. Count Mosca's long Machiavellian disquisitions on the inner workings of the court are no longer as fascinating this time around. The book also feels like an uneasy commingling of two traditions: the French psychological novel (from *La Princesse de Clèves* down to *Adolphe*) and the Italian tale, with farcical elements of opera libretti and commedia dell'arte. In my youth I had accepted this mix of genres as an enrichment; this time I balked, because I was less willing to submit to the novel as a waking dream.

It could be that worldliness itself, the initial spellbinding attraction of *Charterhouse*, no longer possesses the same allure, the same meaning for me. That attribute is no longer so unattainable: I have it—or as much as I am ever going to have.

I now distrust Stendhal's brief for romantic love. His skepticism is more credible to me than his romanticism. *Charterhouse* plays as a conflict between reason and passion. Stendhal admired passion but, I think, didn't really believe in it. He needed it, though, to advance the plot, so that he wouldn't get bogged down again, as had happened with *Lucien Leuwen*, in observation without an engine to drive it. He also needed a magnetic hero, and here we come to my central complaint. Fabrizio is a bore, a cipher, unfit to hold the focus of such a complex novel. His raptures by the lake, his mooning over Clélia in prison, all these passages dragged for me.

How could I have not seen this when I was younger?

I went back and read my college paper. What impressed me was my patience with Fabrizio. Of course I was also largely unformed, largely unconscious at the time, and willing to grant him the benefit of the doubt. For all my underlying malice against this lucky pup, the younger me still accorded him the respect of a legitimate leading man. I was curious, rather than irritated, about why Stendhal chose him as his narrative vessel, and even went to the trouble of developing a literary theory around that choice. What has happened to me over the years that I have gotten so dismissive? Is it that, aging and balding, I no longer have even minimal patience for hearing stories about the troubles of privileged youths? Or has experience taught me that we were all golden boys, golden girls, once upon a time, and therefore the archetype has lost its envious fascination?

I was particularly taken with Fred Dupee's penciled comments on the first page: "Thorough and well reasoned essay—on a fruitful topic. I only think that you might distinguish more between F's unconsciousness and the consequences of it for his temperament; his being able to 'live happily in the moment,' as Stendhal says. Isn't it this last that makes him great, rather than unconsciousness itself?" Living happily in the moment has proven not to be my forte. I think I suspected it would not be even at twenty, and was already mounting defenses against its lack. My old professor was gently pointing to that blind spot.

Dupee himself was, I think it safe to say, bisexual, in his longings if not in practice. He had, in fact, a crush on my friend Jon, which the latter told me about. It may be that the homoerotically inclined retain more of a lifelong enchantment with the youthful Adonis figure, which would enable them to appreciate better the comedy of the superior, older Gina fainting in anguish at the indifference of the younger Fabrizio. It may be that great artists, be they Mozart or Stendhal or Shakespeare, always possess something of the hermaphrodite in their character. I am just speculating here. In any case, Stendhal believed in Italy, in happiness, in dolce far niente, in a way I no longer could. And to that extent, the novel could no longer work as well for me.

Nevertheless, because I knew I was wrong in my judgment, I went back and read parts of it again. With surprising pleasure. Taken a little at a time, like some poisons or homeopathic substances, *The Charterhouse of Parma* remains—delicious.

Coda:
The Life of the Mind

1.

My writing office is on the third floor of a brownstone where my wife, daughter, and I have lived for the past fifteen years. When I look out the window in summertime I am aware of a generalized green from several old trees; in autumn the leaves turn auburn and fall off, and I can see much more clearly my neighbors' brownstones across the street. I've never put up curtains or window shades, and I am never sure how much my neighbors can see into my study, which is why I don't write at my desk in the nude (or not very often).

It is fortunate we are not yet living in an age when our thoughts can be mind-read; otherwise, my neighbors on the block would probably come after me with pitchforks. As it is, I have learned to offer a bland if brusque façade, which serves, just barely.

Our street, in Carroll Gardens, is a quiet one and used to be 90 percent Italian but now is more mixed-gentrified, with Chinese, Arabs, Jews, and whatnot: retirees, firemen, architects, shrinks, law professors, realtors, welfare clients, ex-criminals, art restorers, graphic designers, mentally ill outpatients, and, inevitably, several writers. I am glad the view from my window is fairly mundane and not breathtaking, as a vista too picturesque might distract me from writing. The old expression for cogitating is "being in a brown study," and the muddy cocoa backdrop of brownstone façades and stoops across the way permits me to stay in my thoughts while I am dimly conscious of the lapping ambience of Brooklyn, the sounds of passing cars and the twittering of leaves. It is as though

I am cocooned in a tree house. The muted colors outside my window are slightly blurred around the edges like a Corot painting (the more so because I am nearsighted and not wearing my glasses at the computer).

On the columnar spaces between the windows facing the street, and on every inch of the other three walls in my study, stand floor-to-ceiling bookshelves, and the spines of other authors' volumes, peripherally glimpsed, act as prods to keep me on task.

2.

There is something about autumn that makes me want to rearrange my bookshelves: a soothing seasonal ritual, like carving pumpkins or burning piles of leaves. This fall, the impulse stole on me unexpectedly. I started to hunt for a book to read, when I noticed my Japanese literature section was overflowing, with excess paperbacks stacked horizontally above the tops of upright hardcovers, and others in danger of slipping behind the front ranks and disappearing from sight. The Italian section, I noticed, had a little extra room. I could consolidate the two—but what connection did Japanese and Italian literature have, other than both countries having been Axis powers that fought against us in World War II? No, it would make more sense to move the Portuguese writers in with the Brazilians, and pair the Japanese shelves with the Chinese . . .

Before I knew it, I was cradling armfuls of books like a wobbly accordion. I tried to keep them in the same order, but whenever a book or two fell from my hands, the whole alphabetical system was endangered, and I would end up having to file every one separately, which was what I secretly wanted to do, because it gave me the chance to handle each volume, to finger the covers, to browse a bit in the pages. Not so much the books I loved as the ones I had neglected. At least one-third of my books I haven't gotten around to reading yet: I stockpile books for a rainy day, but if it were to rain continuously from now until I am ninety I might still not be able to finish every title. I have the unfortunate habit of going on book-buying binges and then forgetting what I have acquired. More than once I've picked up a classic (some Dickens, say, which I haven't read yet) in a used bookstore or stoop sale on one of my walks, only to discover that I already owned a copy at home.

These rearranging sessions serve to reacquaint me with my stock, and revive the desire to tackle previously daunting titles. I set these aside in a separate pile, an ambitious stack of miscellaneous items like Wittgenstein's *Tractatus Logico-Philosophicus*, Nabokov's *Ada*, Pirenne's *Medieval Cities*—books which I approach with an expectation more to better myself than to receive pleasure. I place them carefully on the end table beside my writing desk, so that visitors may notice them and admire my intellectual rigor; in time, however, they become an invisible part of the furniture, and I return them to the bookcase regretfully unread.

But I am getting ahead of myself: back to the original organizing task. In a throwback to my childhood play with toy soldiers, I now control the movements of nations by dictatorially dispersing their literatures. Having rearranged the globe, hitched Spain to Greece and returned India to England, I am ready to tackle subtler diasporas. My books are distributed not only by nationality but by subject matter and genre, including categories such as movies, poetry, architecture, social science. Delicate decisions must be made. Once, to honor Freud's felicitous writing style, I paid him the compliment of putting him in German literature along with Rilke and Mann, rather than in the social sciences, where I had relegated such eminences as Max Weber. But then, I had never read much Max Weber, perhaps I was being unfair, so in the end I moved Freud back in with the psychologists and sociologists.

There are also certain sets, such as my complete Charles Lamb, that I want to feature, because I like their bindings, or their tallness requires a higher shelf, or their authors are favorites of mine. This caprice has wreaked havoc with the alphabetical system. At times I will take into consideration the writer's own feelings about whom he or she might wish to lie next to, and will match-make, placing Emily Dickinson at last beside Thomas Wentworth Higginson. In other instances I can be quite brutal about following a rigorous alphabetical schema, deriving sadistic sport at the thought of forcing antagonists in life or aesthetic manner to rub covers together.

The main principle of organization, I am embarrassed to admit, comes down to snobbery. I promote certain writers or national cultures that fascinate me at the moment, or that seem the gold standard of quality, while demoting others to the remoter shelves. Chilliest Siberia is a bookcase just outside my study in the hallway next to the bathroom, which holds those contemporaries of mine, rivals who have somehow managed to win wide public approval. Curious like everyone else, I had bought their books, read them with a mixture of disappointment and relief, and consigned them to the nether regions.

The beauty of my system is that nobody coming into my house and glancing at its library would suspect how sensitively the ordering reflects my discriminations. They would see a somewhat random assortment of books, whereas I perceive the fanaticism, pettiness, malice, and good taste of the person who has put the collection together.

3.

One day I was idly going through new messages in my e-mail when I came upon a request to contribute an essay to a volume, the proceeds of which were to go to the Save Darfur Coalition. The book's premise was that each contributor should expatiate on some risk he or she had faced as a writer. Reluctant as I am to write anything without being paid, and averse to boasting about my alleged nobility in overcoming fears, it nevertheless struck me that during my busy, preoccupied life I had neglected to save the people of Darfur. So I rolled up my sleeves and composed the following:

Every time I momentarily lose orientation, like asking myself in the midst of some domestic family squabble what am I doing here or who am I (such moments of vagueness do not decrease with aging), I think back to the last piece I wrote and tell myself, "Aha, I am the author of ———." It could be a lengthy tome, or a book review or a semihack article I wrote last week, doesn't matter, the point is that I experience an instantaneous congealing of self-confidence. Sometimes as I roam about on a break from writing I tell myself, like a parent reassuring a child, that I am the author of a whole shelf of books; it was always my dream to take up a shelf in the library, and I'm almost at that point, having written maybe a dozen titles, edited a half dozen more, and contributed ten more introductions to photography books or other authors' reissued texts that get my name put in however small type on the cover. You would think that anyone who had already generated so prolific a corpus (we will defer the question of quality for the moment, or indefinitely) would be mature enough not to have to resort to such petty incantations, but such is not the case. I need to pat myself on the back constantly, because without this reminder of my literary output I fear I would vaporize.

The negative corollary of this phenomenon is that every time I finish a book, I become quite morbid and think I am going to die soon. It is as though, having cleared the desk, I no longer have an excuse to live. Actually, even before finishing a book, when I am still in the final stages, I begin to have the hit-by-a-truck fantasy: walking through the streets of Brooklyn, I ask myself if my manuscript has reached a point sufficiently far along that, *were* I hit by a truck and killed instantly, it could still be published, with a short note, of course, by my widow or editor explaining the circumstances. I brood about where I left my manuscript, and if it is in an obvious enough place on my desk or the piles of papers beside the desk so that my wife could find it, after she has gone through the necessary grief-and-burial period, or so that she could locate it on my computer, and initiate the search for a publisher, assuming she liked it enough not to suppress it (one can never be sure about such things). Then the day comes when I have definitely finished the manuscript, for better or worse, and it is a book, or potential book. I take it to the photocopy shop and have three copies made. I give one to a friend and another to my agent. The third I leave with my wife. And I begin to think of death.

Sometimes these thoughts take the form of fantasizing approaching some friend, and asking him to become my literary executor. This fantasy of the chosen friend is shot though with Hawthorne-Melville unconsummated homoeroticism, except the brunt of this romanticized turn in the relationship will start from the moment I die, necrophilia-cally, so to speak: Who will love me enough, once I become a ghost, to put up with the bother of being my executor? First I have to perform a rigorous analysis of all my friends and ask which one of them I trust the most. Many have let me down in the past; these are easily eliminated; but I must also cross off the list those dependable friends who are older than myself and who might not be around long enough to agitate to keep my books in print or, what is even more arduous a task, get the out-of-print ones reissued. There is also a large stack of my uncollected work (journalism, film criticism, book reviews, ephemeral poems, juvenilia), which a really alert, industrious literary trustee might find a way to see into print. How to locate all that material? To gather all my unpublished work together, the chosen literary executor would have to burrow into my files, a process that could easily take half a year. What matters is that, if the friend is successful, he will have added to my library shelf, which is all I care about.

The irony is that I have still not gotten around to composing a will, though my wife and my mother-in-law regularly nag me that it is my responsibility to do so. Writing a will is certainly practical, but this step would entail envisioning my extinction, and while I am happy to do so as an exercise in self-pity or an act of gothic imagination, I am less drawn to the idea of making life easier for those who will survive me. Let them suffer. Oh, I am sure in due course I will make out a will, but the prime motivation for it will be to settle this question of my literary executor.

When I finish a book I am dead, empty. It is at such junctures that I wish I had a knack for living. E. M. Cioran once wrote a book with the beautiful title *The Temptation to Exist*. I, too, have frequently been tempted to exist, but I am no good at it, and so I plod through the hours of leisure with a pretense of graceful participation which does not fool for a second those closest to me (my wife and daughter), and I wait im-patiently for the next opportunity to sit at my desk and write. Anything. For it is only when writing that I begin to exist. In that sense I take no risks by writing: intensely honest self-exposures come easily to me, the most provocative positions that clash with conventional morality are a breeze, complex researches and ambitious structural challenges are finally child's play, next to the difficulty of getting through daily domestic life, trying to love one's family members on a consistent basis (despite the lack of respect they show me compared to the literary community), listening to the neighbors' small talk, and deciding which telephone company provides the best service package.

Acknowledgments

Some of these essays appeared, in similar or altered form, in the following journals and anthologies: *The American Scholar, The Common, Double Take, Family Therapy Networker, Film Comment, Gulf Coast, The Harvard Review, The Hopkins Review, Lapham's Quarterly, The Nation, The New York Times, The Normal School, The Oxford American, Pequod, Preservation, River Teeth, Salmagundi;* and *Loss Within Loss: Artists in the Age of AIDS* (edited by Edmund White), *At the End of the Day: Selected Poems and an Introductory Essay, Brothers* (edited by Andrew Blauner), *By the Waters of Manhattan* by Charles Reznikoff, *Dedicated to the People of Darfur* (edited by Luke and Jennifer Reynolds), *Genesis: Contemporary Writers on Our First Stories* (edited by David Rosenberg), *The Poem That Changed America: "Howl" Fifty Years Later* (edited by Jason Schinder), and *Wanting a Child* (edited by Jill Bialosky and Helen Schulman).

I am supremely grateful to the following friends and editors who read these pieces in earlier drafts and often made suggestions for improvement, which I usually failed to take, to my detriment: Thomas Beller, Carmen Boullosa, Jill Bialosky, Robert and Peg Boyers, Adam Braver, Anne Fadiman, Lynn Freed, Patricia Hampl, James Harvey, Jonathan Lethem, Leonard Lopate, Sandy Macintosh, Honor Moore, David Rosenberg, Adam Shatz, Lynne Sharon Schwartz, Vijay Seshadri, Gavin Smith, Mark Street, Benjamin Taylor, and Bill Zavatsky.

Profound thanks to Civitella Foundation for a month in Italy. I can't thank enough my literary agent, Wendy Weil, for her lifelong (forty years') support. She passed away tragically in September, but not before she found me the exquisitely tactful and sage book editor, Millicent Bennett, and her trusty assistant, Chloe Perkins.

Finally, no words can do justice to the steady and largely benign influence of my wife, Cheryl, and daughter, Lily, whose love, forbearance, and patient instruction have sought to guide me at every turn.

About the Author

Phillip Lopate is the author of *Against Joie de Vivre, Portrait of My Body,* and *Being with Children,* among other books. He is a recipient of the Guggenheim and National Endowment for the Arts fellowships, and his works have appeared in *Best American Essays, The Paris Review, The New York Times,* and many other publications. He lives in Brooklyn, New York, with his wife and daughter, and teaches writing at Columbia University, where he directs the graduate nonfiction program.